SURVIVING TRAUMA

SURVIVING TRAUMA
Loss, Literature and Psychoanalysis

David Aberbach

YALE UNIVERSITY PRESS
NEW HAVEN AND LONDON
1989

Library of Congress Catalog Card Number 89-050650
ISBN 0-300-04557-3

Set in Linotron Palatino by Best-set Typesetter Ltd, Hong Kong
and printed and bound in Great Britain by The Bath Press, Avon

Contents

Foreword

The first task for a psychotherapist is to see the world through the eyes of the person he is trying to help, to put himself into the other's shoes. Only then can he hope to share, if only in small measure, the problems of his patient or to understand why he thinks and feels as he does. The reason is clear. Our own outlook has been shaped by that unique pattern of family relationships that we happen to have encountered during our life, not least during the early years, whereas our patient's outlook has been shaped by some other equally unique pattern. Although sometimes there is overlap between the patterns, more often they are quite different, perhaps to an extreme degree. Those fortunate enough to have lived their years of childhood and adolescence in a stable and reasonably happy family will find it difficult to imagine what it is like to grow up amid the distorted or hostile relationships that occur in some families or amid the emotional devastation of others. Similarly, someone who has had experience of one version of distorted relationships will find it difficult to imagine what it is like to have experienced some other version. Each of us sees the world through his own private spectacles and finds it hard to believe other peoples' spectacles are not the same.

Hitherto the clinical literature has not been very helpful. Much of it is empty of relevant accounts; and, even when a clinician recognizes the need to record the world his patient lives in, too frequently his pen is not equal to the task. This is where the artist scores. As a person whose primary task it is to describe what it feels like to be in some carefully defined human situation, he has both the time and the skill to recreate the situation and to tell us how one person was affected by it – how he thought and felt at the time, how he acted, how he extricated himself or failed to extricate himself, and how perhaps it permanently altered his ways of thinking and feeling about other people. Whether in prose or poetry, the great names in literature are those who are able to give us insight into the worlds of other human beings, as well perhaps as into our own.

Nevertheless, complementary though the study of literature is to the study of personality development and psychotherapy, few in either field are well-versed in the other, whilst systematic efforts to bridge the divide are fewer still. The work of the Scottish psychologist Alexander Shand in *The Foundations of Character* first published in 1914 remains a conspicuous exception. Seeking to understand the emotional roots of human personality, Shand drew on the work of British poets and French prose writers, and in doing so wrote a remarkably insightful chapter on grief and mourning. It was reading this chapter many years ago when I was first working on the psychological processes following separation and loss that led me to realize that a disbelief that death has occurred and an urge to search for and recover the lost person are integral features of normal mourning. Since this profound truth had hitherto escaped clinicians, the field of psychology and psychotherapy are thus deeply indebted to literature.

David Aberbach's book, I believe, will go a long way towards repaying that debt. Deeply steeped in literature of many and diverse kinds, he is familiar also with the findings of current clinical studies of how human beings, both young and old, are affected by separation and loss, and with the different circumstances that either mitigate the adverse effects or else aggravate them. Thus equipped, he is able to show how varied is the creative writing that has been influenced by loss – the loss of a parent during childhood or adolescence, the loss of a spouse, the loss of a brother or sister, or the loss of a child – and also how devastating can be the effects of mass disasters, of which in living memory none compare to the Holocaust. Creative writing, he points out, can attempt many things – to express feelings that are almost inexpressible, to understand what is almost unintelligible, to accept what is at the limit of the bearable, or to restore in symbolic form what cannot be restored in another way. Even in its expression of despair creative writing expresses a search for a way forward.

For some readers the chapters tracing the effects of loss on the ideas expressed by well-known philosophers and mystics will hold special interest. As the author points out, even if the ideas themselves were not born of loss, the tendency of those who have suffered loss to emphasize certain ideas in preference to others can hardly be due to chance. Another chapter with broad social implications is the one in which light is thrown on the personal backgrounds of those whom circumstances throw up to become charismatic characters.

For many readers, including clinicians, the results of

Aberbach's researches will provide a revealing insight, not readily available elsewhere, into how deeply, how adversely, and for how long a time, a human being can be affected by the loss of parental care during childhood or adolescence. In the examples quoted one author after another records either explicitly or implicitly, but always vividly and movingly, his personal experiences. For those who have themselves sustained a loss, to read of the experience of others may be of help, if only by the assurance that they are not alone in how they think and feel. For those more fortunate reading this book may give a glimpse of how the world looks through another's spectacles.

John Bowlby

Preface

'The poets and philosophers before me discovered the unconscious. What I discovered was the scientific method by which the unconscious can be studied.'

Sigmund Freud

Freud's writings on bereavement in the latter part of his career, which have in recent years spawned a considerable and growing literature on the subject, were largely anticipated by creative writers, and, in fact, there is hardly a single idea in the clinical work on loss that does not have some precedent, usually far better expressed, in creative literature. Though there has been some work on loss in literature, much of it has been done by psychologists and psychotherapists, such as Alexander Shand, Anthony Storr, George Pickering, Malcolm Fraser, George Pollock, and Eileen Simpson, rather than by literary scholars— notable exceptions include Edmund Wilson and Andrew Brink. The dearth of literary studies on loss is not surprising when one considers that the clinical study of loss is itself a relatively recent phenomenon. Colin Murray Parkes forcefully drew attention to this omission in his standard work on *Bereavement*, the first edition of which appeared in 1972:

'I know of only one functional psychiatric disorder whose cause is known, whose features are distinctive, and whose course is usually predictable, and that is grief, the reaction to loss. Yet this condition has been so neglected by psychiatrists that until recently it was not even mentioned in the indexes of most of the best-known general textbooks of psychiatry' (1986, p. 26).

A number of important studies have been devoted to the survivor (e.g. Des Pres, 1976; Bettelheim, 1979; Bergmann & Jucovy, 1982), to creativity (e.g. Koestler, 1964; Pickering, 1974; Arieti, 1976), as well as to the subject of loss (e.g. Bowlby, 1980;

Raphael, 1984; Parkes, 1986); yet there has been relatively little inter-disciplinary work in these three areas. Loss as a possible motivation in creativity has been examined by Rochlin (1965), Storr (1972), Wolfenstein (1973), Brink (1977), Pollock (1978), and Aberbach (1983), among others, but the creativity of survivors has been largely neglected in these works. Critical works on literary responses to the Holocaust, such as those of Steiner (1967), Langer (1975), Rosenfeld (1980), Bilik (1981), Mintz (1984), and Roskies (1984), are valuable chiefly for their analyses of the methods and literary devices by which atrocities and their impact are depicted and for setting this literature in a wider literary or historical context; but there has so far been no serious attempt to place survivor literature in the context of the clinical work on grief. Similarly, clinical studies of survivors rarely give sufficient attention to the creative writing of survivors. What insights does the literature by and about the survivor give into the nature of grief and creativity, and particularly into the ways in which grief might spur creativity?

The present work is the first full-length thematic study of loss in literature. Though I had previously worked on the subject as a graduate student in Oxford, in 1975–80, the actual writing of this book began in 1980–2, while I was working in various London day nurseries as a trainee in child psychotherapy at the Tavistock Clinic. At this time, I met Dr John Bowlby whose research on bereavement, while still somewhat controversial, is generally accepted as valid and important, and whose personal encouragement in the writing of this book has meant a great deal to me. John Bowlby's monumental three-volume study, *Attachment and Loss* (1969–80), as well as the work of his research associates, James and Joyce Robertson and especially Colin Murray Parkes, together with that of colleagues such as Dorothy Burlingham and Anna Freud, René Spitz, Michael Rutter, Peter Marris, Michael Balint, Erna and Robert Furman, and Beverley Raphael, provide the clinical background for this book.

The aim of the book was first summarized in an article in the *Times Higher Education Supplement* (9.9.81), in which I suggested that there is a need for closer links between the humanities and the social sciences: a book on clinical and creative literature on loss would help to bridge the two disciplines.

However, the book has expanded into comparative areas largely neglected both by clinical researchers and by literary scholars, such as the role of loss in creativity, particularly of Holocaust survivors, the role of loss in dreams and memories, in mysticism and charisma, and also, to a lesser extent, in philosophical ideas, and in literature depicting psychological disorder and suicidal thoughts and feelings. Loss is presented here as one of many possible forces and subjects of creativity. There is no intention of dealing comprehensively with any one theme or author, or of competing with other existing interpretations of the literature under discussion.

Parts of this book have been published previously: the chapters on 'Creativity and the Survivor', 'Loss and Dreams' and 'Grief and Mysticism', as well as parts of 'Loss and Childhood Memories', first appeared in the *International Review of Psycho-Analysis*; the material on Bialik and on Hitler, in *Encounter*; and the section on Agnon is based largely on a chapter from my book, *At the Handles of the Lock*. Translations from the Hebrew are my own, unless indicated otherwise.

As well as Dr Bowlby, I thank Dr Colin Murray Parkes together with Professor John Carey and the late Professor Richard Ellmann for kindly reading and responding to the book in draft form. I am very grateful to my editors, Robert Baldock and Mary Carruthers, and to readers for Yale University Press – David Nokes, Naomi Segal, Bennett Simon, and Anthony Storr – whose criticisms were of considerable help in the final stages. In addition, I am thankful to Professor Ron Baker and the late Professor Shamai Davidson for help with the chapter on loss and the survivor, and to Sir Isaiah Berlin and Dr Patrick Gardiner for advice pertaining to the chapter on loss and philosophical ideas.

To the British Academy, the Humanitarian Trust, and McGill University, I am grateful for grants which facilitated the writing of this book.

Most of all, I thank my wife, Mimi, whose love made this book possible.

Finally, I have used the universal 'he' when referring to the general person. Without wishing to offend or to be exclusive, I have found this to be preferable to the rather cumbersome alternatives of 'she or he', 's/he', or 'one'. I hope all readers will find this acceptable.

This book is dedicated to Rachel Aberbach (1890–1974) and to Jonathan Solomon Skelker (1943–1963).

1

CREATIVITY AND THE SURVIVOR

Ready for parting, as if my back were turned,
I see my dead come toward me, transparent and breathing.
I do not accept:
one walk around the square, one rain,
and I am another, with imperfect rims, like clouds.
Gray in the passing town, passing and glad,
among transitory streetlamps,
wearing my strangeness like a coat, I am free to stand
with the people who stand at the opening of a moment
in a chance doorway, anonymous as raindrops
and, being strangers, near and flowing one into another.

Ready for parting, waiting a while in the archway
for the signs of my life which appear in the chipped plaster
and look out from the grimy windowpane. A surprise of roses.
Bursting out and already future, twisted into its veins—
a blossoming to every wind. Perhaps
not in my own time into myself and from myself and onward
from gate within gate I will go out into the jungle of rain,
free to pass on like one who has tried his strength
I will go out
from the space in between as if from the walls of denial.

Dan Pagis, 'Ready for Parting'

Writings by and about survivors, of the Holocaust as of other
collective catastrophes, often present with rare clarity the characteristics of grief and may, therefore, be treated as paradigmatic of
creative responses to loss. In this literature, one is faced with the
paradox that the experiences of survivors cannot be reduced to
literature or compared with the experiences of others, for they
suffer not just from individual trauma but also from collective
trauma and must carry an often-unbearable weight of grief. They
mourn family, friends, and the communal bonds which have
been violently torn apart; they mourn the cheapening of their
lives, their lost dignity and humanity; they mourn all that might

1

have been and was not. And although the symptoms associated with so-called 'survivor syndrome' all have parallels in other forms of grief, in their particular configurations and intensity they are unique. Yet, the fact that survivor grief can at all be compared with normal grief is proof that the survivors have not been totally robbed of their humanity, that they remain in this respect recognizably human. There is another side to this paradox–all griefs are both alike and dissimilar, and for this reason clinical and creative literature on the survivor are mutually enhancing and enriching: clinical studies teach the universality of grief reactions, while creative responses bring home the uniqueness of each grief.

The purpose of this chapter is twofold: to compare within a clinical framework expressions of grief in the literature of survivors and of those bereaved in more normal conditions, and to explore the role of creativity as a response to personal and collective loss.

The function of creativity in the wake of traumatic loss is illumined by observations of Freud's in *Beyond the Pleasure Principle* (1920). Here Freud argues that the repeated nightmares of shellshocked soldiers constitute a violent attempt on the part of the unconscious to master the trauma in all its horror and to overcome it. Children's games played in the shadow of a loss may serve a similar function: 'in their play children repeat everything that has made a great impression on them in real life, and in doing so they abreact the strength of the impression and, as one might put it, make themselves master of the situation' (SE, XVIII, pp. 16–17).[1] The same may be true of creativity in general, as D.H. Lawrence wrote some years before Freud after completing his novel *Sons and Lovers*: '. . . one sheds one's sicknesses in books, repeats and presents again one's emotions to be master of them' (Letters, II, p. 90).

The struggle for mastery over grief-ridden trauma is particularly evident among survivors who use creativity to confront and bear witness to the past and to find meaning in continued life. Trauma, far from opening the wellsprings of creativity, can in fact destroy the survivor's power to fantasize and thus greatly diminish spontaneity and individuality. The sheer scale of losses and the forced delay in mourning may make grief exceptionally hard, if not impossible, to bear. Massive exposure to death and dehumanization, together with hunger, terror, cold and illness, may drastically reduce the power to mourn; in such times, grief can endanger survival and must be dammed up. In his memoir of Auschwitz, *Night*, Elie Wiesel recalls that his main preoccupation was not mourning his lost relatives but his stomach: 'Bread, soup – these were my whole life. I was a body. Perhaps less than that even: a starved stomach...I could feel myself as two: my body and me. I hated it' (1960, pp. 69, 105).

Creativity, the affirmation of the wholly individual ability to imagine, may act as a vital part of survival, of the re-emergence of the whole and unique human being. The poem 'Ready for Parting' quoted above vividly enacts the creative struggle against the reductive impact of massive trauma. Its author, the Hebrew poet Dan Pagis, survived the Holocaust and went to Israel as a boy. He learned Hebrew rapidly (his native language had been German) and by the late 1940s began to publish Hebrew poetry. However, twenty years passed before he could bring himself to write openly about the Holocaust. He did not feel that language could be adequate to the horror, and his Holocaust poems, when they did come, were heavily understated, oblique and ironic. 'Ready for Parting' treats the barrier encountered by the survivor in grieving, for he is psychologically imprisoned in the past, haunted by the dead (who to him are still living and breathing), incapable yet of accepting what he has lost. Yet the signs of imagination which enter the poem almost by accident – 'A surprise of roses/ Bursting out and already future, twisted into its veins –/ a blossoming to every wind' – appear to give hope to the poet that he will someday undergo the change needed in order to come to terms with the trauma and to emerge to freedom from within its walls. This hope is no less real for being tinged with ironic evanescence. The irony is underlined in the word 'parting': the survivor must be constantly ready for the incursions of past separations into his consciousness and also for future, unexpected losses and separations (as well as for his own death); but he also hopes that he will someday 'part' with the trauma of loss and its denial.

The role of creativity among survivors may be compared with that of the bereaved in more usual circumstances, especially those who endure loss in childhood. The inhibition or blockage of fantasy as a result of incomplete mourning may find its compensation or antidote in creative self-expression. Through creativity, the artist may confront and attempt to master the trauma on his own terms and, in so doing, complete the work of mourning. The unresolved elements of grief may thus themselves be both motive and substance in creativity: this holds true of all forms of loss and creativity. In particular, a child who loses a parent and has poor conditions for mourning is in this respect little different from

3

the survivor of collective catastrophe. Bowlby compares the unresolved grief of such a child with recurrent physical illness, and the same analogy is true of the survivor:

In a young child an experience of separation from, or loss of, mother-figure is especially apt to evoke psychological processes of a kind that are as crucial for psychopathology as inflammation and the resulting scar tissue are for physiopathology. This does not mean that a crippling of personality is the inevitable result; but it does mean that, as in the case, say, of rheumatic fever, scar tissue is all too often formed that in later life leads to more or less severe dysfunction (1980, p. 22).[2]

A child emotionally crippled by loss who later tries to express and master the unresolved grief creatively might well compare himself or herself with the survivor of concentration camps: a striking example is Sylvia Plath, in poems such as 'Daddy' and 'Lady Lazarus'.[3]

To what extent is the grief expressed in the creativity of survivors comparable with that found in the creativity of others? Psychological responses to survival, as to all forms of loss, vary greatly from person to person. They depend not only on the duration and intensity of the trauma and the conditions for mourning, but also on the individual's make-up, particularly his early family history which may predispose him to react in certain ways under stress. Yet there is hardly a single element of grief which appears in the literature by and about survivors – numbness, yearning and searching, denial, anger, guilt, idealization, identification, depression and despair – which does not have a parallel in creative literature generally as well as in clinical studies of grief.

The parallels may be shown by juxtaposing passages from survivor literature with those depicting grief in more normal conditions. The illustrations from survivor literature which follow are taken from Jewish writings on the Holocaust, in French, German, English, Yiddish, Hebrew and Italian. This literature is a largely secular continuation of an ancient religious-literary tradition, beginning already in the Hebrew Bible, of confronting and coming to terms with collective disaster. It is therefore unusually well suited to expressing both the distinctive character of Jewish suffering and the universal plight of the grief-stricken victim. Most of the writers – Dan Pagis, Aharon Appelfeld, Elie Wiesel, Paul Celan and Primo Levi – were imprisoned in camps, and all suffered the loss of family and friends.

4

The writings of survivors depict and themselves enact a pronounced absence of grief. The novels and stories of Aharon Appelfeld, for example, leave the reader with the disturbing feeling that the emotions of the survivors whom he depicts have been sunken under water or buried behind a great wall of cotton: Appelfeld's muted, understated style contributes to this impression. This phenomenon is all too well known to those who must deal with post-traumatic stress disorder. 'The survivor's main defence against death anxiety and death guilt', writes Lifton, 'is the cessation of feeling' (1967, p. 500). The numbing of feeling beyond normal bounds is a necessary anaesthetic, enabling the survivor to function under severe stress. This numbing exacts a high price: for the gates of feeling are closed not only to the trauma but also, to some extent, to the sources of life and growth and happiness.

Even before the mass-murders in the death camps had begun, on 4 May 1942, the extent of loss was literally unbelievable, and numbing. The historian Lucy Dawidowicz, in *The War against the Jews 1933–45*, writes of the fate of the Soviet and Polish Jews in the months following the German invasion of the Soviet Union in June 1941:

> In Bialystok some 7,000 Jews were killed by the Einsatzgruppen in July: in Kovno, some 6,000 to 7,000; in Vilna, 20,000 or more – nearly half the city's Jewish population – swallowed up in the death pits at Ponary, a desolate village ten kilometres from Vilna. 'How can one write about this? How can one assemble one's thoughts?' Herman Kruk asked in his diary on 4 September 1941, recording the eye-witness reports. The reports were hard to believe; once believed, they were still harder to assimilate. They stunned the mind: they numbed sensibility. The Jews underwent a mass psychic occlusion, the normal flow of their emotions and energies shut off by shock and withdrawal, the business of their daily existence managed with a stringent economy of thought and feeling (1983, p. 251).

In *Night*, Wiesel writes of the all-prevasive numbness of the camp inmates at Auschwitz in response to the loss of their families and friends as well as the conditions of their imprisonment: 'Those absent no longer touched even the surface of our memories. We still spoke of them – "Who knows what may have become of them?" – but we had little concern for their fate. We were incapable of thinking of anything at all. Our senses were blunted; everything was blurred as in a fog' (p. 51).

This blunting of feeling is comparable to the numbness felt in normal grief; but this phase of grief generally occurs only at the start of the grieving process, lasting for as little as a few hours and no more than a week or so (Bowlby, 1980). The American writers James Agee and Delmore Schwartz might be quoted here by way of contrast as much as of comparison. Agee, in the autobiographical novel *A Death in the Family* (1957), tells of the death of Jay Follett and the effect of this death upon his family, particularly his son Rufus and wife Mary. In the scene in which Mary first hears that Jay has been in a road accident and might be dead or dying, Agee describes her mute shock as she goes to the bathroom and stares at herself in the mirror: 'with her wet hands planted in the basin of cold water she stared incredulously into her numb, reflected face, which seemed hardly real to her' (1980, p. 136). Schwartz, similarly, in the autobiographical 'The Brother Poem', recalls his initial absence of feeling at the time of his father's death when he was fifteen:

> Upon the blackboard of my pillowed eyes
> I saw a circle drawn in thick white chalk,
> And this was a hole and in this hole, deep down,
> I saw my father lying in his coffin, and I
> Felt nothing.

(Atlas, 1977, p. 33)

Numbness following a loss gives way to yearning and searching for the dead. As anaesthesia fades, the pain of grief is felt. The poetry of Nelly Sachs, who escaped from Germany to Sweden in 1940, conveys this yearning through inanimate objects associated with the dead, for which the mourner searches, hopelessly questioning. In the futility of seeking the dead in such objects as a stone or a bit of metal lies the motive and essence of the poetry; the very act of creation gives form and significance to this futile yearning and, to an extent, masters it:

> If I only knew
> On what your last look rested.
> Was it a stone that had drunk
> So many last looks that they fell
> Blindly upon its blindness?
>
> Or was it earth,
> Enough to fill a shoe,

And black already
With so much parting
And with so much killing?

Or was it your last road
That brought you a farewell from all the roads
You had walked?

A puddle, a bit of shining metal,
Perhaps the buckle of your enemy's belt,
Or some other small augury
Of heaven?

Or did this earth,
Which lets no one depart unloved,
Send you a bird-sign through the air,
Reminding your soul that it quivered
In the torment of its burnt body?

(1971, p. 84)

During the period of yearning and searching for the dead, which even in normal conditions may last for months or even years (Bowlby, 1980), the searcher still commonly believes, or half-believes, that the dead can be found and recovered. This irrational hope stirs up anxiety which may find a creative outlet. Yearning and searching may involve the actual person lost or animate, inanimate or abstract substitutes, and these, as in Nelly Sach's poetry, may furnish both the motivation and the substance of art. Among survivors, searching must often be postponed: a study of the survivors of Theresienstadt concentration camp (Kral, 1951), for example, revealed that after the war many made lengthy, futile searches for the graves of lost persons. As with grief in normal conditions when mourning is not delayed, such seemingly useless acts may serve a vital function in enabling the bereaved to make his peace with the dead.

An illustration of yearning and searching after a loss in normal circumstances is Thomas Hardy's 'The Voice', written in December 1912, a few weeks after the death of the poet's first wife. The longing for the dead woman, who lives on in the poet's imagination, is not dissimilar from that in Nelly Sachs' poem; inanimate objects – the shoe, the gown – are catalysts for the poets' yearning. The failure to master the grief in 'The Voice' is apparent in the rhythm, which begins in ballad-like fashion but falters and dissolves to listlessness in the final stanza. The broken

7

lines here, as in Nelly Sachs' poem, suggest the poet's heart-broken state:

> Woman much missed, how you call to me, call to me,
> Saying that now you are not as you were
> When you had changed from the one who was all to me,
> But as at first, when our day was fair.
>
> Can it be you that I hear? Let me view you, then,
> Standing as when I drew near to the town
> Where you would wait for me: yes, as I knew you then,
> Even unto the original air-blue gown!
>
> Or is it only the breeze, in its listlessness
> Travelling across the wet mead to me here,
> You being ever dissolved to existlessness,
> Heard no more again far or near?
>
> Thus I; faltering forward,
> Leaves around me falling,
> Wind oozing thin through the thorn from norward,
> And the woman calling.

Among the phases of the grief process, yearning and searching is, perhaps, particularly conducive to creativity. During this phase, there is sufficient distance from the loss to recollect and assimilate emotions deriving from the lost person, yet the burden of grief might still be so pressing that it seeks a creative outlet. In this state of incomplete mourning, when disbelief and denial of the loss commonly oscillate with acceptance, denial might be expressed in a 'living' work of art, a form of 'holding on' to the lost person or persons, while acceptance might find expression in the form of a memorial to the dead.

The very process of creation involves searching for things which can (in theory) be found: ideas, inspiration, technique, and ultimately for the perfection of the whole. Searching is in any case an expression of the normal human impulse to explore and create, and bereavement may give especial force and direction to this impulse. Among artists who have known severe loss, the 'search' for a work of art might be compared with – or, in some cases, even take the place of – the search for the lost person. The attachment to the lost person might thus be displaced on to works of art. At times, the urge to create characters in fiction, poetry, and certainly in biography, might be rooted in the wish to find, recreate, or destroy a lost person. It is intriguing, too, that aspects of yearning and searching, such as a state of heightened arousal and tension, restlessness, sleep disturbance, loss of interest in everyday matters and in personal appearance, are similar to behaviour often associated with periods of creativity.

We have mentioned that the denial of loss is a part of grief. Denial is inherent in the phases of numbness and of searching, for it shields the bereaved from overwhelming shock and pain. Among survivors, as for instance in 'Ready for Parting', quoted above, this denial can become a barrier preventing the return to a normal life: it is portrayed creatively as it is experienced, as being prolonged and distorted. Aharon Appelfeld, for example, is noted for the depiction of characters in whom whole sectors of emotion have been sealed off in response to trauma, though they might learn to live without them as with a paralyzed limb.[4] The Hebrew poet Abba Kovner is another Holocaust survivor who confronts the impossibility of accepting massive collective loss. Kovner survived by hiding in the forests of Poland, fighting for the Jewish partisans. To the survivor-poet in *Ahoti Ketanah* (My Little Sister, 1967) words are inadequate for a horror too great to be absorbed:

> You have not seen a city thrust on its back
> like a horse in its blood, jerking its hooves
> unable to rise.
>
> Bells are ringing.
>
> City.
> City.
> How mourn a city
> whose people are dead and whose dead are alive
> in the heart.
>
> I vow by you today.
> We will not speak, for better or for worse,
> of a world that went to ruin. Oh terror –
> how will this passage of our lives
> be told now.

(1971, pp. 40, 64)

The denial of collective loss is not incomparable with the denial precipitated by the loss of one loved person: both forms of loss may lead to creativity as a means of overcoming denial and of accepting the loss or losses. In Agee's *A Death in the Family*, Rufus Follett, aged seven, is a loose self-portrait of the author, who also lost his father at seven. Rufus is described at breakfast the morning after he hears of his father's death, and as the father's presence is still so strong and fresh in his mind, Rufus cannot yet believe that he is gone forever. Instead, like other children who are similarly bereaved,[5] he imagines his father joining the family for breakfast:

> Now maybe in just a minute he would walk right in and grin at her and say, 'Good morning, merry sunshine,' because her lip was sticking out, and even bend down and rub her cheek with his whiskers and then sit down and eat a big breakfast and then it would be all fun again and she would watch from the window when he went to work and just before he went out of sight he would turn around and she would wave but why wasn't he right here now where she wanted him to be and why didn't he come home? Ever any more. He won't come home ever any more. Won't come home again ever. But he will, though, because it's home (1980, p. 257).

The child's disbelief – 'it was not true' – is not dissimilar from the survivor's response – How mourn a city/ whose people are dead and whose dead are alive/ in the heart.' The child's denial of his loss stems partly from his ignorance of death's permanence, yet this denial persists irrationally even among adults who know full well that the loss is forever. As in Pagis' 'Ready for Parting', in which 'I see my dead come towards me, transparent and breathing', Kovner's dead are alive still 'in the heart'.

A mood of dark resignation mingled with cautious hope engulfs much Holocaust literature, and the anger which is a normal part of the grief process is often either muted or completely absent. The anger of the survivor is likely to be particularly complex and intense as it has so many potential targets: the perpetrators; those who could have helped but did nothing; other victims, including the dead; the survivor himself, for his own helplessness or shameful ineffectuality; and, most tragically, his own family and even his children. For this reason, the anger which should be mastered in the grief process often remains unresolved, distorted or suppressed.

An exception is found in the Hebrew poetry of Uri Zvi Greenberg, whose family was destroyed in the Holocaust and who later wrote an extraordinary series of dirges for European Jewry in

Rehovot ha-Nahar (Streets of the River, 1951). These poems are streaked with anger, often expressed through irony or sarcasm, directed at the perpetrators and, at times, at the victims. Greenberg's poems of wrath suggest that the increased militancy of the Jewish people from 1942, when news of the extermination of the Jews first reached the free world, and onwards was in no small measure a function of mourning. The violent anger in his poetry is presented in the context of mourning the dead and of preparing to begin a new life in Israel. The creative expression of this anger, again, may be seen as a means of giving form and obtaining mastery over vast, inchoate emotions as well as over the terror of living in a Godless, malevolently disordered world. The following lines are taken from the poem *Tahat Shen Maharashtam* ('Under their Ploughtooth'), in which 'there' refers to the killing fields of eastern Europe:

The snow has melted there again...
    the murderers turn back to farmers.
Out they go to plough, in the fields of my dead!
If the ploughtooth rolls out from the furrow
        a skeleton, mine,
The ploughman will have no sorrow or fear.
He'll smile...He knows it...for the blow of his tool
        he'll see again.

Springtime again in the country: flowerbulbs, lilac, singing birds
Sheep lie down in the shallow stream...
No longer the wandering Jews, beards and sidelocks,
In the inns no longer, with *talit* and *tzitzit*,
No longer in shops, with trinkets, cloth, groceries,
No longer in workshops, in the trains, in the market
        in synagogues;
They lie under the ploughtooth of Christians.
God has visited his Gentiles with munificent grace - -

The smouldering rage in this poem might easily be regarded as a thing apart from the grieving process and, indeed, anger after loss is often mistakenly separated from grief; in fact, it is a natural part of grief (Parkes, 1986). It may be aroused by the dead themselves, who are blamed, sometimes unconsciously, for dying; by the perpetrators, either real or imagined; by the frustration of searching in vain; by the injustice of the loss; by its finality. Anger, like denial, appears to be especially strong during the periods of numbness and yearning, when the bereaved has not

11

yet accepted the loss but clings anxiously and irrationally to the hope that the lost person can be brought back and punished for 'deserting' (Bowlby, 1980).

An espisode in Saul Bellow's novel *The Dean's December* shows how disturbing anger can be to the bereaved, even if conditions for mourning are fairly good. Minna Corde, an astrophysicist, and her husband, Albert, a dean of small American college, visit Rumania. During their stay, Minna's mother, a high-ranking Communist official, dies. Although she has not seen her mother for many years, Minna is overwhelmed by anger at her mother for dying: 'I wake up in the night, and everything good in my life seems to have leaked away. It's not just temporary. I feel as if it can never come back. It's black in the room, and even blacker and worse outside. It goes on and on and on, out there. I'm mourning my mother but I also feel terrible things about her. I'm horribly angry' (1982, p. 252–3). The dean tries to console her by saying that he felt similarly in his adolescence when his mother died: 'I remember being sore, too, feeling abandoned when my own mother died' (p. 255). But inwardly he feels that he is called upon, as he puts it, to bail out his wife's inundation of grief with a kitchen cup of psychology: '"It's supposed to be normal, not a sign that there's no love but just the reverse. But I guess the clinicians would say it wasn't the kind of love we'd feel if we were everything we should be. Well, that's standard psychiatry." To himself he added, That's what bothers me about it' (p. 257).

Anger after a loss may be turned inward in the form of guilt, and creativity may serve, again, to confront and master this guilt. No survival, writes Lifton (1967), can occur without severe guilt; but during the Holocaust, the Germans consistently forced the Jews to make agonizing moral choices in which a maximum of guilt would arise. In the ghetto of Vilna, the vast majority of Jews were murdered by the end of 1941. Those who survived had been given yellow cards, work permits. The Germans had not distributed these cards themselves, but forced the Jews to do so. For about a year and a half after the liquidations, writes Dawidowicz, the ghetto went through a period of 'normality'. The survivors gathered up the fragments of their broken lives:

> The normality that they reconstructed was external, part bulwark against the nightmares of the past, a grotesque ordinariness to combat memory. For the ghetto was haunted by 47,000 spectres. Each survivor was burdened by an intolerable weight of guilt feelings, created by the circumstances of the yellow

permits. Everyone who survived felt that his life had cost someone else's, a response common to survivors of all kinds of disasters. In Vilna the mathematics of survival were so simple and stark that self-reproach was the most common denominator (1983, pp. 350–1).

Long after the trauma, survivors may suffer guilt at having survived. Their natural sense of relief and triumph can blight their well-being. Questions gnaw at them: Why was I saved? Why did others die in my place? Why did I not help others more? This guilt may be interpreted as a significant part of the meaning of survival, a testimony to a humanity which has not been destroyed (Bettleheim, 1979). However, survivors themselves rarely speak of their guilt in an affirmative sense, and this is reflected in the literature by and about survivors.

In the play *Children of the Shadow* (1963) by the Israeli poet and playwright, Ben-Zion Tomer, the problem of survivor-guilt is the central theme. The young hero, Yoram, has escaped the clutches of the Nazis and come to Israel where he lives on a kibbutz and marries an Israeli. On the surface, he leads a well-integrated life. Yet, inwardly he is troubled by the past, by guilt at having survived. This guilt is raised to pathological pitch when members of his family, whom he thought dead, unexpectedly arrive in Israel. His guilt at not having shared their suffering is exacerbated by his contempt towards them, and his reluctance to know of their agonies. Their very existence is an affront to his fragile identity as an Israeli. He feels guilt, too, at his anger towards the victims for not having resisted their murderers. The sense of collective guilt, suppressed for many years, now rises up to condemn and imprison him: 'Their black tales make me the accused. Accused without accusation. Then I am sealed. Like a fortress. And as much as they try to burst inside me I am sealed even more. I am sealed – guilt rises in me. Guilt rises in me – I am sealed. What am I guilty of? What?...' Tr. Glenda Abramson (Abramson, 1979, pp. 126–7).

The survivor's guilt at simply living on is expressed with almost prosaic starkness and resignation by Karen Gershon in the poem 'I Was not There'. The repetition of phrases such as 'I was not there to comfort them' suggests that they have run over and over in the mind of the survivor:

The morning they set out from home
I was not there to comfort them
the dawn was innocent with snow

13

in mockery – it is not true
the dawn was neutral was immune
their shadows threaded it too soon
they were relieved that it had come
I was not there to comfort them...

Both my parents died in camps
I was not there to comfort them
I was not there they were alone
my mind refuses to conceive
the life the death they must have known
I must atone because I live
I could not have saved them from death
the ground is neutral underneath

But the atonement can be that of murderer as well as victim. Implicit in Pagis' 'Written in Pencil in the Sealed Railway Car' is the idea that all mankind shared the same origin and, therefore, bears collective responsibility and guilt:

here in this carload
i am eve
with abel my son
if you see my other son
cain son of man
tell him that i
(1981, p. 23)

It is cruelly ironic, nevertheless, that the degree of guilt felt by the survivors and their children is generally far greater than that felt by the perpetrators.

The survivor's guilt is exceptional in its severity, and in fact it is not at all unusual for a bereaved person to hold himself to be at least partly to blame for the loss; guilt, like anger, is a normal part of the grief process (Parkes, 1986). Guilt may arise from the hatred of the dead person, felt either while alive or as a result of dying, or both. The bereaved may have wished at some time for the death, or fantasized it, and consequently feels responsible: bereaved children are particularly likely to feel such guilt, all the more so if they do not receive convincing explanations and reassurances. In *A Death in the Family*, Agee draws attention to the common sense of guilt experienced after a loss in his brief description of Andrew, brother-in-law of the dead man, who feels 'absurd, ashamed, guilty, almost of cheating, even of murder, at

14

being alive' (1980, p. 153). A more profound guilt is described by the Italian poet Giuseppe Ungaretti in poetic fragments entitled *Giorno per Giorno* ('Day by Day'), written after the death of his nine-year-old son Antonietto in 1939. Antonietto had died of appendicitis after faulty medical treatment, and Ungaretti blamed himself:

> Will I always recall without remorse
> A bewitching agony of the senses?
> Blind man, listen: 'A spirit has departed
> Still unharmed by the common lash of life...'
>
> Will I be less cut down to hear no more
> The living cries of his innocence
> Than to feel almost dead in me
> The dreadful shudder of guilt?

The idealization of the dead is yet another part of the grief process which might find a creative outlet among Holocaust survivors as well as among those bereaved in more normal circumstances. In Paul Celan's *Espenbaum* ('Aspen Tree'), the poet's mother, who was murdered by the Nazis, is idealized in a series of associations with beautiful objects – an aspen tree, a dandelion, a rain cloud, a star. These images (which ironically echo the lyrics of the great German Romantics), appear to mitigate, and to make more bearable and controllable, the horror and pain of loss.[6] The dead mother is herself depicted as bewailing the communal tragedy: it may be that Celan is implying, again, the impossibility of mourning the victims of the Holocaust, that the dead must mourn themselves.

> Aspen tree, your leaves glint white into the dark.
> My mother's hair was never white.
>
> Dandelion, so green is the Ukraine.
> My fairhaired mother did not come home.
>
> Rain cloud, do you linger over the well?
> My gentle mother weeps for all.

Parallel instances of idealization of the dead are often found in creative literature – this aspect of mourning is familiar in normal grief: 'Memories of the negative aspects of the dead are easily lost', writes Parkes, 'and idealization is carried out by most bereaved people and encouraged by society (1986, p. 89). In particular, anger and guilt may arouse the mourner's need for restitution: the idealization of the lost person may counterbalance the anger and overcome the guilt and ambivalence. The recollection of the dead person's good qualities, and the suppression of his bad attributes, may ease the process of grief: in time idealization is dulled and is eventually replaced by a more balanced view. Milton's 'Lycidas', written in memory of his drowned friend Henry King in 1637, contains imagery of idealization – the tree, the flower, the star, as well as the shepherd and the vine – not dissimilar from that of Celan. In both poems, there is an implicit ironic contrast between the death and the continuation of life in the natural world. In 'Lycidas', however, there is the consolation of faith, whereas in Celan there is none.

> Thee shepherd, thee the woods, and desert caves,
> With wild thyme and the gadding vine o'ergrown,
> And all their echoes mourn.
> The willows and the hazel copses green,
> Shall now no more be seen,
> Fanning their joyous leaves to thy soft lays.

In the course of grief, the mourner may come to identify himself with the dead person, sometimes even going so far as to adopt his characteristics or the symptoms which led to his death. Among survivors this part of the grief process may be greatly distorted by guilt at living on or by the wish to die. An extreme form of identification with the dead may be found in Elie Wiesel's harrowing account, in *Night*, of the innocent child who is hanged in Auschwitz. This hanging sets the seal on the author's loss of belief in God: he becomes a kind of spiritual cannibal living on at the expense of the dead.

> For more than half an hour he stayed there, struggling between life and death, dying in slow agony under our eyes. And we had to look him full in the face. He was still alive when I passed in front of him. His tongue was still red, his eyes were not yet glazed.
> Behind me I heard the same man asking:
> 'Where is God now?'
> And I heard a voice within me answer him:
> 'Where is He? Here He is – He is hanging here, on this gallows...'
> That night the soup tasted of corpses (1960, pp. 82–3).

Later, in describing the forced march to Buchenwald towards the end of the war, Wiesel again states his identification with the dead; this, too, may signify his own closeness to death, if not his readiness to give up his life in despair:

We were outside. The icy wind stung my face. I bit my lips continually to prevent them from freezing. Round me, every-thing was dancing a dance of death. It made my head reel. I was walking in a cemetery, among stiffened corpses, logs of wood. Not a cry of distress, not a groan, nothing but a mass agony, in silence. No one asked anyone else for help. You died because you had to die. There was no fuss.

In every stiffened corpse I saw myself (p. 109).

The Yiddish poet Abraham Sutzkever, who survived the Vilna ghetto and went to Israel after the war, describes in the poem *Farfroyrene Yidn* ('Frozen Jews') a similarly horrifying identifica-tion of the survivor with the victims. The symmetry of the couplets laid out almost like the bodies which they describe might itself betoken the creative struggle to master the trauma:

I and blue carrion, face to face.
Frozen Jews in a snowy space.

Marble shrouds my skin.
Words ebb. Light grows thin.

I'm frozen, I'm rooted in place
like the naked old man enfeebled by ice.

Tr. Cynthia Ozick (Howe *et al.*, eds., 1987, p. 680).

Alongside of scenes such as these, the depiction of identifica-tion with the dead as a normal part of the grief process may seem paltry. Yet, there is a similarity: widows, for example, not uncom-monly feel a temporary sensation of identification with their lost husbands, and in some cases this might include a sense of seeing themselves in their husbands or of having their husbands inside them (Parkes, 1986).[7] The creative function of identification with the lost person is well expressed by Proust in *Remembrance of Things Past*. After the death in a riding accident of his mistress Albertine, Marcel observes that just as an artist lives in his work, so also a lost person may remain alive within the mourners, who graft the memory, as it were, on to their hearts:

It is often said that something may survive of a person after his death, if that person was an artist and put a little of himself into his work. It is perhaps in the same way that a sort of cutting

17

taken from one person and grafted on to the heart of another continues to carry on its existence even when the person from whom it had been detached has perished (1981, III, p. 534).

The following lines from John Donne illustrate a grafting of this sort, by which the bereaved may commonly identify himself with the lost person:

She is dead; and all which die
    To their first elements resolve;
And we were mutual elements to us,
    And made of one another.
My body then doth hers involve,
And those things whereof I consist, hereby
In me abundant grow, and burdenous,
    And nourish not, but smother.

'The Dissolution'

You that are she and you, that's double she,
    In her dead face, half of yourself shall see;
She was the other part, for so they do
    Which build them friendships, become one of two...

'To the Lady Bedford'

The mourner's identification with the lost person is gradually overshadowed by depression and despair, through which the bereaved may come to terms with the reality of the loss and begin a new life (Bowlby, 1980). The apathy and low-spirits associated with this phase of grief should not be a potentially fatal luxury, but this was the case among concentration camp inmates.[8] For many who underwent the horrors of transport and selection, the will to live was severely undermined. That, according to Bettelheim, 'is why the victims could be herded to the gas chambers without resisting: the transport had turned many of them into walking corpses' (1979, p. 101). For many of the transport survivors, the period of grief which followed was too much. The vast majority of those who died at Buchenwald, writes Bettelheim, died soon after arrival. Those who mourned their lost family and friends, not to speak of their past lives, and their human dignity, put their lives at risk: they were more likely to survive by suppressing grief. After the war, survivors were often assailed with greater vehemence by the emotions which should have been worked through at the proper time, years earlier.

An extreme distortion of the normal phase of grief may be seen in Primo Levi's account, in his memoir of Auschwitz *If This is a Man* (1947), of those inmates who, overwhelmed and exhausted by death and dehumanization, by hunger and cold, by terror and illness, committed a form of spiritual suicide, continuing to function like lifeless automatons. Levi describes these presences crowding his memory, threatening to turn him into one of them, and it may be that by describing them he keeps this identification at bay:

> ...they, the *Muselmänner*, the drowned, form the backbone of the camp, an anonymous mass, continually renewed and always identical, of non-men who march and labour in silence, the divine spark dead within them, already too empty to really suffer. One hesitates to call them living: one hesitates to call their death death, in the face of which they have no fear, as they are too tired to understand.
>
> They crowd my memory with their faceless presences, and if I could enclose all the evil of our time in one image, I would choose this image which is familiar to me: an emaciated man, with head dropped and shoulders curved, on whose face and in whose eyes not a trace of a thought is to be seen (1979, p. 96).

Most attempts to depict the normal phase of depression after the loss of one loved person must pale alongside of this infamous picture. Yet, again, an underlying similarity may be detected between these hollow men and the severely bereaved who have reached the end of their tether. Perhaps the closest to these in literature is Job, with whom survivors are often compared. In despair at the sudden, arbitrary loss of his family as well as of his health, honour and property, Job asks beseechingly why life is given to those who shun it. He may be asking to die, yet his ability to question shows that the spark of life is still in him:

> Why is light given to him that is in misery,
>   and life to the bitter in soul,
> who long for death, but it comes not,
>   and dig for it more than for hid treasures;
> who rejoice exceedingly,
>   and are glad, when they find the grave?
> Why is light given to a man whose way is hid,
>   whom God has hedged in?
> For my sighing comes as my bread,
>   and my groanings are poured out like water.
>   (*RSV*, iii, 20–4)

Job achieves nothing concrete through his complaints and argu-
ments, and when finally answered by the voice of God from the
storm, can only resign himself to God's will, 'and repent in dust
and ashes'. Yet Job's outrage and self-pity, fashioned with rhy-
thmic power and masterful imagery, take on a life of their own in
a realm of art beyond grief and physical suffering, Significantly,
in the final chapter of the book, Job's transformation from the
angry, self-justifying and despairing questioner to the honoured,
prosperous and contented patriarch is marked by a turn from
poetry to prose. In much the same way, an artist motivated by
grief which can be overcome, should be able to turn to other
things once he has expressed it in his art.

To the survivor-artist, in contrast, the trauma more often than
not continues as the dominant force in his art; and, in general, the
creative expression of grief appears to take on particular importance as a means of confronting and attempting to master delayed
grief. Art may enable the artist not just to depict the grief process,
or parts of it, but also, up to a point, to fill in the lacunae of his
mourning, and in doing so creatively, to find meaning in the
midst of grief. Specific functions might thus be ascribed to the
creative expression of grief: for example, by portraying depression, the survivor might attempt to overcome or mitigate despair;
by depicting the identification with the dead, he might give them
a form of posthumous life; through the expression of idealization,
guilt, and anger, he may struggle to achieve restitution with the
dead; and through denial, to accept; through the creative depiction of yearning, he may attempt to 'find' and recover the dead;
and through numbness, to feel.

Among many survivors, however, as among many who suffer
particularly cruel bereavements in normal times, the mastery of
the trauma is a virtual impossibility. Although the survivor may
wish to be ready for parting, he cannot easily do so. The reasons
are clear in the following poem by the Hebrew poet Natan Zach,
'Against Parting':

> My tailor is against parting.
> That's why, he
> said, he's not going away;
> he doesn't want to part
> from his one daughter. He's definitely
> against parting.
> Once, he parted from his wife, and
> she he

saw no more of (Auschwitz).
Parted
from his three sisters and
these he never
saw (Buchenwald).
He once parted from his mother (his father
died of a fine, and ripe age). Now
he's against parting.

Tr. Jon Silkin (Silkin, ed., 1973, p. 168)

The function of creativity when mourning is impossible might include the expression of this impossibility. Tadeusz Borowski, who survived Auschwitz only to commit suicide after the war by gassing, describes the coagulation and stiffening of his physical sensibilities which he attempted, futilely, to reverse through his writings:

I take out fresh paper, arrange it neatly on the desk, and closing my eyes try to find within me a tender feeling for the workmen hammering the rails, for the peasant women with their ersatz sour cream, the trains full of merchandise, the fading sky above the ruins, for the passers-by on the street below and the newly installed windows, and even for my wife who is washing dishes in the kitchen alcove; and with a tremendous intellectual effort I attempt to grasp the true significance of the events, things and people I have seen (1976, p. 180).

Through creativity, the survivor may attempt not merely to comprehend what he has gone through, but also to invest his life with meaning. For the act of creation, which is also an act of testimony, may be perceived as the purpose for which he has been granted life. Viktor Frankl, a psychotherapist who was imprisoned in Auschwitz, relates a memory of the camp:

. . . two people sat before me, both resolved to commit suicide. Both used a phrase which was a stereotype in the camp: 'I have nothing more to expect of life.' Now, the initial requirement was to have the two undergo a Copernican reversal such that they should no longer ask *what they could expect of life*, but were made aware of the fact that *life was awaiting something from them* – that for each of them, indeed for all, somebody or something was waiting, whether it was a piece of work to be done or another human being (1973, pp. 102–3).

In the act of creation, of testimony, survivor-artists may show

how strongly they feel that life is awaiting something from them: it may be that, in general, creativity deriving from loss, while lacking the intense sense of mission which animates much Holocaust literature, has for its underlying purpose the investment of life with meaning through the salvaging of truth and beauty from the pain and the waste time.

2

LOSS AND CREATIVITY

What are the roles of creativity in the wake of loss? We have seen that creativity may help to express, to master and work through the grief process; it might give the bereaved greater control over his life by enabling him to test and even form the new reality after the loss; it might act as a memorial of the lost person, or even represent a victory of sorts over death, the love and care lavished upon the work of art serving as a permanent testimony to the artist's attachment to the lost person. Creativity may also serve to confront and attempt to resolve emotional conflicts and heal wounds caused by the loss itself, or by unhappy elements in the relationship which the loss revives. The satisfaction of creating a thing of beauty may palliate the artist's grief, and the distancing of the self from grief through art may be similarly therapeutic. We possess art, wrote Nietzsche, so that we shall not perish of truth.

Why do some people express grief in art while the majority do not? It may be that for most people it is enough to feel grief and that to record its pain is superfluous, or other outlets may be available, in family and friends, work and recreation. The artist might, to some extent, be cut off from these outlets, or find them insufficient, falling back on inner creative resources. In some cases, a severe bereavement may silence the artist: the Hebrew poetess Yocheved Bat-Miriam ceased writing after the death of her son. Among other writers, such as Walt Whitman, a loss may galvanize a mediocre talent and transform it to greatness.

Whitman's poetry throws into sharp relief the question whether, or to what extent, loss might account for the mystery of the creative gift. Whitman's fame rests almost entirely on one book of poems, *Leaves of Grass*, which he wrote in his Brooklyn home as his father lay dying in another room. (The father died a few days after the publication of the first edition of *Leaves of Grass* in 1855.) It is estimated that a full two-thirds of Whitman's output was written in the year before and the year after this loss. His poetry evidently served as a catharsis, a means of working through the grief process and of recreating himself. The originality of *Leaves of Grass* is astonishing when considered alongside

23

Whitman's previous writings. Though he wrote short stories and poems before, he was little more than a competent hack journalist, an 'ordinary American man with no visible talents' (Zweig, 1984, p. 4). Virtually nothing hints at the flourishing of his genius in *Leaves of Grass*. Did the father's death create Whitman's gift or free it?

Whitman's poetry was bound up with the evolution of his new identity during and after the death. In his poetry, as in life, he saw himself as a father-healer, and even before the father died he seems to have organized his life around a fantasy of being father to his younger brothers and partner to his mother (Black, 1975, p. 31). Why this should have been the case is not entirely clear, but when the father became a helpless, dying invalid, Whitman made this fantasy real: he took over his father's role, supporting the family, caring for his mother, overseeing the life of his siblings, paying the bills. At this time he began his life's work.

Whitman's poetry is a prescription of health and Eros and an antidote to disease and Thanatos. To Whitman, all life, and death too, is good: 'To die is different from what anyone supposed, and luckier.' Whitman's new identity was that of America come-of-age, powerful, confident, creative, heir to the European tradition, the 'corpse' that had fathered the New World. In the preface to *Leaves of Grass*, he wrote: 'America...perceives that the corpse is slowly borne from the eating and sleeping rooms of the house...that its action has descended to the stalwart and well-shaped heir who approaches.' Zweig notes the possible psychological link between the idea of America replacing Europe and Whitman taking his father's place and, in so doing, identifying himself with America: 'The son's self-willed rise had paralleled his father's decline, as if the empty place left by the father provided room for the son to change his life' (p. 237).

Parkes (1986) has written that to gain a new identity after a loss is an integral part of the grief process and there is no doubt that Whitman's poetry illustrates and, indeed, enacts such a transformation. Still, Whitman's circumstances and experiences are duplicated in thousands of lives for whom creativity is not an outlet and it is rarely possible in any case to say why an artist struggling to depict grief should choose or form a particular technique or transform certain aspects of his experience, rather than others. Where is the line between truth and fiction in creativity deriving from loss? In order to explore this question, we will take illustrations of poetic license in depictions of loss by John Donne, Tennyson, James Joyce and Eugene O'Neill where the falsehoods in each case are created in the service of deeper truths.

Donne's *Anniversaries* (1611–12), for example, are patently insincere as a commemoration of Elizabeth Drury, to whom they are dedicated. Elizabeth Drury was the fourteen-year-old daughter of a wealthy London landowner, Robert Drury, who may have commissioned the poems. Ben Jonson's famous criticism of the poem – 'If it had been written of the Virgin Mary, it had been something' – is entirely apt especially as Donne had never met Elizabeth Drury. Yet, the poem is utterly genuine and deeply moving in its expression of grief, and it is right to ask if Donne might have been thinking of a personal loss or losses:

> Sick world, yea dead, yea putrefied, since she
> Thy intrinsic balm, and thy preservative,
> Can never be renewed, thou never live. . .
> The sun is lost, and th' earth, and no man's wit
> Can well direct him where to look for it. . .
> She, she, is dead; she's dead: when thou know'st this,
> Thou know'st how wan a ghost this our world is. . .

> (I, 56–8, 207–8, 369–70)

This seemingly exaggerated grief for Elizabeth Drury might be ascribed in part to Donne's loss of three sisters before he was ten: the first, who died when he was about five, was named Elizabeth. It may be that, as in the case of De Quincey after the death of his sister Jane,[1] Donne was too young properly to mourn Elizabeth at the time of her death. The death of Elizabeth Drury – no matter that he did not know her personally – may have opened long-sealed wellsprings of grief for his sister, or sisters, and found expression in the *Anniversaries*.

Another prominent illustration of the use of poetic license in a creative response to grief is Tennyson's *In Memoriam*, which, like Donne's *Anniversaries*, is an elegy the emotion of which appears to be in excess of the facts. The poem was triggered off by the death of Tennyson's friend, Arthur Hallam, a fellow undergraduate at Cambridge, in mid-1833. The poem was begun shortly afterwards and is dedicated to Hallam, but it can hardly be understood as a reaction to Hallam's death alone. For one thing, it went on far too long – nearly two decades were spent in writing it. It may be that with Hallam's death, as Martin writes, Tennyson lost his most important anchor to reality and virtually gave up the will to live: 'His one remaining resort was to poetry, used as a narcotic for an existence made temporarily meaningless' (1980, p. 184). Yet, over a year prior to Hallam's death, Tennyson had entered 'a desperately long period of discontent and restlessness' (p. 149). *In Memoriam* is a record of this time, exploring the emotional upheavals and griefs which came from a variety of causes. Chief among these, probably, was the death of Tennyson's father, though there is virtually nothing in his poetry indicating the depth of his feeling for his father, who had been an alcoholic, epileptic, and drug addict. After his death, Martin writes, Tennyson 'was probably the one of the family who suffered most' (p. 132). These circumstances might help to explain why the poet's mourning after his death lasted for such a long time. The grief focused creatively on Hallam rather than on the father as it was the more manageable, and the poem took so long to develop as the grief for the father was slow to be resolved. As in the *Anniversaries*, a relatively minor loss sets off a creative response to other, deeper and harder griefs.

The line between truth and fiction in the depiction of grief is similarly blurred in James Joyce's *Ulysses* (1922). In 1908, Joyce's wife suffered a miscarriage (two previous babies had been born normally), and she had no more children: 'This miscarriage', writes Richard Ellmann, 'helped to make Bloom's chief sorrow in *Ulysses*, the death just after birth of his son Rudy' (1982, p. 269). The effects of this loss, however, are given a significance in *Ulysses* which they did not have in Joyce's own life. For the death of Bloom's son has brought on a 'limitation of fertility', and has, in effect, made Bloom impotent. Tucked away in an obscure corner of the 'Ithaca' section of *Ulysses* is the clinical revelation that since Rudy's death, 'there remained a period of 10 years, 5 months and 18 days during which carnal intercourse had been incomplete, without ejaculation of semen within the natural female organ' (1973, p. 657). Bloom's impotence is bound up with grief for his son. His delayed mourning is central to the plot of *Ulysses* as it furnishes the background to many of Bloom's fantasies, his wife's affair with another man, and his empathetic attachment to Stephen Dedalus, which is governed in part by his frustrated desire for a son.[2]

The distinctions between author, implied author, and protagonist, whether narrator or character (Booth, 1961), must often be taken into account in assessing the use of creative license in the depiction of grief. At times, poetic license may be used blatantly in order to heighten the biographical significance of a work of art: an example is found in O'Neill's play *Long Day's Journey Into Night* (1956), which has for its background the death of O'Neill's brother, Edmund, several years before O'Neill's birth in 1889. (The play, completed in 1940, was so searingly personal that O'Neill forbade its publication before his death.) The character based on O'Neill himself is called after the dead child, Edmund, while the dead child is given O'Neill's name, Eugene. The mother, a morphine addict since Edmund's painful birth, confesses her self-blame and guilt over Eugene's death: 'I blame only myself. I swore after Eugene died I would never have another baby. I was to blame for his death' (p. 87). Apart from the changing of the names, O'Neill's characterization seems to have been largely factual, though no doubt altered at times, or sifted through the reminiscences of others, in order to serve his dramatic purposes. The details of Edmund's death and the mother's response are presented in the play. O'Neill's mother, Ella, was absent when in 1885 her eldest child, Jamie, who had measles, entered the baby's room. Edmund contracted measles and died. The mother never forgave herself, nor did she cease mourning for Edmund. She did not want another child and had a series of brought-on abortions before Eugene's birth: 'Ella was upset at the thought of another child blurring her memories of Edmund and replacing him in her heart; she felt it her duty, as a form of penance, to keep the dead child forever enshrined in her thoughts' (Sheaffer, 1968, p. 21). O'Neill's license in giving himself his dead brother's name is symbolic of his identification with his brother, for his existence was bound up and tortured by this loss. In the play, Edmund speaks for O'Neill when he confesses his lifelong sense of alienation from others and his morbidity, which lie at the root of his artistic vocation: 'It was a great mistake, my being born a man, I would have been much more successful as a sea gull or a fish. As it is, I will always be a stranger who never feels at home, who does not really want and is not really wanted, who can never belong, who must always be a little in love with death!' (pp. 153–4).[3] O'Neill's play is a reconstruction of a set of relationships many years after they have come to an end. Perhaps more revealing of the impact of loss upon creativity are works written at the time of a loss, in which grief is not merely the substance and meaning of the art but its course is substantially affected by the act of creation: Thomas Hardy's poems of 1912–13, S.J. Agnon's stories of 1908–11, and D.H. Lawrence's works of 1910–12. Although these writings have been subjected to extensive literary analysis,[4] they have not previously been studied in the context of loss and creativity, and for this reason a brief discussion of the general relationship between clinical and creative writings on grief may be useful at this point.

Modern research on loss, a good survey of which is given by Bowlby (1980), has organized and clarified much that was already known or suspected: it has distinguished between normal and pathological grief; analyzed similarities between the mourning of children and of adults; emphasized the importance of the conditions for mourning in determining the course of grief; showed that grief can last far longer than some like to think, for one does not 'get over' a loss so easily; and, finally, has made clear that a number of reactions not generally regarded as part of normal grief, such as 'seeing' the lost person or being angry with him or her, are in fact not uncommon.

Nevertheless, this research has not described the components of grief more effectively than creative artists, and does not attempt to do so. While it is true that each grief has its own emphases and length, and circumstances may lend grief many unpredictable shades, twists and intensities, in a general way a number of phases and characteristics appear universally to mark the progress of grief: all of these are depicted in literature and most have been discussed in the previous chapter. In normal grief four main phases may be identified, although these may oscillate or overlap with one another (Bowlby, 1980; Parkes, 1986). First, on suffering the loss there is a sensation of numbness, which may last for as little as a few hours and generally passes within a week or so. Second, the bereaved yearns and searches for the lost person – this may last for months or even years. Third, despairing of the possibility that the lost person will return, the bereaved undergoes depression, and this too may last for long periods. Fourth, and finally, he will come to terms with the loss and reorganize his life in accordance with the changed circumstances.

Within these phases, in addition, a number of prominent grief characteristics may also appear. During the early phases of grief, the bereaved is often unable to believe that the loss is final and will deny the loss. In some cases he may feel an inexplicable sensation of triumph and feelings of anger and guilt are not uncommon. The bereaved may perceive of the lost person in a distorted fashion, excessively hated or idealized, before arriving at a more balanced image in the latter part of grief and, as part of the healing process, he may eventually come to feel that he has taken on a new identity. Normal grief involves gradual change and the mitigation of pain as the bereaved returns to everyday life; abnormal grief (creative expressions of which are the subject of Chapter Eight below) means that some part or parts of the grief process are not worked through but remain in a chronic, often distorted form.

Against this clinical background, in which grief is perceived

28

as a dynamic process bringing the mourner back to normal life, the creative responses to loss of Hardy, Agnon, and Lawrence may be more clearly understood. Some of the phases and characteristics of grief are more pronounced in one writer than the others, but this is in the nature of grief and of creative license.

Hardy's *Poems of 1912–13* were written after the death of his wife, Emma, in November 1912. Even allowing for transmutation in the creative process, it seems that, to a large extent, Hardy's mourning is depicted faithfully. The poems, which are mostly arranged in chronological order, are a unique testimony, moving beyond words, to the evolution of grief in the first months. Most of the chief elements of grief are found in these poems: the poet's numbness at the unexpectedness of the loss, his remorse and anger, denial and searching – he frequently imagines his wife's voice or presence – his depression and despair, his desire to join her in death, and his eventual movement towards recovery, all spur Hardy's creative impulse and enter the fabric of his poetry. As one can trace the line of impact of stone on shattered glass, so also one can see the shock in Hardy's poems giving way to bitterness at lost happiness and the longing to relive the past, and his despair, in turn, giving way to acceptance and restitution as he became fascinated by memories of his courtship and marriage forty years previously.

After a romantic, happy start, the marriage had foundered – 'Things were not lastly as firstly well', Hardy confesses in 'After a Journey'. As the years passed, Emma Hardy suffered increasingly from mental illness, and the couple, while continuing to live together, moved emotionally apart. In her later years, Emma, to Hardy's distress, was afflicted with the delusion that she was being conspired against and followed. She convinced herself that she, and not Hardy, had written the Wessex novels. According to Hardy's second wife, the couple were about to separate at the time of Emma's death (Millgate, 1982, pp. 489–90).

The unexpectedness of the loss is alluded to in the poem 'Your Last Journey', written the month after Emma's death. In this poem, Hardy recalls that just eight days before her death, Emma had passed the very spot in which she was to be buried. In a deeper sense, though, Hardy had lost her long before: his regret over the suddenness of her passing is mingled with remorse at having lost touch with her in recent years, as she became less stable, for he was no longer close enough and, perhaps, no longer cared, to see her decline:

29

I drove not with you...Yet had I sat
At your side that eve I should not have seen
That the countenance I was glancing at
Had a last-time look in the flickering sheen,
Nor have read the writing upon your face,
'I go hence soon to my resting place...'

'Without Ceremony' touches again on the harsh abruptness of the death:

...now that you disappear
For ever in that swift style,
Your meaning seems to me
Just as it used to be:
'Good-bye is not worth while!'

The immediate impact of the loss on Hardy is visible also in 'The Prospect', dating from December 1912. The poet depicts the winter landscape with its icy air, 'a numbing that threatens snow', as the image of his wan future, dead and cold. Winter numbness mirrors the poet's numbness in the throes of grief.

As the weeks wore on, Hardy's grief became an all-consuming obsession in his poetry. In 'The Going', written at the same time as 'Your Last Journey' and 'The Prospect', Hardy reveals further traces of his remorse and anger at Emma's passing, as well as his searching for her:

Why do you make me leave the house
And think for a breath it is you I see
At the end of the alley of bending boughs
Where so often at dusk you used to be;
  Till in the darkening dankness
  The yawning blankness
Of the perspective sickens me!

Just as in 'The Haunter', the poet speaks to his dead wife, so also, in 'The Voice', he imagines her calling to him.[5] In this poem, Emma's presence is called up, again, by the sound of the wind, this time with strong intimations of the finality of her absence:

Woman much missed, how you call to me, call to me...
Or is it only the breeze, in its listlessness
Travelling across the wet mead to me here,
You being ever dissolved to existlessness,
Heard no more again far or near?

The poet's searching for his wife, his denial of her death and his remorse towards her mark the other poems written during this period and later: she appears to him as a 'faithful phantom' ('The Haunter'), a 'phantom figure' ('At Castle Boterel'), a 'thin ghost' whom the poet frailly follows ('After a Journey'). In one poem, the poet meditates upon a scene of his courtship and wonders if the loss can truly be permanent: 'Shall she and I not go there once more now March is nigh?' ('On Beeny Cliff'). In another poem, a moth tapping at a window-pane makes him think that his wife is knocking, and he sees her face and hears her calling him to join her ('Something Tapped'). In yet another poem, a lock of her hair which she gave him during their courtship arouses in him the hope, irrational he knows, for her to be restored to life:

> Yet this one curl, untouched of time,
> Beams with live brown as in its prime,
> So that it seems that I even could now
> Restore it to the living brow...

'Rain on a Grave', dated 31 January 1913, conveys both the poet's wish for the restoration of his wife and his stronger wish to join her in death:

> Would that I lay there
> And she were housed here!
> Or better, together
> Were folded there away
> Exposed to one weather...

The turning point in Hardy's grief was his visit in March 1913 to Cornwall, where he had courted Emma, and particularly to the church of St Juliot where he had first met her: 'much of my life claims this spot as its key' ('A Dream or No'). The poems written during this visit, including 'At Castle Boterel' and 'After a Journey', mark the high point of Hardy's art. What distinguishes these poems, apart from their technical excellence (which in Hardy one almost takes for granted), is their evocation of the way in which the past lives on in the present, mirroring, nourishing and consoling it. Painful as Hardy's visit was, it revived all that was most alive and beautiful in his love for Emma and which had, in the intervening years, been worn down and tainted.

The consolatory nature of Emma's memory is alluded to already in 'The Haunter', apparently written prior to the Cornwall visit. Here, the presence of the dead wife is itself comfort for the loss. She is the speaker in the poem:

If he but sigh since my loss befell him
  Straight to his side I go.
Tell him a faithful one is doing
  All that love can do
Still that his path may be worth pursuing,
  And to bring peace thereto.

In 'After a Journey', Hardy's climactic poem of restitution, the wife's presence is all-pervasive, 'facing round about me everywhere'. Yet, by fixing his mind on memories of affirmation, the poet can overcome the dark night of his grief:

Ignorant of what there is flitting here to see,
  The waked birds preen and the seals flop lazily;
Soon you will have, Dear, to vanish from me,
  For the stars close their shutters and the dawn
  whitens hazily.
Trust me, I mind not, though Life lours,
  The bringing me here; nay, bring me here again!
    I am just the same as when
Our days were a joy, and our paths through flowers.

Agnon's stories written at the time of his mother's death in 1909 provide an equally remarkable inner portrait of the writer's grief as experienced at the time.[6] Whereas Hardy's *Poems of 1912–13* are the work of a man of over seventy, Agnon's stories of 1908–11 heralded a precocious start to his career: he was a full half-century younger than Hardy. At this time, in the spring of 1908, he left his birthplace, the east European town of Buczacz, and went on his own to Palestine. He had written a great deal prior to his departure, in Yiddish more than in Hebrew, and had shown literary promise, but little more. Arnold Band, in his definitive critical study of Agnon, *Nostalgia and Nightmare*, points out that 'the Buczacz stories would hardly lead us to the suspicion that S.Y. Czaczkes [Agnon adopted his pseudonym in 1908, with the publication of the story 'Agunot'] had the same literary potential as S.Y. Agnon of Jaffa. The advance in writing ability is unusual' (1968, p. 67).[7]

After landing in Jaffa, Agnon underwent an artistic metamorphosis. His story 'Agunot', composed only a few months after his arrival, is a soaring achievement, stamped with a distinctive style, filled with delicate shades of feeling and music, an unmistakable triumph for a man barely into his twenties. Some credit for Agnon's blossoming as an artist must go to the cultural milieu of his new home, where Hebrew, however imperfectly used, was a living and inspiring language. But can the change in environment alone explain Agnon's artistic leap forward?

Agnon left home in a time of crisis. His mother, Esther, was seriously ill with a heart condition. Her precarious health must have stirred up his guilt at leaving her. Perhaps for this reason he would sometimes claim to have arrived in Jaffa in the late spring of 1909, after her death: in fact, he had arrived a full year beforehand.[8]

Judging from the content of the stories written at this time, it seems likely that the final illness and death of Agnon's mother precipitated his astonishingly rapid maturity as an artist. Agnon's grief found an outlet in the realm of art, where a monument to the dead may be erected, where the relationship may be gone over and the trauma of loss confronted.

As the eldest of five children, Agnon had a special place in his mother's affections. They were drawn even more closely together by the frequent absences of her husband on business (he was a furrier) and by her infirmity. She spurred her son's literary ambitions, introducing him to the classics in world literature, stimulating him to be an artist.

The stories which Agnon wrote during his mother's final illness and after her death – 'Agunot', 'The Well of Miriam', 'The Outcast', 'The Sister', and others – act as inadvertent milestones of the progress of his mourning. 'Agunot' was written several months before the death, and it reflects his grief over the separation from her. He had never before been away from home for any length of time. He must have suspected also, and feared, that he would never see her again. Even so, 'Agunot' is not simply disguised autobiography for there are clear signs here (as in later stories) that even at this time Agnon was acutely conscious of the need for artistic distance. A woman, not a man, suffers the loss of her mother. At the same time, a man – in this story, the artist Ben Uri – though he does not seem directly touched by this loss, is afflicted with grief, remorse and guilt, as if he, too, were bereaved.

'Agunot' is a central work in the Agnon canon. Set in nineteenth-century Jerusalem, it tells of the wealthy Ahiezer who betrothes his daughter, Dinah, to a young rabbi for whom he builds a house of prayer and study. He hires Ben Uri to carve the Holy Ark, without which the building is like a soulless body. Ben Uri is attracted to Dinah, but his absorption in his art is such that he neglects her. His frame of mind after finishing the Ark, his masterpiece, is similar to that of a bereaved person: he feels 'like an empty vessel', 'a limb torn from his body', it is 'the end of his spiritual life', 'he was overcome by misery and began to cry unawares'. His love for Dinah is reawakened to no avail: 'it was hard and troublesome for him and he had great longings...if only he could see that lovely girl, Dinah, and pour out his heart to her...but she had already disappeared' (1908, p. 56).[9]

The introduction of the motif of the dead mother is by no means essential to the plot. Yet, Dinah's dead mother enters the story after Dinah, enraged with jealousy, pushes over Ben Uri's Ark. She feels bitter remorse for this deed for by tainting herself with sin, she no longer resembles her mother:

> On her couch at night Dinah lies. Her heart beats mercilessly with remorse. Her wickedness is great, her sin unendurable. She buries her head in the pillow, tormented with shame – she cannot cry. Her sin stands before her like an angel with sword drawn, about to do her harm...Dinah leaped from the bed, lit a taper – and saw the large mirror on the wall. The mirror had belonged to her mother, but now it held nothing of her good-ness. Dinah knew that if she stood in front of it, it would only show her own face, the face of a sinner, a rebel...'Mother, mother!' her heart cried out, for she longed to pour her sorrow out – but she found no one (p. 57).

Dinah's guilty feeling of being judged and her contrition, though brought on by the act of violence against the Ark, resembles the emotions often felt by the bereaved towards the dead. Her anger, too, is not unusual after a death.

From 'Agunot' onwards, the Agnon hero cannot fully detach the memory of his dead mother from other women to whom he becomes attached. In 'The Well of Miriam', written shortly after the death of Agnon's own mother, the grief and almost frantic despair at the loss of the beloved are so great that art appears to be overcome by autobiography. Three stories are contained in one: the frame story of Hemdat's journey to Palestine, his yearn-ing for a young woman, Miriam, and his worry for his mother's health and then the two stories which he writes, one entitled 'Luz', about himself and the dying Zohara whom he loves, and the second about Raphael the scribe and his wife Miriam (this was the seed of Agnon's later story, 'The Legend of the Scribe'). The three stories have this in common: each tells of an artist whose beloved is ill and dies before her time. In each case, the grief is expressed in art. Raphael writes a scroll in memory of his wife 'who passed away in the prime of her days'; Hemdat, after Zohara's death, writes the story 'Luz' in her memory; and in the frame story he describes the imminent death of his mother.

Agnon's grief is an integral part of these and other, more sophisticated, works written at this time and later. 'The Outcast', for example, was begun at the time that Agnon wrote 'Agunot' and 'The Well of Miriam'. This story describes a young man, Gershom, who lives in an east European town in the last century. The premature death of his mother drives Gershom to an infantilism which prevents him from separating her memory from the image of his financée. Lying in his mother's bed, he imagines himself a baby by his mother's side, then he thinks of his fiancée: 'Childishness overcame him, as it he were a baby by his mother's side. Sleep enveloped him sweetened with passages from the *Song of Songs* and with the image of his betrothed' (*Collected Works*, II, p. 37). Objects belonging to his mother are charged with meaning for him: her prayer book becomes almost an extension of her, an object of semi-erotic veneration and longing: 'How he desired to embrace and kiss his mother's prayer book. When she, of blessed memory, had prayed, her hands would embrace the covers as the hands of Moses had grasped the two Tablets of the Law' (p. 32). Gershom's grief breaks his heart, and the story ends with his death. In this story Agnon is clearly exploring the direction in which his grief was taking him at one point, but which he overcame, perhaps largely thanks to his art.

Like 'The Outcast', 'The Sister', published in 1911, tells of a young man, again a thinly-disguised self-portrait of the author, who has recently lost his mother and is living in Jaffa; he enters his sister's room and watches her unseen, deeply moved by her resemblance to their mother: 'She sat by the window. His mother, of blessed memory, would do the same...the same trembling shoulders, the same bent head, the same peculiar sadness enveloping those who approached her' (III, p. 406). The sister is reading a novel which had belonged to her mother and, like her, she leaves it unfinished.[10] Overcome by the memory of his mother, the young man kisses his sister passionately.

Agnon's preoccupation with the ailing or dead mother or mother-figure recurs in several of his important later works. In some of these, such as 'Iddo and Enam', the mood of loss and searching prevails, but in an ethereal form, as if the hurt has shrunk, leaving a mist of grief, a scar hidden at their centre. Yet, the clearest, most forceful expressions of the shock of bereavement and the process of grief appear in the early stories written at the time of the mother's death. Crude as these stories are in some respects – they are, after all, the work of a very young man struggling to create his own artistic voice – they are impressive for their beauty and emotional conviction. Agnon's separation from his mother, her final illness and death, were among the chief catalysts in his rapid growth in artistic maturity, bringing to the surface conflicts and preoccupations which haunted him to the end of his life.

D.H. Lawrence belonged to the same generation as Agnon and came to artistic maturity at about the same time, also during the emotional crisis of his mother's death, in December 1910. Unlike Agnon, he was at home, in Eastwood, Nottinghamshire, at the time, and he nursed his mother as she was dying of cancer in the autumn of 1910. His response to this, the greatest blow of his life, was to explore his grief, confronting it again and again until he emerged from it some two years later. He, too, had been unusually close to his mother, and his shock and despair when he realized that she was dying found an immediate outlet in creativity: while he sat by her bed he wrote poems and began the first draft of *Sons and Lovers*.[11] Lawrence's awareness of the importance of his mother's death in his creative life is stated in the poem 'The Inheritance', in which the mother bequeaths her son the 'gift of tongues', the power of his art:

I am dazed with the farewell
But I scarcely feel your loss.
You left me a gift
Of tongues, so the shadows tell
Me things, and the silences toss
Me their drift.

The years 1910–12, from the death of his mother until and after his elopement with Frieda Weekley, saw an extraordinary outpouring of creativity when he wrote most of the poems in *Amores*, *Love Poems*, *New Poems*, the novel *The Trespasser*, drafts of most of the stories in *The Prussian Officer*, including 'The Vicar's Daughter', and crowning this achievement, the novel *Sons and Lovers*. As in Agnon's case, Lawrence's style changed in the process of his grief, from the awkward, imprecise romanticism of his youth to a more mature and distinctive style, sharper and freer, and more realistic emotionally.

The period after the mother's death was also a turning point in Lawrence's physical health, and the beginning of his serious illness can be traced to the effects of his grief. In a cancelled passage in the 1928 preface to his *Collected Poems*, Lawrence wrote of his 'sick year', when 'for me, everything collapsed, save the mystery of death, and the haunting of death in life. I was twenty-five and from the death of my mother, the world began to dissolve around me, beautiful, iridescent, but passing away substanceless. Till I almost dissolved away myself, and was very ill' (1972, p. 851). In some of his poems, he describes the physical effects of his grief:

My chest gapes open sometimes
　At the wound's gaping cicatrice

'Bereavement'

What is the heavy, hot hand
That is always grasping me;
I can always feel it on my chest.

'Loss'

His relentless obsession with his loss at this time may be gauged by the titles of these poems and others such as 'My Mother Dead' (later changed to 'The End'), 'The Dead Mother' (later 'The Bride'), and 'My Love, My Mother' (later 'The Virgin Mother'). It may be too that Lawrence changed the titles as the obsession appeared to be too glaring. The openings of some of these poems – 'Since you did depart' ('The Inheritance'), 'Since I lost you...' ('Silence') – give further testimony to the depth of Lawrence's grief.

In the 1928 preface to his *Collected Poems*, Lawrence acknowledged that 'many of the poems are so personal that, in their fragmentary fashion, they make up a biography of an emotional and inner life' (1972, p. 27). The content of these poems later found its way into *Sons and Lovers* and other works: the main difference between the poetry and the prose is that the poetry is often an immediate creative reaction to grief, perhaps even written down at the time, whereas the prose explores this grief, amplifying and adapting it in the dynamic context of family bonds, with the mother in particular. From the poems alone, the reader would have hardly an inkling of the abnormal attachment and conflict between mother and son, created by the mother's troubled marriage, by the father's distance from the family by

37

virtue of being a rough, uneducated miner, by the older brother's death when Lawrence was sixteen, and by his own weak constitution. All this conspired to bring him firmly under his mother's control,[12] and together with his consequent struggle for self-realization, is central in the novel, in which the account of the Morel family is essentially that of Lawrence's own family.

In *Sons and Lovers*, Gertrude Morel, frustrated by her bad marriage, transfers her affections from her miner-husband to her sons, first William, then Paul. William's death robs her for a time of the will to live but soon after, Paul comes down with pneumonia and his mother recovers, nursing him through his illness. Mother and son, having saved each other, are now firmly, almost incestuously, bound together. In a powerful scene, Lawrence describes Gertrude Morel nursing her son at night and sleeping in Paul's bed when the crisis of his illness comes:

> 'I s'll die, mother!' he cried, heaving for breath on the pillow.
> She lifted him up, crying in a small voice:
> 'Oh, my son – my son!'
> That brought him to. He realized her. His whole will rose up and arrested him. He put his head on her breast, and took ease of her for love.
> 'For some things,' said his aunt, 'it was a good thing Paul was ill that Christmas. I believe it saved his mother.'
> Paul was in bed for seven weeks. He got up white and fragile. His father had brought him a pot of scarlet and gold tulips. They used to flame in the window in the March sunshine as he sat on the sofa chattering to his mother. The two knitted together in perfect intimacy. Mrs. Morel's life now rooted itself in Paul (ch. 6).

With knowledge of his background, the reader understands clearly why Paul should be so unusually grief-stricken after the mother dies. This background knowledge is mostly absent in the poetry, yet the elements of grief for the mother are virtually identical in the poetry and in the prose. There is, for example, the idealized picture of the dead bride-like mother in the poem 'The Bride' and in *Sons and Lovers*:[13]

> She looks like a young maiden, since her brow
>   Is smooth and fair,
> Her cheeks are very smooth, her eyes are closed.
>   She sleeps a rare
> Still winsome sleep, so still, and so composed.

Nay, but she sleeps like a bride, and dreams her dreams
   Of perfect things.
She lies at last, the darling, in the shape of her dream;
   And her dead mouth sings
By its shape, like the thrushes in clear evenings.

She lay like a maiden asleep. With his candle in his hand, he bent over her. She lay like a girl asleep and dreaming of her love. The mouth was a little open, as if wondering from the suffering, but her face was young, her brow clear and white as if life had never touched it (ch. 14).

Similarly, in the depiction of the absence of feeling after the loss, the prose and the poetry are intertwined. In the poem 'The End', Lawrence echoed a letter of 12 December 1910, three days after his mother's death, in which he expressed his numbness in the aftermath of the loss – 'I have died, a bit of me . . .' (I, p. 199):

And oh, my love, as I rock for you tonight
And have not any longer any hope
To heal the suffering, or to make requite
For all your life of asking and despair,
I own that some of me is dead tonight.

In *Sons and Lovers*, Paul Morel's loss of feeling after his mother's death is placed in the context of his search for meaning amidst his grief: 'The first snowdrops came. He saw the tiny drop-pearls among the grey. They would have given him the liveliest emotion at one time. Now they were there, but they did not seem to mean anything' (ch. 15).

The sense of detachment from others and from life generally, common after a bereavement,[14] also appears both in the poetry and in the prose. In the poem 'Blue', the poet is afflicted by his feeling of alienation from the sources of life:

I who am substance of shadow, I all compact
Of the stuff of the night, finding myself all wrongly
Among the crowds of things in the sunshine
   jostled and racked.

Paul Morel, similarly, is tormented by the barrier between himself and the world, created by the loss of his mother: 'He saw the face of the barmaid, the gabbling drinkers, his own glass on the slopped, mahogany board, in the distance. There was something between him and them. He could not get into touch' (ch. 15). He no longer knows where he belongs in the world, amid 'the vastness and terror of the immense night. . . Where was he? – one tiny upright speck of flesh, less than an ear of wheat lost in the field' (*ibid.*). This question recurs in the poem 'The Chief Mystery', in which the poet, in a similar scene, stands in the dark of night and perceiving the grass, the wind and clouds about him, asks: 'But I, where among them am I?'

The acute yearning and searching for the mother is expressed most movingly in the poetry as in the prose through symbolic association, and this was not just a literary device as Lawrence indicates in a letter dated five days after his mother's death:

> I'm so miserable about my 'matouchka'. When I am not in good health my mind repeatedly presents me a picture: no matter what my thoughts are, or what I am doing, the image of a memory floats up. This afternoon, it is just the winsome, wavy grey hairs at my mother's temple, and her hand under her cheek as she lay (*Letters*, I, p. 202).

Thus, a yellow leaf blown in the wind rouses him sharply from a dream in which the poet relives his mother's final agony ('Brooding Grief'); a piece of paper swiftly blown away by the wind recalls to Paul Morel the swiftness of his mother's passing (ch. 15); the sound of a woman singing takes the poet back to childhood and the memory of his mother singing hymns at home on Sunday: 'my manhood is cast/ Down in a flood of remembrance, I weep like a child for the past' ('Piano'); a wisp of cigarette smoke evokes the thin grey strands of the mother's hair during her last weeks:

> Why does the thin grey strand
> Floating up from the forgotten
> Cigarette between my fingers,
> Why does it trouble me?
>
> Ah, you will understand;
> When I carried my mother downstairs,
> A few times only, at the beginning
> Of her soft-foot malady,
>
> I should find, for a reprimand
> To my gaity, a few long grey hairs
> On the breast of my coat; and one by one
> I watched them float up the dark chimney.

'Sorrow'

'He [Paul Morel] sat in the kitchen, smoking. Then he tried to brush some grey ash off his coat. He looked again. It was one of his mother's grey hairs. It was so long! He held it up, and it drifted into the chimney. He let go. The long grey hair floated and was gone in the blackness of the chimney' (ch. 13).[15]

In the poetry, as in the prose, the presence of the mother remains as the mourner has not yet fully accepted the fact of her death:

I see each shadow start
With recognition...

> 'The Inheritance'

I feel your silence touch my words as I talk
    And hold them in thrall.

> 'Listening'

Who could say his mother had lived and did not live? She had been in one place, and was in another; that was all. And his soul could not leave her, wherever she was. Now she was gone abroad into the night, and he was with her still. They were together (ch. 15).

The urge for union with the mother, to incorporate her, in life or in death, is also found in the poetry as well as in the prose. In 'The End', Lawrence gives immediate expression to this desire at the time of the death:

If I could have put you in my heart,
If I could have wrapped you in myself
How glad I should have been!

In *Sons and Lovers*, this wish is linked with the wish for death which is overcome by the consolation, frequently felt by mourners, that the dead lives on in the survivors. Paul Morel engages in an inner dialogue in which his will to live is tested:

'She's dead. What was it all for – her struggle?'
That was his despair wanting to go after her.
'You're alive.'
'She's not.'
'She is – in you.'
Suddenly he felt tired with the burden of it.
'You've got to keep alive for her sake,' said his will in him (ch. 15).

The sense of emotional depletion, of being small and helpless in a cruel, despairing world, is conveyed in the overriding symbol of the night; faced with this abyss of despair, Lawrence found an assurance and power of expression which he had not previously known:

I with the night on my lips, I sigh with the silence of death;
And what do I care though the very stones should cry me
                              unreal, though the clouds
Shine in conceit of substance upon me, who am less
                    than the rain.

                                        'Blue'

On every side the immense dark silence seemed pressing him, so tiny a spark, into extinction, and yet, almost nothing, he could not be extinct. Night, in which everything was lost, went reaching out, beyond stars and sun. Stars and sun, a few bright grains, went spinning round for terror, and holding each other in embrace, there in a darkness that outpassed them all, and left them tiny and daunted. So much, and himself, infinitesimal, at the core a nothingness, and yet not nothing.
    'Mother!' he whispered – 'mother!' (ch. 15).

This haunting of death in life aroused an unambiguous wish for death, and in one poem, 'In Trouble and Shame', the poet compares his body to a useless piece of lumber which he would like to cast off. The poem 'Call into Death' is another in which the drift to death is strong:

And I am willing to come to you now, my dear,
As a pigeon lets itself off from a cathedral dome
To be lost in the haze of the sky; I would like to come
And be lost out of sight with you, like a melting foam.

For I am tired, my dear, and if I could lift my feet,
My tenacious feet, from off the dome of the earth
To fall like a breath within the breathing wind
Where you are lost, what rest, my love, what rest!

Yet, in other poems, 'Brother and Sister' for example, the movement towards restitution and recovery is apparent:

Let us not cry to her still to sustain us here,
Let us not hold her shadow back from the dark!
Oh, let us here forget, let us take the sheer
Unknown that lies before us...

Similarly, at the end of *Sons and Lovers*, the conflict between the wish to die and the life force is resolved in favour of life:

> She was the only thing that held him up, himself, amid all this. And she was gone, intermingled herself. He wanted her to touch him, have him alongside with her.
> But no, he would not give in. Turning sharply, he walked towards the city's gold phosphorescence. His fists were shut, his mouth set fast. He would not take that direction, to the darkness, to follow her. He walked towards the faintly humming, glowing town, quickly.

Lawrence described the novel as 'the bright book of life': in *Sons and Lovers*, more clearly and fully than in the other works written in the aftermath of his mother's death, he portrays his reaction to this loss. Conspicuous by its absence, however, is any expression of anger at the mother for dying – in view of Lawrence's close dependence upon her, one would expect this. There are hints, as in the poem 'Elegy' – 'The night you closed your eyes for ever against me' – and, in *Sons and Lovers*, in Paul's rejection of Miriam which, as Daleski (1965) has suggested, is a backhanded rejection of the mother, and in Paul's self-destructive behaviour after the death. Yet the absence of anger and the preponderance of idealization may be taken as signs of an emotional problem which Lawrence never fully overcame and which he kept returning to in his writings until the end of his life.[16]

'The death of a parent,' writes Kermode, 'often signals mysterious upheaval and change in the personal life, but the totality of Lawrence's break with the past is very striking' (1973, p. 34). As in the case of Whitman and Agnon, the emergence of Lawrence's mature creative voice appears to have been part of the changes effected by the grief process. These changes are not usually so dramatically visible, but they are often a major factor in creativity as we shall see further in the next chapter, on dreams. Our starting point here is *The Interpretation of Dreams*: Freud's personal experience of loss, most significantly the death of his father, had a decisive impact upon the writing of this trailblazing book.

3

LOSS AND DREAMS

Sigmund Freud began writing *The Interpretation of Dreams* after the death of his father in 1896. He wrote at the time to his friend and colleague Wilhelm Fliess, 'I feel now as if I had been torn up by the roots' (1954, p. 170). In the preface to the second edition (1908) of *The Interpretation of Dreams*, Freud admitted that the book was 'a portion of my own self-analysis, my reaction to my father's death – that is to say, to the most important event, the most poignant loss, of a man's life' (1900, p. xxvi). In addition, at least three major childhood experiences of loss or separation emerged in the course of Freud's self-analysis, and these also figure, directly or indirectly, in the book on dreams. These are the loss of his brother, Julius, in infancy, the abrupt dismissal of his nanny for theft when he was 2½ years old, and separations from his mother in childhood owing to illness – she had tuberculosis.[1]

Freud's discovery of the effects of loss on his dreams was a crucial factor in the development of psychoanalysis, but he made little use of this discovery in evolving a theory of loss and separation. Rather, he incorporated the results of his self-analysis into a general theory of the Oedipus complex. Only towards the end of his life, in *Inhibitions, Symptoms and Anxiety* (1926), did he revise his theory and give a central position to loss and separation, but by this time, the impetus of his work on loss and dreams had been lost. The large body of clinical literature on loss and separation which has built up in recent years takes virtually no account of dreams. In addition, although Freud and his followers attached the highest importance to creative literature as a source of insight into human nature, relatively little attention has been paid to the abundant literary material on dreams and loss. The aim of this chapter, accordingly, is to examine the possible role of loss in the dreams of writers – of Dante, Descartes, Milton, De Quincey, Nerval, Cocteau, and Jung – and to consider the impact of loss and separation in Freud's life, and also to determine in particular why Freud waited a quarter of a century to develop a theory of loss when he had the evidence, his own dreams and self-analysis, at the time of writing *The Interpretation of Dreams*.

Most of the dreams below pre-date Freud and with the exception of Milton and Jung, all the dreamers suffered the loss of at least one parent in childhood. Their dreams, while often relating to more immediate losses (or other crises) in adult life, frequently reflect the childhood bereavements as well, and show once again how the imagination may struggle to confront and master grief. Their transformation into art may be seen as a further stage in this struggle. From this point of view, it does not matter if the dreams were actually dreamt or imagined. The first dream, of Dante's, appears in *La Vita Nuova*, written around 1390–5, during the period after the death of the poet's beloved Beatrice:

> In my room I seemed to see a cloud the colour of fire, and in the cloud a lordly figure, frightening to behold, yet in himself, it seemed to me, he was filled with a marvellous joy. He said many things, of which I understood only a few; among them were the words: *Ego dominus tuus* [I am your master]. In his arms I seemed to see a naked figure, sleeping, wrapped lightly in a crimson cloth. Gazing intently I saw it was she who had bestowed her greeting on me earlier that day. In one hand the standing figure held a fiery object, and he seemed to say, *Vide cor tuum* [Behold your heart]. After a little while I thought he wakened her who slept and prevailed on her to eat the glowing object in his hand. Reluctantly and hesitantly she did so. A few moments later his happiness turned to bitter grief, and, weeping, he gathered the figure in his arms and together they seemed to ascend into the heavens. I felt such anguish at their departure that my light sleep was broken, and I awoke (1980, pp. 31–2).

Dante's depiction of Beatrice, both in *La Vita Nuova* and in *The Divine Comedy*, is characterized by intense idealization. He relates that from the moment he first set eyes on Beatrice, when he was nearly nine and she just turned eight, she was the apogee of holiness to him, and Love, the 'lordly figure' in the dream, ruled him. Later he goes so far as to compare her with the Virgin Mary, the Church, Divine Grace, Christ himself; and by the end of the Paradiso, she is the revelation of God's presence on earth. 'The moment I saw her', he writes in *La Vita Nuova*,

> I say in all truth that the vital spirit which dwells in the inmost depths of the heart, began to tremble so violently that I felt the

vibration alarmingly in all my pulses, even the weakest of them. As it trembled, it uttered these words: *Ecce deus fortior me, qui veniens dominabitur mihi* [Behold a god more powerful than I who comes to rule over me]. At this point, the spirit of the senses which dwells on high in the place to which our sense perceptions are carried, was filled with amazement and, speaking especially to the spirits of vision, made this pronouncement: *Apparuit iam beatitudo vestra* [Now your source of joy has been revealed]. Whereupon the natural spirit, which dwells where our nourishment is digested, began to weep and, weeping, said: *Heu miser! quia frequenter impeditus ero deinceps* [Woe is me! for I shall often be impeded from now on]. From then on indeed Love ruled over my soul, which was thus wedded to him early in life, and he began to acquire such assurance and mastery over me, owing to the power which my imagination gave him, that I was obliged to fulfil all his wishes perfectly. He often commanded me to go where perhaps I might see this angelic child and so, while I was still a boy, I often went in search of her; and I saw that in all her ways she was so praiseworthy and noble that indeed the words of the poet Homer might have been said of her: 'She did not seem the daughter of a mortal man, but of a god' (pp. 29–30).

Even taking into account the literary conventions of Dante's age when, in the tradition of courtly love, women were frequently placed on a religious pedestal, this idealized image is unusually intense. As we have seen, idealization of the dead is not infrequently a part of the grief process (Parkes, 1986), and it may be that Dante's idealization of Beatrice was connected with delayed grief for his mother who had died some three or four years before he first saw Beatrice. His description of his attitude towards Beatrice contains a number of other elements which may be associated with mourning for the mother: a part of him (the 'natural spirit') feels grief at the sight of Beatrice; she is an object of yearning and he often goes 'in search of her'; she is carried up to heaven – the bereaved child undoubtedly believed that his mother was in heaven; and, although Beatrice was younger than Dante, he invariably adopts a filial position towards her. Thus, on his reunion with her in the *Purgatorio*, Dante likens himself to a little boy overcome by the presence of his mother:

And even as a little boy may think
His mother formidable, I thought her so...
(Canto 30)

Similarly, on seeing Beatrice in all her splendour in the *Paradiso*, Dante compares himself to a baby wishing to be breast-fed:

> No little infant mouthes as readily
> Towards his mother's breast, if he awake
> Much later than his hour is wont to be...
> (Canto 30)

If Beatrice called up such a response in life, although Dante hardly knew her, how much more did she in death: when she died, Dante's unresolved grief for his mother may have been revived, and his dream in *La Vita Nuova* may reflect this grief. In Dante's account, the dream took place shortly after she greeted him for the first time, nine years after he first set eyes on her. Dante admits that during these nine years he had longed for Beatrice, but had never sought her love or even spoken to her, perhaps he had purposefully avoided her. The dream helps to explain why. Love, to the poet, is a source of fear, pain and guilt. He feels an insurmountable barrier between himself and his beloved, and her bestowal of greeting arouses the terror of desertion. This fear is far more than the normal adolescent anxiety at being turned down: the woman eats his heart and disappears. Where does this fear come from? It may well be the poet's terror at being hurt and abandoned as his mother 'abandoned' him by dying, or a fear of his own suppressed hostility at her for dying, or of the imagined retaliatory anger of the lost person.[2] For these reasons, it seems, he must keep Beatrice at a distance. Even his distant, unreal vision of Love is fraught with pain; how much more is actual earthly love a source of deep anxiety to him.

Unlike Dante's dream, the following dream of Descartes' does not relate directly to the loss of a person, but reveals characteristics of the dreamer which may plausibly be connected with childhood loss. Descartes' original account of the dream is lost, but it was recorded by Baillet in 1691, some forty years after the philosopher's death:

> The moment Descartes had fallen asleep he believed he saw certain phantoms and was frightened by their appearance. He believed he was walking in the streets and was so terrified by the apparition that he bent over (*renverser*) to his left side to get to the place he was headed for, because on his right side he felt a great weakness and he could not stand upright. Embarassed

by having to walk like this, he made an effort to straighten himself out, when he felt a strong wind. The wind seized him like a tornado, so that he whirled three or four times on his left foot in a circle. But even this was not the thing that frightened him. To advance was so difficult that he expected to collapse at each step. At last he noticed on the road a *Collège* which was open, and he entered to find refuge in his trouble. He tried to reach the church of the *Collège* and his first thought was to say a prayer, when he suddenly noticed he had passed an acquaintance without greeting him and he wanted to turn back to show his politeness. However, he was prevented forcibly by the wind which blew in the direction of the Church. At that moment he saw in the middle of the courtyard of the *Collège* another man. This one addressed Descartes politely and amicably by name, and told him he had something to give him to take along in case he was going to see Mr. N. Descartes believed it to be a melon which someone had brought from an exotic country. He was most astonished to see that the people who had gathered around him with this man, to chat, were all able to stand upright and firmly on their feet while he was still bent over and staggering, although the wind which had threatened to knock him over had diminished considerably (Stern, 1966, pp. 80–1).

This is the first of three dreams dreamt by Descartes on the night of 10 November 1619 at the age of twenty-four, and they heralded his decision to devote his life to a quest for philosophic Truth. The instability and apparent irrationality of the dreamer are in striking contrast to the later certainty and rationality of the philosopher. For underlying Cartesian philosophy is the belief that true science rests on axiomatic principles, from which by use of rational rules irrefutable conclusions can be drawn. However, the fixities of Descartes' philosophy, notably the axiom 'I think, therefore I am', were arrived at only by means of profound uncertainties which led him to doubt the reality of the material world, to reject the prevailing beliefs of the day, the authority of tradition, faith and dogma, and to bring everything before the bar of reason. The extreme chaotic insecurity underlying the need for such intellectual certainty may be found in the dream.

The best-known illustration of Descartes' distrust of the evidence of his senses and the evolution of his method of reasoning, appears in the *Second Meditation* (1641), in the example of the piece of wax:

Let us take, for example, this piece of wax: it has been taken quite freshly from the hive, and it has not yet lost the sweetness of the honey which it contains: it still retains somewhat of the odour of the flowers from which it has been culled; its colour, its figure, its size are apparent; it is hard, cold, easily handled, and if you strike it with the finger, it will emit a sound. Finally all the things which are requisite to cause us distinctly to recognize a body, are met with in it. But notice that while I speak and approach the fire what remained of the taste is exhaled, the smell evaporates, the colour alters, the figure is destroyed, the size increases, it becomes liquid, it heats, scarcely can one handle it, and when one strikes it, no sound is emitted. Does the same wax remain after this change? We must confess that it remains; none would judge otherwise. What then did I know so distinctly in this piece of wax? It could certainly be nothing of all that the senses brought to my notice, since all these things which fall under taste, smell, sight, touch, and hearing, are found to be changed, and yet the same wax remains.

Perhaps it was what I now think, *viz.* that this wax was not that sweetness of honey, nor that agreeable scent of flowers, nor that particular whiteness, nor that figure, nor that sound, but simply a body which a little while before appeared to me as perceptible under these forms, which is now perceptible under others. But what, precisely, is it that I imagine when I form such conceptions? Let us attentively consider this, and, abstracting from all that does not belong to the wax, let us see what remains. Certainly nothing remains excepting a certain extended thing which is flexible and movable. But what is the meaning of flexible and movable? (1970, I, p. 154).

Descartes concludes that the basic nature of the wax cannot be grasped by his imagination: 'We must then grant that I could not even understand through the imagination what this piece of wax is, and it is my mind alone which perceives it' (p. 155). Truth for Descartes is to be found not in sensory perceptions of the animate or inanimate world, but in the world of the mind.

What was the cause of this insecurity which led him to search so relentlessly for Truth? A number of psychological studies, by Wisdom (1947), Feuer (1963), Stern (1966), Storr (1972), Eisenbud (1978), and Dyer (1986), have placed the strongest emphasis on the loss of Descartes' mother as an infant. Until he was nine, he was raised by his father and stepmother, then sent to a Jesuit boarding school. The confusion, weakness, isolation, the sense of being whirled about by irrational forces beyond his control, the fear of physical and mental collapse which might have followed in the wake of loss, come out in the dream.

In general, loss in early childhood may lead to profound distrust, both of human beings and, by extension, of objects. The growth of 'basic trust' (Erikson, 1963) comes through consistent, loving care in infancy and the baby's growing perception that it is 'in good hands'. Loss or separation in infancy may lead to a state of chronic distrust, or what Laing (1969) describes as 'ontological insecurity'.

Descartes' dream might, therefore, be interpreted as evidence of 'ontological insecurity' deriving, in part at least, from the loss of his mother. The intensity of his search for Truth in science may reflect an unresolved (and perhaps unresolvable) phase of grief after his mother's death; the melon and the church may be maternal objects of searching, offering nourishment, shelter and comfort, to which he is driven by the fury in his mind which threatens him with collapse. His system of thought, while having an objective value of its own, may be seen as an attempt to overcome this insecurity, to hold on to something after his mother's death, to discover what is real and true, and to convince himself that the world is stable and reliable after all.[3] Descartes evidently struggled to control and master his world intellectually, by achieving an intricate knowledge of its mechanics. The split between thought and feeling in his philosophy may be understood, on a psychological level, as his defence against overwhelming fears aroused by loss whose power is symnbolized by the tornado-like wind.

Whereas the dreams of Dante and Descartes illustrate long-lasting consequences of loss, the following dream of Milton's is of a type not unfamiliar in the first months after a loss:

> Methought I saw my late espoused saint
>   Brought to me like Alcestis from the grave,
>   Whom Jove's great son to her glad husband gave,
>   Rescued from death by force though pale and faint.
> Mine as whom washed from spot of childbed taint,
>   Purification in the old Law did save,
>   And such, as yet once more I trust to have
>   Full sight of her in heaven without restraint,
> Came vested all in white, pure as her mind:
>   Her face was veiled, yet to my fancied sight,

Love, sweetness, goodness, in her person shined
So clear, as in no face with more delight.
But O as to embrace me she inclined
I waked, she fled, and day brought back my night.

Sonnet 19

Both Milton's first wife, Mary Powell (d. 1652) and his second wife, Katherine Woodcock (d. 1658) died shortly after giving birth, and it is not known to which wife Milton is alluding in this sonnet.[3] In referring both to pagan myth and to the 'old Law' of the Jewish tradition (specifically the laws of the purification of women after childbirth, in *Leviticus*, xii, 4–8), Milton underscores the universal nature of his loss. In the Greek myth, adapted by Euripedes, Alcestis gives her life to save her husband, Admetus. Hercules ('Jove's great son' in Milton's sonnet) brings her back from the grave and restores her to her husband. However, Milton, unlike Admetus, is a 'glad husband' again only in his dream. His 'seeing' his wife is equally poignant. His waking forces him to be conscious not only of his wife's death but also of the loss of his sight.

Even in waking life, however, it is not unusual for a bereaved person to imagine that the lost person is present and can be seen from time to time (Bowlby, 1980; Parkes, 1986). In his letter of 1 November 1820, Keats writes that he still 'sees' Fanny Brawne after their final separation; likewise, C.S. Lewis writes of the presence of his dead wife, 'the impression of her *mind* momentarily facing my own' (1974, p. 57). Among fictional illustrations, one of the best-known is that of Madame Aubain in Flaubert's 'A Simple Heart', who 'sees' her dead husband and daughter. Another is that of Countess Natalia Rostov in Tolstoy's *War and Peace* (1865–8) who, after the death of her youngest son, Piotr, in the French invasion of 1812, has hallucinations that Piotr has returned: 'How glad I am my boy has come. You are tired. Would you like some tea...You have grown so handsome and manly' (1987, p. 1279). In Dickens' *Great Expectations* (1861), Pip describes the effect on him of his sister's death:

> The figure of my sister in her chair by the kitchen fire haunted me night and day. That the place could possibly be, without her, was something my mind seemed unable to encompass; and whereas she had seldom or never been in my thoughts of late, I had now the strangest idea that she was coming towards me in the street, or that she would presently knock at the door.

In my rooms too, with which she had never been at all associated, there was at once the blankness of death and a perpetual suggestion of the sound of her voice or the turn of her face or figure, as if she were still alive and had been often there (ch. 35).[4]

Milton's sonnet may be taken to anticipate the writing of *Paradise Lost*. The poet's grief for his lost marital paradise and the women who brought death into his life may be echoed in the Biblical story of the fall from innocence and happiness and the woman who brought death into the world. Adam's first words to Eve – these have no precedent in the Bible but are original to Milton – surprise the reader with their elegiac tone:

> Return fair Eve,
> Whom fly'st thou? Whom thou fly'st, of him thou art,
> His flesh, his bone; to give thee being I lent
> Out of my side to thee, nearest my heart
> Substantial life, to have thee by my side
> Henceforth an individual solace dear;
> Part of my soul I seek thee, and thee claim
> My other half...

(iv, 481–8)

Adam, in a heartfelt cry after the Fall of his longing for reunion with Eve, alludes to a biblical passage (*Genesis*, ii, 23) in an altered context – 'bone of my bone and flesh of my flesh' appears in the account of Eve's creation, and there is no mention in the biblical narrative of Adam's grief at the prospect of Eve's death. Adam's powerful expression of yearning might therefore betray Milton's own grief for his wife and his struggle through art to master this grief:

> How can I live without thee, how forgo
> Thy sweet converse and love so dearly joined,
> To live again in these wild woods forlorn?
> Should God create another Eve, and I
> Another rib afford, yet loss of thee
> Would never from my heart; no, no, I feel
> The link of nature draw me: flesh of flesh,
> Bone of my bone thou art, and from thy state
> Mine never shall be parted, bliss or woe.

(ix, 908–16)

In contrast with Milton's expressions of yearning and searching, which are explicable as direct reactions of a husband after the death of his wife, De Quincey's account of his dreams of searching after adult loss, shows that this grief was rooted in childhood loss. De Quincey himself recognized this. In his introduction to the *Suspiria de Profundis* (1845), the unfinished sequel to the *Confessions of an English Opium Eater* (1821), De Quincey writes that his purpose in the *Confessions* was to show how his childhood experiences, particularly of loss, affected his dreams and acted as major causative factors in his opium addiction. De Quincey appears, in fact, to have been the first to attempt a study of loss and dreams (or what emerged as that, to a large extent), predating Freud by almost eighty years. The effects of childhood loss on De Quincey are visible in the following dream from the *Confessions*, as well as some of the causes of his 'perpetual sense of desertion' and his 'chronic passion of anxiety' – phrases with which he described himself – and his need to numb these feelings with opium:

I thought that it was a Sunday morning in May, that it was Easter Sunday, and as yet very early in the morning. I was standing, as it seemed to me, at the very door of my own cottage. Right before me lay the very scene which could really be commanded from that situation, but exalted, as was usual, and solemnized by the power of dreams. There were the same mountains, and the same lovely valley at their feet; but the mountains were raised to more than Alpine height, and there was interspace far larger between them of meadows and forest lawns; the hedges were rich with white roses; and no living creature was to be seen, excepting that in the green churchyard there were cattle tranquilly reposing upon the verdant graves, and particularly round about the grave of a child whom I had tenderly loved, just as I had really beheld them, a little before sun-rise in the same summer, when that child died. I gazed upon the well-known scene, and I said aloud (as I thought) to myself, 'It yet wants much of sun-rise; and it is Easter Sunday; and that is the day on which they celebrate the first-fruits of resurrection. I will walk abroad; old griefs shall be forgotten today; for the air is cool and still, and the hills are high, and stretch away to heaven; and the forest-glades are as quiet as the churchyard; and, with the dew, I can wash the fever from my forehead, and then I shall be unhappy no longer.' And I turned, as if to open my garden gate; and immediately I saw upon the left a scene far different; but which yet the power of dreams had reconciled into harmony with the other. The scene was an oriental one; and there also it was Easter Sunday, and very early in the morning. And at a vast distance were visible, as a stain upon the horizon, the domes and cupolas of a great city – an image or faint abstraction caught perhaps from childhood from some picture of Jerusalem. And not a bow-shot from me, upon a stone, and shaded by Judean palms, there sat a woman; and I looked; and it was – Ann! She fixed her eyes upon me earnestly; and I said to her at length: 'So then I have found you at last.' I waited: but she answered me not a word. Her face was the same as when I saw it last, and yet again how different! Seventeen years ago, when the lamp-light fell upon her face, as for the last time I kissed her lips (lips, Ann, that to me were not polluted), her eyes were streaming with tears: the tears were now wiped away; she seemed more beautiful than she was at that time, but in all other points the same, and not older. Her looks were tranquil, but with unusual solemnity of expression; and I now gazed upon her with some awe, but suddenly her countenance grew dim, and, turning to the mountains I perceived vapours rolling between us; in a moment all had vanished; thick darkness came on; and, in the twinkling of an eye, I was far away from mountains, and by lamp-light in Oxford-street, walking again with Ann – just as we walked seventeen years before, when we were both children (1966, pp. 97–8).

Though this dream, set in Grasmere, is dated June 1819, it had recurred in many variations for years beforehand. The two parts of the dream refer to two of the most distressing losses of De Quincey's adult life: Kate, Wordsworth's daughter, to whom De Quincey had been deeply attached, and who had died in 1812 at the age of four; and his accidental separation from Ann, a fifteen-year-old prostitute who had befriended him during his impoverished time in London in the winter of 1802–3.

De Quincey's grief reactions to these losses went beyond normal bounds. After Kate Wordsworth died, he suffered such grief that he often spent whole nights lying on her grave in Grasmere. To cope with his depression, he took heavy doses of opium and, according to Lindop (1981), the girl's death may have been the decisive factor in turning him into an addict. Similarly, in *Confessions*, De Quincey described his separation from Ann exaggeratedly, as the 'heaviest affliction' of his life. His account of yearning and searching for her for many years afterwards belies the fact that he had known her for a bare few months:

> If she lived, doubtless we must have been sometimes in search of each other, at the very same moment, through the mighty labyrinths of London; perhaps even within a few feet of each other – a barrier no wider in a London street, often amounting in the end to a separation for eternity!...I have looked into many, many myriads of female faces, in the hope of meeting her. I should know her again amongst a thousand...(1966, p. 56).

What caused De Quincey's susceptibility to such extreme grief reactions? In his autobiographical writings he strongly suggests that these had their roots in childhood loss. His first knowledge of death came at 4½ when his sister Jane died. He writes movingly of his ignorance of the meaning of death, and of his disbelief that the loss was permanent:

> I knew little more of mortality than that Jane had disappeared. She had gone away; but, perhaps, she would come back. Happy interval of heaven-born ignorance! Gracious immunity of infancy from sorrow disproportioned to its strength! I was sad for Jane's absence. But in my heart I trusted that she would come again. Summer and winter came again – crocuses and roses, why not little Jane? (1966, p. 125).

In contrast with Jane's death, the illness and death of his sister Elizabeth, when he was seven, was a blow whose effects he felt for the rest of his life. De Quincey's mother was rather cold and aloof (he wrote of her: 'She delighted not in infancy, nor infancy in her'), and Elizabeth had mothered him and was his favourite companion. News of Elizabeth's impending death consequently set off an unusually powerful grief reaction in which, no doubt, the long-bottled-up mourning for Jane was also expressed: 'Rightly is it said of utter, utter misery that it "cannot be *remembered*". Itself as a rememberable thing, is swallowed up in its own chaos. Blind anarchy and confusion of mind fell upon me. Deaf and blind I was, as I reeled under the revelation' (p. 128).

He describes how he would search the inanimate world for some sign of his sister (the intensity of this searching brings to mind his later searching for Ann):

> Into the woods, or the desert air, I gazed, as if some comfort lay hid in *them*. I wearied the heavens with my inquest of

beseeching looks. Obstinately I tormented the blue depths with my scrutiny, sweeping them for ever with my eyes and searching them for one angelic face that might, perhaps, have permission to reveal itself for a moment (p. 137).

De Quincey's wish to restore the lost persons, and his failure to accept their deaths, may be seen also in the dream, with its biblical allusions to salvation and resurrectiion. The appearance of Ann, 'the tears were now wiped away', may refer to the passage in *Isaiah* telling of the eradication of death: 'He will swallow up death for ever, and the Lord God will wipe away tears from all faces' (xxv, 8). Another biblical allusion is his description of Ann among the Judean palms, 'not a bow-shot from me', which recalls Hagar and Ishmael driven into the desert: 'When the water in the skin was gone, she cast the child under one of the bushes. Then she went, and sat down over against him a good way off, about the distance of a bowshot; for she said, "Let me not look upon the death of the child"' (*Genesis*, xxi, 15–16). De Quincey seems to have hoped for divine intervention such as that which saved the two outcasts.

De Quincey's circumstances for mourning in childhood had been particularly unfavourable. His father died not long after the death of Elizabeth. Utterly devastated, he had no one to turn to, and became increasingly solitary and withdrawn. Lindop has astutely noted: 'It was not so much the shock of Elizabeth's death as Thomas' inability to complete his mourning that conferred on the event a lasting significance' (1981 p. 12). The unresolved grief was apparently displaced on to Ann and Kate Wordsworth later in life, and emerged in his dreams.

Another nineteenth-century harbinger of Freud was Nerval, who treated his dreams with utmost seriousness, describing them as 'études de l'âme humaine'. Nerval's attempts to probe and come to terms with the effects of his childhood loss are a central preoccupation in his dreams, such as the following one from *Aurélia* (1855).

I suddenly found myself in a room which formed part of my grandfather's house, only it seemed to have grown larger. The old furniture glowed with a miraculous polish, the carpets and curtains were as if new again, daylight three times more brilliant than natural day came in through the windows and the door, and in the air there was a freshness and perfume like the first warm morning of spring. Three women were working in the room and, without exactly resembling them, they stood for relatives and friends of my youth. Each seemed to have the features of several of them. Their facial contours changed like the flames of a lamp, and all the time something of one was passing to the other. Their smiles, the colour of their eyes and hair, their figures and familiar gestures, all these were exchanged as if they had lived the same life, and each was made up of all three, like those figures painters take from a number of models in order to achieve a perfect beauty.

The eldest spoke to me in a vibrant, melodious voice which I recognized as having heard in my childhood, and whatever it was she said struck me as being profoundly true. But she drew my attention to myself and I saw I was wearing a little old-fashioned brown suit, entirely made of needlework threads as fine as a spider's web. It was elegant, graceful, and gently perfumed. I felt quite rejuvenated and most spruce in this garment which their fairy fingers had made, and I blushingly thanked them as if I had been a small boy in the presence of beautiful, grown-up ladies. At that moment one of them got up and went towards the garden.

It is a well-known fact that no one ever sees the sun in a dream, although one is often aware of some far brighter light. Material objects and human bodies are illumined through their own agencies. Now I was in a little park through which ran long vine arbors, loaded with heavy clusters of black and white grapes; and as the lady, guiding me, passed beneath these arbors, the shadows of the intertwined trellis-work changed her figure and her clothes. At last we came out from these bowers of grapes to an open space. Traces of the old paths which had once divided it cross-wise were just visible. For some years the plants had been neglected and the sparse patches of clematis, hops and honeysuckle, of jasmine, ivy, and creepers, had stretched their long clinging tendrils between the sturdy growths of the trees. Branches of fruit were bowed to the ground and a few garden flowers, in a state of wildness now, bloomed among the weeds.

At distant intervals were clumps of poplars, acacias and pine-trees, and in the midst of these were glimpses of statues blackened by time. I saw before me a heap of rocks covered with ivy, from which gushed a spring of fresh water whose splashes echoed melodiously over a pool of still water, half-hidden by huge water lilies.

The lady I was following stretched her slender figure in a movement that made the folds of her dress of shot taffeta shimmer, and gracefully she slid her bare arm about the long stem of a hollyhock. Then, in a clear shaft of light, she began to grow in such a way that gradually the whole garden blended with her own form, and the flowerbeds and trees became the patterns and flounces of her clothes, while her face and arms imprinted their contours on the rosy clouds in the sky. I lost her thus as she became transfigured, for she seemed to vanish in her own immensity.

'Don't leave me!' I cried. 'For with you Nature itself dies.'

With these words I struggled painfully through the brambles trying to grasp the vast shadow that eluded me. I threw myself on a fragment of ruined wall, at the foot of which lay the marble bust of a woman. I lifted it up and felt convinced it was of *her*...I recognized the beloved features and as I stared around me I saw that the garden had become a graveyard, and I heard voices crying: 'The universe is in darkness' (1958, pp. 130–1).

Nerval's dream may be compared with that of Dante in *La Vita Nuova*: in both a beloved woman disappears, leaving the poet in a state of anguish. Nerval's dream, like that of Dante, appears to have at its root the loss of the mother in infancy. Shortly after Nerval's birth, his father, an army doctor, left home with his wife for army service in the Napoleonic wars. Nerval was left in the care of a peasant wet-nurse at Loisy in the Valois. Two and a half years later, his mother died, and he passed into the care of his mother's uncle in the nearby village of Mortefontaine. When he was seven his father reappeared and took Nerval into his home in Paris. In later life, Nerval suffered from severe manic-depression, and was eventually confined in a mental hospital in Passy. The works he wrote while in care, of which *Aurélia* is the last before his death (it is likely that he committed suicide) provide a unique inner portrait of a man tormented by the effects of childhood loss, yet able to describe these objectively in art.[5]

As background to his dream, Nerval tells of his rejection by a woman named Aurélia, which he regards as punishment for some unpardonable crime. Having described his current emotions, Nerval goes on to connect these with memories and dreams of his childhood. The setting is his home in the Valois, which he remembered as a lost paradise: it is spring, everything is new and fresh and in bloom, the light is 'three times more brilliant than natural day'. The features of the three women are those of the dreamer's relatives and friends, but the single image of 'perfect beauty' which they make up may well be that of the mother. (This image brings to mind the vision of the goddess who appears to the poet later in *Aurélia* and tells him, 'I am the same as Mary, the same as your mother, the same being also whom you have always loved under every form'.) The suit which is sewn for the poet could, accordingly, symbolize the garment of the psyche, the maternal bond which, elegant and graceful as it is in spring, is too delicate for harsher seasons.

The walk through the garden might represent the period of transition before the departure of Nerval's mother. At this time, she made her tumultuous decision to join her husband and leave her son in the care of the wet-nurse. Her preoccupation may have led to the neglect of the baby (possibly symbolized by the neglected plants and the blackened statues), and caused him anxiety which found expression in his following and clinging to her. (This anxiety, as well as the other feelings of the dreamer, may also be connected with later experiences of separation, both in childhood and in adult life, notably his abandonment by the actress Jennie Colon.) The expansion of the woman before vanishing and her metamorphosis into the natural world suggests the way a baby might perceive his mother as 'the whole world' upon whom he is totally dependent. The loss of the mother may, therefore, be equated in the mind of the baby with the death of all nature.[6] If he could talk, he would say, as the dreamer does, 'Don't leave me! For with you Nature itself dies.'

Children separated from their mothers show a marked increase in aggressive and destructive acts (A. Freud & Burlingham, 1975; Heinicke & Westheimer, 1966): this is illustrated in pathological form in Nerval's fantasies of omnipotence and violence towards women, which counterpart the idealized image in the dream. The fluctuations of idealization and violence may be regarded as part of the manic-depressive cycle. The crime for which the poet has allegedly been rejected by Aurélia may be found in fantasies such as these:

I thought I was in the midst of some vast charnel-house where the history of the universe was written in characters of blood. Opposite me was painted the body of an enormous woman; but various parts of her had been sliced off, as if by a sword: on the other walls, other women of different races, whose bodies dominated me more and more, made a bloody jumble of limbs and heads, ranging from empresses and queens to the humblest

peasants. It was the history of all crime,and I only had to keep
my eyes on any one spot to see depicted there some tragic scene.

'There,' I told myself, 'is what has resulted from power
bestowed on man. Man has little by little destroyed and cut up
the eternal type of beauty into a thousand little pieces, so that
his races are more and more losing strength and perfection...'
And indeed, on a line of shadow creeping in through a chink
in the door, I saw the descending generations of future races'
(p. 171).

The exaggeration in the size of the woman in this fantasy, as in
the dream of the vanishing lady, may reflect the distortion of an
infant's feelings after the loss of his mother.[7] As in the case of
Dante, Nerval's idealization of women, in *Aurélia*, *Les Filles des
Feu*, and elsewhere, appears to originate partly in violent impulses stirred up by the loss of the mother. Idealization keeps
women at a distance in order to avoid hostility, pain and guilt,
and is seen in Nerval's pastoral fantasy 'Sylvie' (1853), in which
the poet rejects 'the real woman' and longs for the love of an
unapproachable goddess.

Nerval's dream leaves little doubt that his disillusionment with
and revulsion at women had their origin primarily in childhood
loss. The utter despair with which the dream closes foreshadows
the poet's death by hanging not long after.

Whereas Nerval's dream anticipates the possibility of his own
suicide, the following dream of Cocteau's looks back to the
suicide of a parent, and it reflects the struggle to make sense of
this loss and to come to terms with it. The dream began shortly
after his father's suicide in 1898 and, if the author is to be taken
literally, it recurred as many as two or three thousand times over
the next thirteen years. It appears in Cocteau's account of his
drug addiction and cure, *Opium* (1930):

I should like some Freudian to tell me the meaning of a dream I
had several times a week beginning when I was ten. The dream
stopped in 1912. My father, who was dead, was not dead. He
had turned into a parrot in the Pré Catalan, one of those parrots
whose squawking is always associated in my mind with the
taste of foamy milk. In this dream my mother and I were about
to sit down at a table in the farm of the Pré Catalan, which
seemed to combine several farms and the cockatoo terrace of
the Jardin d'Acclimatation. I knew that my mother knew, and

that she didn't know that I knew, and it was clear to me that she was trying to discover which of the birds it was that my father had turned into, and why he had turned into that bird. I awoke in tears because of the expression on her face – she was trying to smile (Steegmuller, 1970, pp. 9–10).

Echoes of this dream reverberate all through Cocteau's astonishingly varied career as poet, dramatist, artist, novelist, ballet designer and film director. The dream prefigures Cocteau's obsession with violent death, with the force of the supernatural, with fantasies of metamorphosis, resurrection and rescue, and with the oedipal theme. The fantastic and haunting sense of loss pervading the dream is present throughout Cocteau's works.

Cocteau was reticent about his father. His reluctance to talk about his suicide or to confront it directly in his art is, perhaps, both a measure of the extent to which it troubled him, and also of his mother's unwillingness to discuss it with him. It seems that she tried to shield him and put on a brave face, but the dream poignantly shows that the boy saw through her. The denial of the loss and the wish to restore the lost person are implicit in the father's metamorphosis (the cockatoo is, no doubt, a play on the family name). The boy's association of the bird's sound with the taste of foamy milk may indicate his recognition of his father as a source of sustenance and support (there may also be a homosexual element here, as the male figure is linked with a female activity). At the same time, the ridiculousness of the father's metamorphosis may be a sign of oedipal denigration of the father and, in general, of the boy's ambivalence towards him both before and after the suicide. The dream suggests the closeness and mutual empathy of mother and son in the wake of loss but also a failure of communication. Her searching and her incomprehension of the full reasons for her husband's suicide may be evident in her attempts to find out which bird he had been turned into and why. The surrealism of this dream may be seen partly as a disguise for the boy's own searching for his father – the bereaved, as Parkes (1986) has pointed out, often put on a 'false face' to hide their grief – and a similar function may be detected in the use of surrealism by the mature artist.

The dream stopped after Cocteau met Diaghilev in 1912. When he said that he wanted to create ballet, Diaghilev challenged him: 'Etonnez-moi!' 'From that moment,' Cocteau wrote, 'I decided to die and be born again' (Steegmuller, p. 82). The discovery of his artistic vocation appears to have freed Cocteau from his dream for, among other things, it gave him the means to struggle with and master the trauma of his father's death.

Cocteau's use of symbols and the supernatural to create a personal myth of loss and recovery may be compared in certain respects with Jung. The following 'mythic' dream of Jung's occurred in January 1923, on the night before his mother's death:

> I was in a dense, gloomy forest; fantastic, gigantic boulders lay about among huge jungle-like trees. It was a heroic, primeval landscape. Suddenly I heard a piercing whistle that seemed to resound through the whole universe. My knees shook. Then there were crashings in the underbrush, and a gigantic wolfhound with a fearful, gaping maw burst forth. At the sight of it, the blood froze in my veins. It tore past me, and I suddenly knew: the Wild Huntsman had commanded it to carry away a human soul. I awoke in deadly terror, and the next morning I received the news of my mother's passing (1961, pp. 344–5).

This dream aroused intense fear because, Jung explains, the Wild Huntsman is Wotan, or the devil: Jung had dreamed, in effect, that his mother (the 'human soul') had been carried off to hell by the devil.

The anticipation of the mother's death (she was by this time old and ill) seems to have revived in full force Jung's childhood ambivalence towards her. In his early years she had suffered from mental illness and been treated in a hospital in Basle. The nature of her illness and the separation had a profound, long-lasting impact on Jung: 'I was deeply troubled by my mother's being away. From then on, I always felt mistrustful when the word "love" was spoken. The feeling I associated with "woman" was for a long time that of innate unreliability" (p. 23). As he grew older, Jung conceived of his mother as having two personalities, one loving and reliable, the other unpredictable and frightening: 'There was an enormous difference between my mother's two personalities. That was why as a child I often had anxiety dreams about her. By day she was a loving mother, but at night she seemed uncanny' (p. 67).

Jung's dual attitude to his mother, formed by her dual personality, was sharpened by his parents' incompatibility: 'My parents' marriage was not a happy one, but full of trials and difficulties and tests of patience' (p. 347). His parents were sleeping apart and Jung was sharing a room with his father when he had a grisly hallucination:

From the door to my mother's room came frightening influences. At night Mother was strange and mysterious. One night I saw coming from her door a faintly luminous, indefinite figure whose head detached itself from the neck and floated along in front of it, in the air, like a little moon. Immediately another head was produced and again detached itself. This process was repeated six or seven times (pp. 33–4).

As the apparition of the beheaded figure comes from the mother's bedroom, it could betray violent impulses and death-wishes towards the mother. The actual death of this Medusa-like mother provoked in Jung conflicting emotions, in response to her own dual nature and its lifelong effect on him. On receiving the news of her death, Jung went home to her:

> ...I had a feeling of great grief, but in my heart of hearts I could not be mournful, and this for a strange reason: during the entire journey I continually heard dance music, laughter, and jollity, as though a wedding were being celebrated...One side of me had a feeling of warmth and joy, and the other of terror and grief...(p. 345).[8]

Jung's reaction of joy, as well as of grief, to his mother's death, could be ascribed to the fulfilment of his unconscious desire for her to die and, indeed, to go to hell.

Jung's dream and his interpretation of it help to clarify not only the nature of his bond with his mother but also some of the personal motivations underlying his psychological system. For at the heart of Jung's thought lies the quest to reconcile opposites, to achieve wholeness and self-realization. Despite the terror aroused by the dream, Jung attempts a reconciliation of sorts, through an affirmative interpretation. For originally, he writes, Wotan was not a devil but a nature spirit, the *spiritus Mercurialis*, sought by the alchemists. Thus, according to Jung, 'the dream says that the soul of my mother was taken into that greater territory of the self which lies beyond the segment of Christian morality, taken into that wholeness of nature and spirit in which conflicts and contradictions are resolved' (p. 345).

The seven dreams related above bear out Freud's belief that poets and philosophers discovered the unconscious. These dreams vividly illustrate the impact which bereavement may have on the unconscious. They confirm Freud's emphasis on loss in

Inhibitions, Symptoms and Anxiety, which was prefigured already in his self-analysis a quarter-century earlier. Freud's own dreams and memories, many of which are recorded in *The Interpretation of Dreams* and in his letters to Fliess, left him in no doubt as to the critical effect on him of loss and separation, both in childhood and in adult life; and this was confirmed further by patients such as Anna O., Emmy von N., and Elisabeth von R., whose hysterical symptoms, related in the *Studies on Hysteria* (1895), were clearly connected with severe loss.

Finally, we may conclude this chapter by returning to our two initial fundamental questions: what was the role of loss in Freud's self-analysis? and why did he not immediately use his discoveries to evolve a theory of loss, rather than wait some twenty-five years before doing so?

As we noted, Freud is known to have suffered at least three major forms of loss or separation in childhood:

1. His brother, Julius, born when Freud was nearly 1½, died about six months later (Krüll, 1986). Freud wrote to Fliess at the time of his self-analysis: 'I welcomed my one-year-younger brother with ill wishes and real infantile jealousy, and his death left the germ of guilt in me' (1954, p. 219).

2. Freud lost his nurse, Resi Wittek, to whom he was closely attached, when he was 2½. He wrote of her to Fliess: 'If...I succeed in resolving my hysteria, I shall have to thank the memory of the old woman who provided me at such an early age with the means for living and surviving' (*ibid.*).

3. According to Jones (1953, p. 17), Freud's mother suffered from tuberculosis when he was a child. She underwent treatment at a spa in Roznau, in Moravia.[9] Her illness had not been cured two decades later. In the available correspondence of Freud's early adult life, he mentions his mother only twice: 'that she was very given to complaining, and that she suffered from a serious tuberculosis of the lung' (*ibid.*, p. 173). It is not surprising, therefore, to learn that Freud was extremely worried about his mother's health.

Some of the effects of the mother's illness may be glimpsed in Freud's self-analysis. He does not write about it openly, but alludes to it obliquely. Anxiety over the mother's health, separations owing to her medical treatment, the symptoms themselves, and the mother's self-preoccupation (of which her persistent complaining was, no doubt, a sign) must, to an extent, have affected the bond with her son. Freud's sibling rivalry and his consequent guilt after his brother's death may have intensified as a result of the mother's illness. In addition, it is likely that her illness, her pregnancy with Julius, her mourning in the wake of his death, and her confinement with a third child (who was born around the time of the nurse's dismissal) heightened Freud's anxiety over separation from her and his dependence on his nurse. For these reasons, the loss of the nurse who, in Freud's extraordinary phrase, gave him 'the means for living and surviving' (die Mittel zum Leben und Weiterleben) – as though his mother did not fulfil this role, or not adequately – was a particularly hard blow. A memory of his from the period shortly after the nurse was dismissed confirms the deep impression that this loss made on him and his anxiety that his mother, too, would disappear. In the memory, he cried bitterly over his mother's absence until finally she reappeared: 'I feared she must have vanished, like my nurse not long before' (1954, p. 223).

Freud's anxiety over the potential loss of his mother is evident also in a dream of his dating from the age of six or seven and related in *The Interpretation of Dreams*: 'I saw my beloved mother, with a peculiarly peaceful, sleeping expression on her features, being carried into the room by two (or three) people with birds' beaks and laid upon the bed. I awoke in tears and screaming, and interrupted my parents' sleep' (1900, p. 583). Anxiety over separation from the mother, either because of her illness or because of the nurse's disappearance, or both, may account partly for the violent, incestuous side of Freud's attachment to his mother: Freud's incestuous feelings for his mother may have been exaggerated by his need to hold on to her in his anxiety that she would disappear. Freud himself interpreted his anxiety in the dream of his mother's death as evidence of his 'sexual craving' for her, rather than of grief at her death.[10]

The impact which his mother's tuberculosis had upon Freud's emotional and intellectual life may have been considerable: medical treatment at the time was primitive and its results unpredictable, and the Freud family must have suffered greatly under the threat of the mother's death. In his essay on 'The Aetiology of Hysteria', Freud compares the origins of hysteria to those of tuberculosis, for just as some who breathe the bacillus are not affected, so also some who recall infantine sexual experience do not become hysterics:

Is not the tubercule bacillus ubiquitous and is it not inhaled by far more people than are found to fall ill of tuberculosis? And is its aetiological significance impaired by the fact that other factors must obviously be at work too before the tuberculosis, which is its specific effect, can be evoked? In order to establish the bacillus as the specific aetiology it is enough to show that tuberculosis cannot possibly occur without its playing a part (1896, p. 209).

That Freud's thinking was deeply affected by his mother's illness is suggested further in his *New Introductory Lectures on Psychoanalysis* (1933), his first major work after his mother's death in 1930, in which he compares psychoanalysis and its long-term treatment with tuberculosis.

Leaving aside somewhat conjectural matters such as these, a single major fact to emerge from a study of Freud's self-analysis (or what is known of it) is that Freud knew, from his experiences of the dismissal of his nurse and his mother's illness, how strongly a child can feel anxiety and longing for a lost loved one. Yet in the formulation of a theory of childhood development in *The Interpretation of Dreams*, he actually plays down the importance of loss and separation to the child, not only if the child's nurse has been dismissed but even if his mother has died:

To children, who are spared the sight of the scenes of suffering which precede death, being 'dead' means approximately the same as being 'gone' – not troubling the survivors any longer. A child makes no distinction as to how this absence is brought about: whether it is due to a journey, to a dismissal, to an estrangement, or to death. If, during a child's prehistoric epoch, his nurse has been dismissed, and if soon afterwards his mother has died, the two events are superimposed on each other in a single series in his memory as revealed in analysis. When people are absent, children do not miss them with any great intensity; many mothers have learnt this to their sorrow when, after being away from home for some weeks on a summer holiday, they are met on their return by the news that the children have not once asked for their mummy (1900, pp. 254–5).

Freud immediately goes on to formulate the Oedipus complex, arguing that dreams of the death of parents occur most frequently with the parent who is of the same sex as the dreamer, 'as though boys regarded their fathers and girls their mothers as their rivals

in love, whose elimination could not fail to be to their advantage.'
In this way, the theory of the Oedipus complex supplanted a
latent theory of loss and separation in *The Interpretation of Dreams.*

Freud waited a quarter-century before giving the role of childhood loss its proper emphasis in his work. In *Inhibitions, Symptoms and Anxiety,* he writes of the effect on a young child of
separation from its mother:

> It cannot as yet distinguish between temporary absence and
> permanent loss. As soon as it loses sight of its mother it
> behaves as if it were never going to see her again; and repeated
> consoling experiences to the contrary are necessary before it
> learns that her disappearance is usually followed by her re-
> appearance (1926, p. 169).

Freud even goes so far as to describe separation as *the* key to
anxiety, an assertion which Bowlby (1973) points out is an over-
statement. Yet, as we have seen, over thirty years previously,
Freud's self-analysis revealed to him the critical importance of
loss and separation in his own early life. Why did he not give
these factors their due in *The Interpretation of Dreams*? Why,
indeed, did he minimize the role of loss and separation in the life
of the child? It may well be that Freud himself did not know how
much importance to attach to his early experiences of loss and
separation. He may have given way to a natural tendency to deny
the trauma and, in effect, to reassure himself that his nurse's
dismissal and separations from his mother would not have
affected him as they did. Denial might have been a particularly
strong temptation in the Victorian era, when it was often believed
that one should 'get over' and forget a loss within a relatively
short time, and that, as Freud himself writes, 'When people are
absent, children do not miss them with any great intensity.' The
carnage of World War One put an end to this naive, self-serving
attitude and brought about far greater public consciousness of the
effects of loss, which is reflected in Freud's post-war writings,
including *Inhibitions, Symptoms and Anxiety.*

It may also be that Freud did not wish to emphasize publicly
the role of loss in his own life as it was too personal (his mother
was alive at the time of writing *The Interpretation of Dreams*), and it
seemed to interfere with or even to contradict the theory of the
Oedipus complex. Freud was juggling with complex and seemingly contradictory ideas during the course of his self-analysis,
and it may be that he did not know how to fit the evidence
pertaining to loss and separation into the theory of the Oedipus

complex. Preferring the more original, dramatic, and 'universal' concept of the Oedipus complex, he found it necessary to down-play loss and separation.

Freud's difficulties in reconciling a theory of loss to the Oedipus complex may be understood more clearly by considering how closely, in his own case, the Oedipus complex appears to have been tangled up with loss. Freud discovered the Oedipus complex in himself at the time of his self-analysis following his father's death (1954, p. 223). With the death of his father Freud experienced the anger, the hatred, and the self-reproach which, as we have seen, are often felt by the bereaved towards the dead and, to some extent, Freud recognized this. In the dream which he had on the night before or after his father's funeral,[11] and which he related to Fliess, he described his guilt towards his father as a universal effect of loss:

I found myself in a shop where there was a notice up saying: 'You are requested to close the eyes.' I recognized the place as the barber's to which I go every day. On the day of the funeral I was kept waiting, and therefore arrived at the house of mourn-ing rather late. The family were displeased with me, because I had arranged for the funeral to be quiet and simple, which they later agreed was the best thing. They also took my lateness in rather bad part. The phrase on the notice-board has a double meaning. It means 'one should do one's duty towards the dead' in two senses – an apology, as though I had not done my duty and my conduct needed overlooking, and the actual duty itself. The dream was thus an outlet for the feeling of self-reproach which a death generally leaves among the survivors (1954, p. 171).

However, what apparently shocked Freud in particular was his discovery that he had unconsciously wanted his father to die, and although such hostile feelings are also not uncommon among the bereaved, Freud interpreted them as a sign of primeval oedipal rivalry rather than as part of the grief process.[12] And so, in the very section of *The Interpretation of Dreams* in which one might expect insight into the effect of loss on dreams, 'Dreams of the Death of Persons of whom the Dreamer is Fond', Freud empha-sizes the role of wish-fulfilment, not even considering the possi-bility that such dreams may act as a means of mastering grief, and immediately after plays down the impact of loss upon the child 'if his nurse has been dismissed, and if soon afterwards his mother has died', going on to formulate the concept of the Oedipus complex!

Freud's grief for his father was almost certainly complicated by childhood attitudes and emotions which were revived by the loss, and in fact what he described as his Oedipus complex had much to do with loss. Thus, Freud's jealous hatred for his father as a rival for his mother's love could have been intensified by his separation anxiety towards his mother as a result of her tuberculosis and her confinements with seven children after him, including the one who died. As in his early years, she was preoccupied with illness, death, giving birth, the care of so many children and the poverty of the family did not make matters easier. She was unable to give her eldest son the consistent, unanxious care which she undoubtedly wished to give him and perhaps for this reason the nurse had to be employed. He reacted by becoming overly-attached to her, fearful of her departure, and suspicious of his father as a rival interfering with his needs. The anxiety towards the mother was heightened by the nurse's dismissal, as Freud was terrified that she, too, would vanish.

As Freud grew older, his mother may have welcomed his excessive attachment to her as he was her first-born and favourite. Her husband was elderly–he was twenty years older than her and, significantly, the marriage had been arranged–and he was somewhat detached by age and temperament from the rest of the family. His orthodox Jewish origins were also a source of friction and animosity.[13] Freud's consequent over-attachment to his mother, in turn, might have added fuel to the sense of rivalry with the father.

So Freud's emphasis on the Oedipus complex in *The Interpretation of Dreams* – an emphasis which studies have shown not to be untrue but exaggerated (Kline, 1972) – may be traced in part to the effects of his grief following his father's death. His equation of anxiety with libido rather than with separation may, similarly, be attributed partly to his preoccupation – revived and, to some extent, intensified by grief – with the problem of rivalry with his father for his mother's love.

Freud's overemphasis on separation as *the* key to anxiety in *Inhibitions, Symptoms and Anxiety* may, likewise, be linked with a personal grief of Freud's following an especially severe loss. In 1923, Freud's favourite grandson, Heinz, died of tuberculosis at the age of four. Freud wrote that he had never experienced such grief as after the boy's death: 'I myself was aware of never having loved a human being, certainly never a child, so much' (1960, p.

349). Heinz's mother, Sophie (Freud's second daughter), had died in 1920 when Heinz was an infant, and Freud had the opportunity to observe the effects of this loss on Heinz.[14] These circumstances might have predisposed Freud to place emphasis on separation as the key to anxiety. But by then he was old and ailing, and his basic theories had taken root and it was too late for him to revise them fully and bring them into line with his later ideas.

Freud's views on dreams and loss, objectively true as they are in some respects, are of course stamped with the vicissitudes of his life experiences and passions – in short, his humanity. Although he did not live to incorporate the concept of loss, with its manifold ramifications, into his psychoanalytic theory, his efforts to record and interpret his dreams after his father's death were the foundation both of his self-analysis and of modern dream analysis. His conviction that dreams are the royal road to the unconscious is borne out in studies of dreams of loss in literature. Each dream, susceptible as it is to various levels of interpretation, reveals the essence of the effect of loss on the dreamer and the dynamics of his relationship with the lost person. Memories, too, may serve a creative function in dealing with loss, for like dreams they can can both screen trauma and express it and, in so doing, enable the bereaved gradually and on his own terms to master it.

4

LOSS AND CHILDHOOD
MEMORIES

Of this, at least, I feel assured, that there is no such thing as
forgetting possible to the mind; a thousand accidents may, and
will interpose a veil between our present consciousness and the
secret inscriptions on the mind; accidents of the same sort will
also rend away this veil; but alike, whether veiled or unveiled, the
inscription remains for ever; just as the stars seem to withdraw
before the common light of day, whereas, in fact, we all know
that it is the light which is drawn over them as a veil – and that
they are waiting to be revealed, when the obscuring daylight shall
have withdrawn.

Thomas De Quincey, *Confessions of an English Opium Eater*

In common with dreams, memories stemming from loss often
confront the trauma indirectly, in a screened, compressed,
symbolic or elliptical form. Literature offers a host of examples of
memories relating to loss, particularly in childhood and amply
reflects the importance which Freud attached to memories as
veiled forms of whole slices of experience (1899, 1901, *et al.*). It
may be that childhood bereavement is more likely than adult loss
to find artistic expression in memories, as childhood grief is often
not worked through at the time of the loss but seeks an outlet
later in life. Memories of childhood may act as a starting point for
such delayed mourning and the creative use of these memories
may serve as a means of confronting and mastering the trauma,
and especially the violent anger stirred up by it.

Judging from the work of the great pre-Freudian writers, it
seems that Freud discovered little that is new about memories.
Rather, he formulated generalizations, within a far-reaching psychoanalytic framework, by which memories can be better understood. Like other memories, recollections of loss, or connected
with loss, may sometimes be interpreted as 'screen memories',[1]
an expression originated by Freud (1899) and as mysterious and

airily intriguing as its German original, *Deckerinnergungen*, is Teutonically weighty and rhythmically gutteral. By this he meant a seemingly innocuous childhood memory retained into adult life and, frequently, reactivated in times of stress. As the personality changes, new memories may be revived which fit the present. Whether or not these memories are true or falsified is beside the point and thus fictional illustrations are as valid as biographical ones. In Dostoyevsky's *The Brothers Karamazov* (1880), for example, the link between a screen memory and childhood loss may be readily inferred in the account of Alyosha, who retains a single memory dating prior to his mother's death when he was three. This memory casts light on Alyosha's later character and on his life as a monk:

> . . . all he remembered was an evening, a quiet summer evening, an open window, the slanting rays of the setting sun (it was the slanting rays that he remembered most of all), an icon in the corner of the room, a lighted lamp in front of it, and on her knees before the icon his mother, sobbing as though in hysterics, with screams and shrieks, snatching him up in her arms, hugging him to her breast so tightly that it hurt, and praying for him to the Virgin, holding him out in both hands to the icon as though under the Virgin's protection, and suddenly a nurse runs in and snatches him from her in terror (1978, p. 17).

Alyosha's almost saintly dedication to the Church, as to a substitute mother, is linked by Dostoyevsky to the loss of his mother, who, knowing that she is about to die, offers her son to the Virgin in a moment of anguish and radiance that virtually determines his life. The full extent of the trauma is screened by this radiance— indeed, it is the sunlight that Alyosha remembers most vividly— but the anguish remains, though mastered in the service of God.

A screen memory may thus be seen as a sign of conflict between the denial of the truth and the facing of it. The fact of its selection is itself important. Screen memories have qualities of dreams, such as repression, symbolization and condensation. As screen memories both confront and avoid, express and disguise, they serve well as vehicles for recalling and working through the yearning and searching phase of grief, in which denial and acceptance commonly overlap, or for expressing a fixation at that phase.

Writers who have suffered childhood loss often seem particularly aware that their childhood memories have altered with time and have accumulated symbolic meaning. Wordsworth writes in this way of his childhood memories in *The Prelude*:

> I cannot say what portion is in truth
> The naked recollection of that time
> And what may rather have been called to life
> By after-meditation.

(1805 edn., III, 645–8)

He compares memory with a view of water from a moving boat. The traveller is confused by the many things reflected, and at the bottom of the deep:

> ...often is preplexed, and cannot part
> The shadow from the substance...

IV, 254–5)

The revelations of Freud have had the effect of making twentieth-century writers even more conscious of the transformations and the potential significance of these memories. In an autobiography which gives a central place to the impact on him of the loss of his mother in childhood, Stephen Spender prefaces his childhood memories with the following remarks:

> I have read that it is impossible to remember things which have happened to one, as they really were. Memories – the argument runs – are only present in our minds because they have been transformed from a past actuality into a present myth, which is a new experience only distantly related to the old. We colour our past experiences with those present ones which give them significance, illustrating what we are and not what they were.
> This may be so (1951, p. 322).

Just as screen memories do not of course invariably screen traumas such as loss, memories of childhood loss do not necessarily act as screens but may register images directly relating to the loss. For example, Richard Steele beating at his father's coffin (Connely, 1934, p. 20); Rousseau voraciously reading his dead mother's books (1977, p. 20);[2] De Quincey collapsing on hearing of his sister's death (1966, p. 28);[3] Martin Buber's being told as a child that his mother, who had disappeared, would never return (1973, pp. 17–18).[4]

The proximity in time of a memory to a bereavement might

indicate that it screens the trauma, expressing it, yet holding it in check. One of the earliest memories of the Hebrew poet Chaim Nachman Bialik was of a fire which took place when he was seven, not long after his father's death. He used this memory in his major poetic work, *The Scroll of Fire* (1905), with its spectacular account of the burning of the Temple in Jerusalem and the defeated God in mourning among the ruins:

> In the middle of the night it seemed the whole world was being destroyed. Everything was lit up – I saw a plain, a synagogue – I heard cries – it was all a game, an entertainment. I remember that I was very happy at the sight, but there was also the fear of God. When I wrote the opening of *The Scroll of Fire*, I recalled the dry trees burning fiercely in a storm of fire, and everything was wiped out, only heaps of coals remained (1935, II, p. 30).

The fire provoked mixed emotions – it was 'a game, an enter-tainment', 'but there was also the fear of God'; similarly, the loss of the father was a lifelong source of ambivalence to the poet.[5] In the opening of *The Scroll of Fire*, however, the dominant mood is one of grief. God is described as sitting with his head buried in his arms, covered by mountains of grief: 'Silent and desolate he sat and stared at the ruins. Eternal wrath darkened his eyelids and the great silence was frozen in his eyes.' Like the ruined natural world in Nerval's *Aurélia*, or the lost Atlantis in the writings of Tolkein and C.S. Lewis,[6] this image of total destruction appears to reflect the poet's chronic sense of personal loss: the death of Bialik's father was the all-consuming tragedy of his early life. It led to the total break-up of his family. His mother was unable to support him and, not long afterwards, sent him to live with his grandparents. From the child's point of view, 'it seemed the whole world was being destroyed...everything was wiped out'.

In the writings of Edmund Gosse, similarly, a memory dating from after a parent's death appears to reflect obliquely the effects of this trauma on the child. The memory dates from the late 1850s, shortly after the death of Gosse's mother, and concerns not an event but a powerful wish, when Gosse was about nine. After his mother's death in London, Gosse moved with his father, a marine zoologist, to the Devonshire coast. At this time, he writes in his memoir of childhood, *Father and Son* (1907), 'a fresh rival arose to compete for me with my Father's dogmatic theology. This rival was the Sea' (1976, p. 71). His great desire was 'to walk out over the sea as far as I could, and then lie flat on it, face downwards, and peer into the depths. I was tormented with this ambition, and, like many grown-up people, was so fully occupied by these vain and ridiculous desires that I neglected the actual natural pleasures around me' (p. 73).

As Bialik does not connect his memory of the fire with his father's death, so also Gosse does not relate this memory to the death of his mother (the immediate effects of which are described in the previous chapter of *Father and Son*); yet the link is implicit. The memory in its context of loss acts virtually as an emblem of Gosse's profound loneliness after her death, as well as his rather morbid introspection at the time – he relates that the favourite topic of conversation between himself and his father at this time was murders. His grief was impeded further by the rigid puritan restraint of his father, who was going through a devastating religious and professional crisis in the aftermath of Darwin's revelations on the origins of species. The boy's wish to peer into the depths of the sea might indicate the power of his yearning and searching for his mother, and his longing for her physical contact is also evident perhaps in his desire to miraculously defy physical laws, and walk Christ-like over the water and lie flat on it.

As Gosse was a leading expert on English literature by the time of writing *Father and Son*, he was probably well aware of the similarity between his own attachment to the sea after his mother's death and that of Paul Dombey in Dickens' *Dombey and Son* (1846–8). Here, too, the yearning for the sea symbolizes the child's yearning for his mother, who had died in giving birth to him. But at the same time it may betray a death-wish – 'The bottom of the sea is cruel', writes Hart Crane in 'Voyages'. Florence Dombey takes her sickly brother to the sea. Paul falls asleep, then suddenly wakes in a start and sits up listening. Florence asks him what he hears:

> 'I want to know what it says,' he answered, looking steadily in her face. 'The sea, Floy, what is it that it keeps on saying?'
> She told him that it was only the noise of the rolling waves.
> 'Yes, yes,' he said. 'But I know that they are always saying something. Always the same thing. What place is over there?' He rose up, looking eagerly at the horizon.
> She told him that there was another country opposite, but he said he didn't mean that; he meant farther away – farther away! (ch. 8).

Later, Paul confesses that he doesn't know 'why the sea should always make me think of my mama that's dead' (ch. 12).

Of all literary childhood memories, perhaps the most famous and elaborate is Proust's fictionalized memory of his mother's kiss at the start of *Remembrance of Things Past*. Proust began this massive semi-biographical novel shortly after the death of his mother in 1905. This loss was the watershed in his life and art, the point at which Time Present became Time Past, for Proust laboured for the rest of his life after her death to recreate his past, and to preserve his mother, in art.

The novel begins with the narrator's memories of his aunt's home in Combray where he spent his holidays as a child. Sickly and sensitive, with a clinging dependence upon his mother, he was deeply upset at having to go to bed early, for he would feel that he had lost his mother until the next day. Her goodnight kiss was his consolation, an eagerly-awaited ceremony necessary to dispel the anxieties which would otherwise prevent him from sleeping. One night during a dinner party, the little boy, aged seven, was sent to bed without his kiss. After an agony of waiting, exacerbated by his mother's failure to respond to the imploring note he had sent her, he heard her footsteps on the stairs. He ran to her and, in a paroxysm of joy and terror, flung himself into her arms. His mother, who 'had never allowed herself to indulge in any undue emotion with me', was apparently annoyed at this display. But the father appeared at this moment and, unexpectedly, seeing the boy's misery, suggested that she spend the night with him. Alone with her, the boy broke into tears – as he described it thirty years later, he could still hear his sobs – 'their echo has never ceased' – and his mother, too, was overcome. She spent the rest of the night comforting him and reading to him. This victorious 'puberty of sorrow', as Proust calls it, became the symbol of defeat in his later life:

> It struck me that if I had just won a victory it was over her, that I had succeeded, as sickness or sorrow or age might have succeeded, in relaxing her will, in undermining her judgment; and that this evening opened a new era, would remain a black date in the calendar. And if I had dared now, I should have said to Mamma: 'No, I don't want you to, you mustn't sleep here' (1981, I, p. 41).

It is interesting to consider Proust's creative blossoming after his mother's death in connection with his reaction to a case involving an acquaintance, Henri van Blarenberghe, who murdered his mother and then killed himself. Several days later,

Proust published an article on the crime, arguing that van Blarenberghe had done violently what other men do gradually, for all men 'kill' their mothers: 'The fact is that we age and kill the heart that loves us by the anxiety we cause, by the uneasy tenderness we inspire and keep in a state of unceasing alarm' (Painter, 1965, p. 70). Proust's empathy with the matricide coming so soon after the crime might be condemned as tasteless and repellent, if not mad. On a deeper level, however, it contains an indirect confession of his own suppressed violence and his sense of guilt over his mother's death. For if he had 'murdered' his mother, she had done the same to him, with her excessive anxiety and uneasy tenderness, turning him (as he no doubt suspected at times) into a semi-invalid, responsible at least in part for his lifelong insomnia and illnesses, his homosexuality and drug-addiction, and his inability to lead a 'normal' life in society, especially where women were concerned. This anger might be foreshadowed in the memory of the mother's kiss and revived with her death, and it may be that 'the child's anger went deeper than his remorse, that the true crux was not her final capitulation, but her initial refusal' (Painter, 1959, p.11). The loss of the kiss and its recovery thus became the first intimation and symbol of the loss of the mother (as well of other losses, such as that of Albertine), and her recovery in art. Behind the screen of art, the bereaved artist struggled to master his consequent guilt and anger.

Anger and sudden violence appear to be especially common in childhood memories which relate to a time of loss or separation. The first memory to which the term 'screen memory' was applied may be cited as an example. It appears in Freud's essay 'Screen Memories' (1899) and is related by one of Freud's patients:

I see a rectangular, rather steeply sloping piece of meadow-land, green and thickly grown; in the green there are a great number of yellow flowers – evidently common dandelions. At the top end of the meadow there is a cottage and in front of the cottage door two women are standing chatting busily, a peasant-woman with a handkerchief on her head and a children's nurse. Three children are playing in the grass. One of them is myself (between the age of two and three); the two others are my boy cousin, who is a year older than me, and his sister, who is almost exactly the same age as I am. We are picking the yellow flowers and each of us is holding a bunch of flowers we have already picked. The little girl has the best bunch; and, as though by mutual agreement, we – the two boys – fall on her and snatch away her flowers (SE, III, p. 311).

Freud's analysis of this memory makes clear, as Jones (1953) and others have long maintained, that the 'patient' was, in fact, Freud himself. The scene is Freiberg, Freud's birthplace and home until the age of three, when his family moved to Vienna. Freud revisited Freiberg only once, when he was sixteen, and stayed with family friends. He fell in love with their daughter, Gisela, but was too shy to tell her: at this time, the memory returned. Freud analyzes the theft of flowers as a screen for a rape fantasy directed both towards his cousin Pauline and Gisela: 'Taking flowers from a girl means to deflower her.'

At the same time, Jones writes, this memory undoubtedly contains undertones of homosexuality and of incest involving Freud's mother; and, as we have seen in the previous chapter, Freud's overly-close bond with his mother was affected by anxiety for her health as she had tuberculosis. In the mid-nineteenth century, this illness was far more serious and frightening than it is today, and it required treatment away from home, which might explain why the mother does not appear in the memory. The illness may have been worsened by the death of her second son, Julius, not long before the events in the memory took place. Another severe loss which occurred around the time of the memory, as we have seen, was the dimissal for theft of Freud's nanny, to whom he was also closely attached, all the more so as a result of his mother's illness. Unlike the mother, the nanny does appear, as the children's nurse chatting by the cottage door. The violent act in the memory might, therefore, reflect anger not only at the mother for her absence (and for being distracted by her illness) but also at the nanny for having 'deserted'.

Anger at a lost person is a normal part of the grief process, and the greater the dependence the more severe this anger is liable to be. Children are therefore especially likely to be angry after a severe loss, but owing to their very dependence often cannot express this anger directly but must do so in a displaced form. The innocent and harmless attack on a little girl who is gathering flowers may be a convenient displacement of this sort. Other instances of childhood memories of violent acts against female objects, in the writings of Bialik and Wordsworth, may be compared with Freud's memory as they too date from a period of loss. The psychological tactic of using such memories both to screen out and to express harsher things, and by doing so to master trauma creatively, is well defined in a fragment of conversation between Freud and his 'patient':

> Freud: It is precisely the coarsely sensual element in the fantasy which explains why it does not develop into a *conscious* fantasy but must be content to find its way allusively and under a flowery disguise into a childhood scene.
> Patient: But why precisely, into a *childhood* scene, I should like to know?
> Freud: For the sake of its innocence, perhaps. Can you imagine a greater contrast to these designs for gross sexual aggression than childhood pranks? (SE, III, p. 317).

This mixture of innocence and experience, revelation and concealment is found in a childhood memory of Bialik's from his semi-biographical memoir, *Aftergrowth* (1903–23). The similarity to Freud's memory is remarkable: here, too, a little boy, the poet, attacks a little girl while she is gathering flowers:

> Feigele in her white dress darts like a bird from plant to plant, picking flowers; I follow her. How many she has picked today; she has a whole sheaf in her arms! Suddenly she starts back. She has just seen a dead snake in the grass. 'Don't be afraid!' I calmed her out of experience. 'He is dead, just look!' And I lift the snake in my hands. I have no fear of snakes. They are to be found in our garden and they do not impress me. 'Drop it, drop it!' she cries out startled, and steps back. 'Throw it away!' A spirit of lighthearted bravado possesses me. I shake the snake at her as if it were a whip. She runs away yelling in fright and I, cruel fellow that I am, pursue her. While running the flowers drop from her hands one by one and scatter – blue, yellow and white. The great radiance of the sunset filters through her thin dress and earlobes; I chase her, snake in hand.
> Suddenly – I do not know how it happens – Feigele vanishes from my sight. She has hidden herself (1939, pp. 123–4).

It is impossible to know how much of this extraordinary memory is real, how much comes from a later time or from the poet's imagination, though in Bialik's posthumous works there is a biographical fragment which indicates that in some form or another the scene described actually took place: 'Once I chased two little girls in a field, a snake writhing in my hand. The sun went down in a flow of blood across the green space' (1971, p. 244).

As in the case of Freud's memory, the poet's memory of 'deflowering' the little girl dates from a period shortly before a major loss and upheaval and the violence here may be seen to be a result of this loss. The memory is set in the Volhynian village of Radi where the poet lived until he was five, when his family moved to the larger town of Zhitomir. This move, which took place in the late 1870s, was later regarded by the poet as a catastrophic loss of his childhood paradise. It set into motion a chain of events culminating in his father's death and his separation from his mother. In a continuation of the memory, the sunset is seen by the child as a theophany reminiscent of *The Scroll of Fire*, terrifying him with its signs of world-consuming conflagration, and possibly alluding to the impending destruction of his childhood.

Another seemingly innocent childhood memory which dates from a period of family break-up is by Wordsworth in the fragment known as 'Nutting'. This memory, like those of Freud and Bialik, is of a sudden, seemingly irrational and unpremediated act of violence against a female object: the poet describes himself as a young boy in Hawkshead in the Lake District, forcing his way through tangled thickets to a nook of hazel boughs unravished by human touch. With voluptuous joy he eyes the bower and plays with its flowers, but then, without warning, he falls upon it and violates it. Exultant in his destructiveness, he then feels guilt and sorrow intruding:

> ...the hazels rose
> Tall and erect, with tempting clusters hung,
> A virgin scene! – A little while I stood,
> Breathing with such suppression of the heart
> As joy delights in; and with wise restraint
> Voluptuous, fearless of a rival, eyed
> The banquet; – or beneath a tree I sate
> Among the flowers, and with the flowers I played...
> Then up I rose,
> And dragged to earth both branch and bough, with crash
> And merciless ravage; and the shady nook
> Of hazels, and the green and mossy bower,
> Deformed and sullied, patiently gave up
> Their quiet being: and unless I now
> Confound my present feelings with the past,
> Ere from the mutilated bower I turned
> Exulting, rich beyond the wealth of kings,

I felt a sense of pain when I beheld
The silent trees, and saw the intruding sky.

This is vintage Wordsworth and it works on many levels. For example, as a metaphor of man's destructiveness, a reprehensible, though perhaps inevitable, product of his civilization, and then specifically, as a reflection of the Industrial Revolution which, by the end of the eighteenth century, when this fragment was written, had already begun to ravage and deform the European countryside and skies. Yet, in the lines 'unless I now/ Confound my present feelings with the past', Wordsworth also exposes his own suspicion that the memory might have a private symbolic meaning. The mutilation of the bower, 'Tall and erect, with tempting clusters hung,/A virgin scene!', might represent rape, violence, or some form of maltreatment of a woman, with consequent pain and guilt. There might be an unconscious allusion here to Wordsworth's feelings over his affair with his French lover, Annette Vallon, with whom he fathered an illegitimate child before leaving her in France during the troubles of 1792: according to Moorman (1957), this was the bitterest experience of his life, and it seems to have left its mark on his writings, especially those telling of violated and deserted women.

But was this the bitterest experience of Wordsworth's life? As we have seen, Wordsworth, like Bialik, was orphaned at an early age, and the destruction of the hazel bower apparently took place not long after his mother died – there is an allusion earlier in the fragment to Ann Tyson, 'my frugal Dame', with whom he lodged while in school at Hawkshead after his mother's death. Again like Bialik, Wordsworth did not suffer the loss of one parent alone but was separated from his surviving parent and experienced by the age of eight the complete disruption of his family life. He then passed into the care of grandparents – again, like Bialik – with whom he was miserable. He thus had good reason to be angry and even violent. Another memory of his, which according to Moorman apparently dates from the time when he lived with his grandparents, may be compared in its sudden, wanton violence to the 'Nutting' fragment:

... while I was at my grandfather's house at Penrith, along with my eldest brother, Richard, we were whipping tops together in the large dining-room... The walls were hung round with family pictures, and I said to my brother, 'Dare you strike your whip through that old lady's petticoat?' He replied, 'No, I won't.' 'Then,' said I, 'here goes'; and I struck my lash through her looped petticoat, for which no doubt...I was properly punished' (Owen & Smyser, eds., 1974, III, p. 372).

This hostility could also be turned inwards: Wordsworth recalled that he once nearly committed suicide by stabbing himself with one of his grandfather's swords but could not bring himself to go through with it (*ibid.*, p. 372).[7] His experience of childhood loss, particularly the death of his mother, accounts in no small part for the torture which he inflicted on himself in later years. Even Coleridge, who was no stranger to inner torment, wrote that Wordsworth, in comparison with himself, had 'more hours that prey upon his flesh and blood' (Griggs, ed., 1966, p. 491).

Wordsworth's extreme remorse during the years immediately following his desertion of Annette Vallon might be interpreted as a reaction to what was, perhaps unconsciously, a case of mimesis: he left Annette as his mother had left him.[8] We have already pointed out that, especially among children, anger and self-blame after a loss are common. Wordsworth's unconscious revenge, if that is what it was, might have brought to the surface unresolved feelings deriving from the loss of his mother. His memory of the hazel bower might, therefore, have acted as a screen for the passion, the sorrow, the destructiveness and the guilt aroused by the death of his mother and revived by Annette Vallon.

The memories of Freud, Bialik, and Wordsworth have in common a violent act against a female object and proximity in time to a traumatic loss. The three writers share an uncommon degree of anxiety over separation from their mothers – Wordswroth and Bialik as a result of their orphanhood, and Freud, because of his mother's illness and consequent separations from her as well as the loss of his nanny. In general, these memories suggest that the dependence caused by separation from the mother or her loss might lead, among other things, to incestuous fantasies; and, as we have seen, the sexual violence in the memories might screen and master creatively the destructive anger at having been 'abandoned' by the mother.

In this chapter, we have looked at ways in which loss, particularly in childhood, may be imprinted upon adult memories. These memories may serve as a gauge, allowing bearable elements of grief to enter consciousness while screening off other elements which are too harsh to be confronted squarely. Further ways of mastering grief through creativity may be discerned in mystical literature, much of which deals with phenomena comparable to the phases and characteristics of grief.

5

GRIEF AND MYSTICISM

The soul cannot be possessed of the divine union until it has divested itself of the love of created beings.

St John of the Cross, *The Ascent of Mount Carmel*

A man does not join himself with the Universe so long as he has anything else to join himself with.

T.S. Eliot, 'Shakespeare and the Stoicism of Seneca'

Hardly a phase or characteristic of grief does not have a parallel in mystical experiences. Mystical experiences vary widely in religious and cultural background. They differ in mode of onset, duration, intensity, in their susceptibility to recall, and meaning. They may be treated as signs of sickness or healing, of weakness or adaptation, of illusion or a higher reality, of breakdown or creativity. Among psychological interpretations, a number of studies have emphasized similarities and differences between forms of mysticism and mental illness (e.g. Laing, 1959; Bateson, 1961; Prince & Savage, 1965; Wapnick, 1969; Scharfstein, 1973; Horton, 1973; Furst *et al.*, 1976; Woods, 1980). Various psychological concepts have been applied to mysticism It has been termed as a defence of the ego by Freud (1930); an expression of the collective unconscious by Jung (1935); a type of infantilism connected with fantasies of bodily incorporation by Riviere (1955); a creative experience akin to or deriving from 'phallic awe', experienced in early childhood by Greenacre (1957); a manifestation of regression in the service of the ego by Prince and Savage (1965). However, among these and other interpretations, none has given due attention to similarities between certain mystical experiences and grief reactions.[1] Both the literature on mysticism (e.g. Otto, 1930; Zaehner, 1957; Stace, 1960; Goodenough, 1965; Parrinder, 1976; Wainwright, 1981) and on loss have largely overlooked this connection. Similarly, the insights of creative writers into the nature of loss and mysticism have been mostly ignored.

At times, the links between loss and mystical calling are fairly clear, as in the autobiography of the sixteenth-century Spanish mystic, Sister Teresa. Teresa's life in the Church began with her mother's death: 'When my mother died, I was twelve years of age or a little less. When I began to realize what I had lost, I went in my distress to an image of Our Lady and with many tears besought her to be a mother to me' (1944, I, p. 12).

In her treatise, *The Interior Castle*, her soul is described allegorically as a castle of many rooms, the innermost of which is inhabited by God. She can reach this room only through solitary contemplation and prayer. A stage of this process is the ecstatic 'Prayer of Quiet'. However, she cautions, one must not regard the ecstasy aroused during this phase as an end in itself, for union with God has not yet been achieved. The imagery used at this point gives further insight into Teresa's need for the mystical life in order to provide a transcendent subsititute for her lost mother: 'For as yet the soul is not even weaned but is like a child beginning to suck the breast. If it be taken from its mother, what can it be expected to do but die?' (1946, II, p. 245).

Yet, what of the mystics whose experiences may not be related to loss, and of the vast majority of those who suffer loss without having mystical experiences? There can be no proof that mysticism necessarily stems from loss or, for that matter, from distorted relationships, illness, trauma, or family break-up, or from such causes alone. To explore possible traumatic roots of mystical experiences is by no means to reduce them to mere illusion, a symptom of illness or weakness in ego structure. Neither does it imply the rejection of mysticism as a form of adaptation, creation and healing, even a life-affirming gift of grace, a source of consolation, hope and joy. Having made these necessary qualifications, we may consider some of the parallels between the processes of mysticism and grief. These include, detachment, yearning and searching, depression (or The Dark Night of the Soul), 'finding', union, transformation, and return to social life.

Mystical traditions throughout history agree that, as Zaehner writes, 'no progress in the inner life is possible without detachment from all things worldly' (1957 pp. 172–3). The general aim of mysticism, union with God, requires withdrawal, silence, meditation, asceticism, purgation of the passions,

The inner freedom from the practical desire,
The release from action and suffering, release from the inner
And the outer compulsion...

T.S. Eliot, 'Burnt Norton'

Hindu mysticism, the most ancient which has come down to us, teaches that the wise man is he who divests himself of affections, for only he can surrender himself to the higher being, Brahman. Buddhist mysticism, likewise, emphasizes that attachments to humans and material things alike are worthless—all is transient, illusory, filled with sorrow. In a similar vein, the anonymous fourteenth-century author of *The Cloud of Unknowing* writes of detachment from others as a necessary condition for achieving union with God: '. . . you must also put a cloud of forgetting beneath you and all creation' (1978, p. 66). The sixteenth-century Spanish mystic, St John of the Cross, uses different imagery to express the same idea: attachments to people are like the chord by which a bird, yearning to fly freely, is held captive.

The following is a description of the mechanism of detachment:

> The deactivation of systems mediating attachment behaviour, thought and feeling, appears to be achieved by the defensive exclusion, more or less complete, of sensory inflow of any and every kind that might activate attachment behaviour and feeling. The resulting state is one of emotional detachment which can be either partial or complete.

This passage, which might be taken for an account of the process of mystical detachment, is by Bowlby (1980, p. 70), and it refers to a phase of grief observed among children bereaved or separated from their parents. Among widows, similarly, social withdrawal is not uncommon (Marris, 1958; Parkes, 1986). Bowlby continues: 'Deactivation of attachment behaviour is especially liable to be initiated during the early years, though it can undoubtedly be increased and consolidated during later childhood and adolescence.' Prolonged or repeated separations, especially during the first three years of life, can severely inhibit attachment behaviour and, in some cases, can lead to indefinite detachment (Bowlby, 1973).

The voluntary detachment of the mystic, which is undertaken as a necessary preliminary to spiritual elevation, cannot be equated with the involuntary withdrawal of the bereaved. At the same time, the two forms of detachment are not entirely dissimilar. There is room for conjecture that, as in the case of Sister Teresa, loss may be an important, even crucial, factor inclining an individual to mystical withdrawal. A bereaved person who, as part of his grief, experiences detachment from others, might be impelled to seek comfort and meaning in the controlled, orderly and elevating process of mysticism, in which detachment is not merely approved but is a *sine qua non*. In this way, he can make a virtue of necessity. Through mysticism the pain of grief is likely to diminish as the bereaved becomes absorbed in the quest for divine union. Thus, mystical detachment might, at times, be a practical and creative response to loss.

The intense reactions of the bereaved are, in all probability, equal to those of the mystic, and the need for detachment may be equally strong in both. The mystical attainment of *apatheia* and the overcoming of passions such as anger might be compared with the social withdrawal of the bereaved which, as Marris (1958) and Parkes (1986) have pointed out, often results from the fear of ungovernable passions such as anger. Mysticism can serve to elevate what could otherwise be a harmful symptom of grief. Both forms of detachment have been interpreted as defences of the ego (Freud, 1930; Bowlby, 1980). Both are part of a process and are harmful if they persist to the exclusion of the healthy goals of mysticism and the working through of grief – the return to normal social life.

The yearning and searching of the mystic, likewise, may often be compared with that of the bereaved. The nature of yearning for the deity is well illustrated in the *Psalms*:

As a hart longs for flowing streams
so longs my soul for thee, O God.
My soul thirsts for God,
for the living God...

(*RSV*, xlii, 1–2)

O God, thou art my God, I seek thee,
my soul thirsts for thee;
my flesh faints for thee,
as in a dry and weary land where no water is.

(*RSV*, lxiii, 1)

Various mystical traditions, including the Hindu, Jewish and Christian, teach the idea of a God in hiding, the *Deus absconditus*, with whom the searcher longs to be reunited. In *The Cloud of Unknowing*, for example, God is hidden but can be preceived and reached; therefore, the author adjures, 'beat away at this cloud of unknowing between you and God with that sharp dart of longing love' (1978, p. 76). Images of searching, as for a lost person with whom the searcher believes he can be reunited, are common in mystical literature. In the teaching of Sister Teresa, the 'wound of love' is caused by the intense longing for the hidden God.

In normal grief, similarly, the bereaved often feels that the lost person is merely in hiding and that he or she can be restored. For this reason, as in the case of mystical detachment, the yearning and searching which are institutional parts of the mystical process might have an especial attraction to the bereaved. As a prominent phase of grief, yearning and searching may last for years (Bowlby, 1980; Parkes, 1986). Among the features of this phase are the alternation between belief and disbelief in the loss, and anger that comforters cannot help and that searching has no use. Bowlby (1973) has corroborated Freud's hypothesis (1926) that where loss is believed to be permanent, the reaction is sadness and pain; where it is thought to be only temporary, the reaction is anxiety. This anxiety, which stems from the futile hope of restoring the lost person, appears to underlie yearning and searching.

When grief follows a normal course, however, the bereaved is at least partly aware that his searching is useless, but, as Parkes points out, 'this does not prevent him from experiencing a strong impulse to search' (1986, p. 64). In his self-observations after his wife's death, C.S. Lewis remarks on the complex network of stimulus and response which now, frustratingly, had no outlet: 'Thought after thought, feeling after feeling, action after action, has H. [Lewis' wife] for their object. Now their target is gone. I keep on through habit fitting an arrow to the string; then I remember and have to lay the bow down' (1974, p. 39). Here again, the use of mystical searching for the bereaved may be inferred: This searching can act as a form of transcendent denial, keeping alive the anxious hope of return and even, perhaps, the pattern of attachment, and easing the depression and pain which are part of the grief process. For the bow of mystical searching, to borrow Lewis' image, is not laid down, but the arrow is aimed at a higher entity. Insofar as mysticism may be a possible response to loss, it offers a mixture of acceptance and denial not unlike that in normal grief: acceptance, in that searching is not aimed, at least not directly, towards the restoration of the lost person; denial, as searching is not given up, but is directed onto a transcendent being which, it is understood, can be 'found'.

In normal grief, again, yearning and searching give way to a recognition of the permanence of the loss and to a phase of depression and despair (Bowlby, 1980; Parkes, 1986). This phase has its mystical counterpart in the Dark Night of the Soul, an expression first used by John of the Cross who also gave the fullest and most remarkable description of this part of the mystic-al process in *The Dark Night of the Soul*. The Dark Night, in brief, is the purgatory between mystical illumination and union with God, a state of death-in-life in which the soul is assailed and annihilated by God in the act of purifying it and preparing it for renewal and union. During this stage, the mystic is tormented by the conviction that he has been abandoned by God. He is cast adrift alone, helpless, unloved, in despair, 'a poor, bare, forked animal', a castaway on a desert island, bereft of all hope of survival.

It is meaningless to speculate whether the Dark Night is more or less intense than the terrible depression which may be endured by the bereaved. Each is a necessary part of a process which can last for years. Each, too, can be overwhelming and can severely hamper the capacity for normal social functioning. Just as de-pression after loss can be a sign of illness if it persists, so also the Dark Night can signify illness if it continues indefinitely. But by the same token, both the Dark Night and depression after loss can be strengthening processes which bring the mystic and the be-reaved respectively back to a normal life within society.

The parallel between the cycle of mystical illumination and the Dark Night of the Soul and manic-depression has been noted by scholars (e.g. Zaehner). This comparison need not imply the equation of the Dark Night with mental illness or the denial of its role in spiritual elevation and creativity. Bearing this in mind, the links between the Dark Night and mourning may be pursued further. The mystical 'dream of perfect harmony' which counter-parts the Dark Night as mania counterparts depression might also be interpreted as an expression of grief. As we have already pointed out, idealization such as this is not uncommon as a grief reaction.

Manic-depression, like the cycle of mystical illumination and the Dark Night, might have its germination in grief, but it can also be transformed to act as a spur to creativity and a defence against mental illness (Storr, 1972). Loss renders the bereaved especially vulnerable to manic-depression: in consequence of loss, Storr writes (pp. 75–6), the manic-depressive is chiefly afraid of the withdrawal of love. Anger, a normal part of grief, is suppressed by the manic-depressive, for, as Storr continues, 'if he does not [suppress his anger], he is in danger of destroying his relation with his loved person for ever' (p. 82). The consequent need for reparation which, in Storr's view, might be a primary motive in creativity,[2] might also underlie qualities of mysticism such as union, harmony, passivity, wholeness, love – indeed, one of the striking features of mysticism is the attempt, explicit or implicit, to eliminate aggression, conflict and destruction. What is true of the depressive might, in this respect, also be true of the mystic, for 'the depressive is trying to replace a world which he feels he has himself destroyed' (*ibid.*). The success of mysticism in denying destructive anger may lie in its power to convince the bereaved that the lost person is not destroyed but can be re-covered transcendentally.

It is possible, at any rate, that grief may incline a bereaved person to the *via negativa*, as this way is already inherent within him as a result of loss. This might certainly have been the case with John of the Cross. Brennan writes of the death of John's father and the poor conditions for mourning which followed: '. . .a few months after Juan's birth, he died of a lingering illness, leaving his widow and three sons in great poverty' (1973, p. 4). The awful sense of abandonment which pervades the Dark Night is likely to be especially strong among those who suffer loss, as John did, in childhood. The greatest affliction of the Dark Night, which John depicts so movingly, is probably little different from the anguish suffered by any child bereaved of a loved father: '. . .the thought that God has abandoned it [the soul], of which it has no doubt; that He has cast it away into darkness as an abominable thing' (1973, p. 89).

The conviction among mystics of 'finding' and being 'found' by the divine presence after passing through the Dark Night also has its equivalent in the grief process. The bereaved often have illusions, hallucinations and dreams of reunion with the lost person.[3] In studies by Marris (1958) and Rees (1971), about one half of widows and widowers interviewed admitted that they had had illusions or hallucinations of their dead spouse. Rees, in interviews with 293 widows and widowers, discovered that 39.2 percent had 'the illusion of feeling the presence of the dead spouse' (p. 38). Others had seen, heard, spoken to, and even touched the lost person. Dreams that the dead spouse is still alive are equally common. Most of these illusions, hallucinations and dreams are reported as being a source of comfort and support, and it appears that these are part of the normative process of grief. However, these phenomena are transient and, with the acceptance of the loss, are generally regarded by the bereaved as imaginary, a sign of denial and of longing for reunion. Their function, according to Parkes (1986), is apparently to ease the process of mourning, to dull death's sting. To the mystic, in contrast, finding the object of the search is a permanent reality.

A number of further observations are relevant in considering the 'visions' of the bereaved and mystical visions. First, in pre-modern societies there was comparatively little organized knowledge of the nature of grief. Superstition abounded and the supernatural element in religious tradition was taken far more seriously than it is today. Mental disturbance was often regarded as a sign of divine visitation. As a result, the 'visions' of the bereaved were often interpreted as mystical phenomena rather than as normal grief reactions.

A second observation regards the susceptibility of bereaved children to 'visions' connected with the lost person. As these are common among bereaved adults, they might be equally (if not more) common among grieving children. Children, being more impressionable, are more liable than adults to persist in the belief that illusions of the lost person are real.[4] Prior to the modern age, those who suffered bereavement in childhood and who had 'visions' as part of the grieving process were far more likely to be regarded as mystics than they are today, and to live out this role with all its social and religious implications.

A third point involves a child observation of Freud's (1920), the only one in his entire *oeuvre*. This observation casts light on mystical 'finding' as a possible response to loss for it indicates how searching for a person who cannot be found might be transformed into searching for an object which can be found. The child was Freud's grandson, Heinz, whom Freud looked after during the child's separations from his mother (Freud's daughter, Sophie). His analysis of the boy's play during these separations has an important place in the evolution of his ideas on loss and separation.[5] At the age of 1½, the child was exceptionally well-behaved, and in spite of his attachment to his mother, never cried when she left him for a few hours. His only game was to throw toys and other objects and retrieve them while crying out 'o-o-o-o.' Once Freud saw him with a wooden reel and a piece of string tied to it:

> What he did was to hold the reel by the string and very skilfully throw it over the edge of his curtained cot, so that it disappeared into it, at the same time uttering his expressive 'o-o-o-o'. He then pulled the reel out of the cot again by the string and hailed its reappearance with a joyful '*da*' ['there']... (p. 15).

Clearly, said Freud, the child had substituted objects which he could control, lose and find at will, for the mother over whom he had little or no control. Mysticism, too, might, in some cases, represent an attempt to substitute objects and aims over which one has a degree of control, can lose and possibly find, such as union with a higher being, for lost persons over whom one has no control and who may be gone permanently. In the use of objects as substitutes, a common element may be detected in play, mysticism and creativity: each may act as a means of escape into fantasy, but can also enhance one's grip on reality.[6]

The climactic stage in the mystical process, union with the divine presence, also has a parallel in the grieving process, in the form of identification with, or in some cases, an actual sense of union with the lost person. Union with the divine is a universal element in mysticism, though it may take many forms, metaphorical and moral as well as metaphysical. In Hinduism this concept is expressed in the saying *Tat twam asi* (This is thou): man, by finding his true immortal self (*atman*), becomes united with Brahman and, in so doing, achieves *nirvana*. In Buddhism, similarly, man must strive to recognize the unity of all within the eternal Buddha, the *dharmakaya*, the absolute truth or reality which transcends human perception. Jewish mysticism teaches *devekut* (adhesion, cleaving, union) with God;[7] Christian mysticism refers to Jesus' words, 'Abide in me and I in you' (John, xv, 4) as pertaining to divine union, which has its concrete expression in baptism and the Eucharist; even Islam, which insists on the absolute transcendence of God, has developed the mystical doctrine of *tawhid* (union). Various metaphors have been used by mystics to describe the *unio mystica*. Among the most beautiful are those of Sister Teresa, who likened it to a spiritual marriage, or to a silkworm transformed into a white butterfly.[8]

As we have noted, a temporary sensation of identification or union with the lost person is regarded as compatible with normal mourning (Bowlby, 1980; Parkes, 1986). In Parkes' study, a minority of widows were conscious of coming to resemble their husbands or of 'containing' them. These sensations tended to alternate with periods when the husband was experienced as a companion. One widow described the following experience: 'At dawn, four days after my husband's death, something suddenly moved in on me – a presence almost pushed me out of bed – terribly overwhelming' (p. 120). From then on, she had a strong sense of her husband's presence, either near or inside her.[9] Another widow spoke of her happiness at having her late husband within her: 'It's not a sense of his presence. He is here inside me. That's why I'm happy all the time. It's as if two people were one' (p. 121). Such language is not dissimilar from that of mystics

– except that they would be speaking not of a lost person but of God. Yet the mystic's belief in the reality of this union is far stronger and more persistent than that of the bereaved, in normal grief at any rate, when the mourner is likely to be aware of the irrationality of his or her reactions to the loss.

In religious doctrine, as in theories on grief, there is controversy whether identification, with the divine presence or with the lost person, is normal or aberrant. In Islam, for example, the idea that man can be identified with God through divine union is heretical. Similarly, the fourteenth-century German mystic, Meister Eckhart, was condemned by Pope John XXII for teaching that man is deified by his awareness that he loves God with His own love. In most mystical doctrines, man may be absorbed by God, but he cannot become God.

The distinction in mystical thought between identifying God *with* or *in* man, and *vice versa*, may be compared with a similar distinction in the location, or mislocation, of a lost person during the grief process. Freud who at first (1917) regarded the identification of the bereaved with the dead (the adoption of their traits and, sometimes, of their ailments) as a symptom of pathological grief, later (1923, 1933), came to regard it as a vital part of grief. Freud's views have been developed by more recent researchers (e.g. Krupp, 1965; Rochlin, 1965). According to Krupp, identification can derive from repeated losses and frustrations in infancy and can represent an attempt to prevent further losses by 'becoming' the lost person. The attraction of absorptive mysticism might, in some cases, have a similar origin. Others (Bowlby, 1980; Parkes, 1986) treat this phenomenon, when transient, as a normal coping mechanism. When persistent, however, it can become a pathological means by which the bereaved attempts to communicate the denial of loss and a disguised striving to recover the lost person (Bowlby, p. 289).

Whether identification is normal or pathological, central or peripheral to loss, the interpretations of this aspect of grief are valuable in considering the possibility that mystical union is, at times, a transcendent expression of grief. In Freud's view, the mystical feeling of 'oneness with the universe' is a form of consolation and defence, 'as though it were another way of disclaiming the danger which the ego recognizes as threatening it from the external world' (1930, p. 72). Influenced by Freud, Jung (1919) at first regarded the longing for mystical union as symbolic of a child's yearning for reunion with its mother, but later came to regard all types of mystical experience as expressions of the collective unconscious (1935). Others, including Riviere (1955), Greenacre (1957) and Winnicott (1971), have followed the early Jungian interpretation which believes mystical union have its roots in infantile phenomena.

The illusory nature of mysticism has been implicitly linked by Winnicott with so-called 'transitional objects' used by the infant in place of its mother in the process of testing reality and learning to differentiate between its inner world and the outer world.[10] Winnicott writes of transitional objects both as a source of health and growth and, if carried to extremes, of illness. As the infantile basis of art and religion (and, by implication, mysticism), they are

> . . . the substance of *illusion*, that which is allowed to the infant, and which in adult life is inherent in art and religion, and yet becomes the hallmark of madness when an adult puts too powerful a claim on the credulity of others, forcing them to acknowledge a sharing of illusion that is not their own (1971 p. 3).

The distinction between the acceptance of illusion as illusion and illusion as reality may be applied to the concept of identification in grief and in mysticism. The difference may be illustrated obliquely in the Jewish joke set in the pietistic world of the nineteenth century East European *shtetl* (village). A merchant visits his rabbi, a venerable and strictly observant sage, to complain about his son-in-law: 'He's a fanatic, he gets up at four in the morning, takes an ice-pick, goes to the river where he knocks a hole in the ice and ritually immerses himself in the freezing water.' 'What's wrong with that?' asks the rabbi, 'You know I do the same.' To which the merchant replies, 'Yes, but he means it seriously.'

Up to a point, then, illusion may be healthy, but beyond that point, if it is taken too seriously, it can become a symptom of illness. The identification of subject and object, according to Winnicott, is a normal, illusory part of infant development. Until the baby learns to distinguish between inner and outer, subject and object, its female part, in Winnicott's view, relates to the mother, particularly the breast, 'in the sense of *the baby becoming the breast (or mother) in the sense that the object is the subject*' (p. 79). This phenomenon is transient, as is the illusion of 'becoming' the lost person in the course of grief, or of mystical union in which subject and object are one.

In some cases, undoubtedly, the mystic and the bereaved use what is ordinarily a transitional phenomenon as a permanent defence. This would indicate a pathological condition. If worked through fully, however, both the process of mysticism and of grief lead to the transformation of the self and to a return to normal social life. Mystics use such words as rebirth, escape, salvation, integration, self-realization, to describe the change which they undergo as a result of divine union. John of the Cross compared this transformation to that undergone by a burning log of wood which becomes pure fire. Nothing as dramatic as this occurs in the process of recovery after loss. Yet, in a manner analogous to the mystic, the old self of the bereaved is consumed by his grief and he emerges a different person. Parkes (1986) describes the reorganization and repair after loss as a process of 'realization' not dissimilar from that of mystics: 'As the old assumptions about the world prove ineffective and a fresh set of assumptions is built up so the old identity dissolves and is replaced by a new and different one' (pp. 122–3).[11] This transformation prepares both the mystic and the bereaved to return to normal social life. The withdrawal of the great mystics was never an end in itself, but a prelude to a thorough immersion in social activity. The success of the mystical process, as of the process of grief, may be gauged by the degree of consequent integration into society, the ultimate goal of mysticism (Woods, 1980) as of grief (Bowlby, 1980).

What conclusions can be reached by comparing mysticism and grief? While there are many differences between the two, the similarities are too striking to be ignored. Mysticism cannot be equated with grief, but it can, in some cases at least, provide an effective outlet for the expression of grief, a means by which the bereaved might struggle to work through the grief process. Mysticism can satisfy the need for an orderly, transcendent, goal-oriented form of grief. Thus, withdrawal after loss might become the withdrawal needed for mystical contemplation. Yearning and searching for the lost person might evolve into yearning and searching for a spiritual being. The anger, confusion, and depression which often emerge in grief might be expressed in the mystical Dark Night of the Soul. 'Finding' the lost person might have its parallel in mystical 'finding' and illumination. Union with the lost person might become union with the divine being. The transformation of the bereaved into a new person might have its counterpart in spiritual rebirth. Finally, the return to normal social life is the ideal end of both the mystical and the grieving processes. One other similarity might be added: both mysticism and grief might be viewed as a measure of love, an affirmation of the love of God as of the lost person. Love, the source of ecstasy in attachments, of consequent pain in loss, is also the balm of grief, as Parkes writes wisely and movingly:

Just as broken bones may end up stronger than unbroken ones, so the experience of grieving can strengthen and bring maturity to those who have previously been protected from misfortune. The pain of grief is just as much a part of life as the joy of love; it is, perhaps, the price we pay for love, the cost of commitment (1986, p. 26).

Insofar as mysticism derives from loss, how might grieving for a lost person evolve into a mystical quest for union with a divine being? In most, if not all, forms of mysticism a religious-cultural structure is present, and deeply influences the nature of the mystical process. In the Judaeo-Christian tradition, for example, the link between loss and the attachment to God as a substitute parent-figure is firmly established. We read in the *Psalms*,

For my father and my mother have forsaken me,
but the Lord will take me up. (*RSV*, xxvii, 10)

Does such a transformation occur spontaneously or in stages, or either, depending on the character of the bereaved? Here we may look for insight to creative literature. Mystical or semi-mystical experiences are not infrequently described in literature, especially, it seems, in the writings of those who suffered loss or severe upheaval in childhood. The feelings expressed by these writers are often no less intense than those of mystics, and this lends support to the view that mystical experiences and sensations (as opposed to the mystical process) are more common than might be thought. As a means of clarifying further the possible links between grief and mysticism, a conjectural evolution of grief to mysticism may be constructed, using illustrations from a variety of writers. We may postulate a number of characteristics or stages, which might oscillate or overlap: the identification of a lost person with animate or inanimate objects; detachment of objects from the lost person; identification and mystical union of the bereaved with these objects; union of the bereaved with the universe, or 'cosmic consciousness'. This model, crude and un-satisfactory as it is, cannot act as a precise, comprehensive de-scription of all instances in which grief is transformed to mystic-ism. No doubt, there is infinite variety in the character, the intensity and the degree of the transformation, the nature of which is dictated largely by the needs and conditions of the bereaved. Yet, if this model casts even a little light onto an obscure subject, it will have served its purpose.

Creative literature offers abundant illustrations of objects belonging to the natural world which come to be identified with a lost person. Three prominent examples in English fiction may be found in Emily Brontë's *Wuthering Heights* (1847), Charles Dickens' *Great Expectations* (1861) and Edgar Allan Poe's macabre short story, 'Ligeia' (1838). In each there may be a strong autobiographical element. [12] Though none is in itself 'mystical', each one suggests how loss might impel a severely bereaved person towards mysticism.

Wuthering Heights tells the story of Heathcliff, an orphan adopted by the landowner, Mr Earnshaw. Earnshaw's daughter, Catherine, and Heathcliff fall in love. When she comes of age, however, Catherine marries someone else and dies in childbirth. For the rest of his life, nearly two decades, Heathcliff tortures himself with her memory, to the point where he starves himself to death for grief. Shortly before his death, he speaks of the natural world as a continual reminder of his loss and his desire for reunion with his beloved in death. It may be that the 'excess of violent emotion', which characterizes Heathcliff, as well as his pathological yearning for Catherine, betray the effects of his childhood loss:

> ...what is not connnected with her to me? and what does not recall her? I cannot look down to this floor, but her features are shaped on the flags! In every cloud, in every tree – filling the air at night, and caught by glimpses in every object by day – I am surrounded with her image! The most ordinary faces of men and women – my own features – mock me with a resemblance. The entire world is a dreadful collection of memoranda that she did exist, and that I have lost her (ch. 33).[13]

The first three sentences of this passage, placed in a different context, could almost be mistaken for the confession of a mystic who perceives everywhere the divine image of the Virgin Mary.

In *Great Expectations*, Pip, like Heathcliff, is an orphan, raised by his sister.[14] He falls in love with Estella, the cruel, beautiful ward of Miss Havisham, but for many years is separated from her. He sees her again when she is about to marry, and confesses to her his continuing love. To Pip, Estella, like Catherine to Heathcliff, is in everything. As in Heathcliff's case, Pip's chronic yearning for Estella may be linked with his experience of childhood loss:

You are part of my existence, part of myself. You have been in every line I have ever read, since I first came here, the rough common boy whose poor heart you wounded even then. You have been in every prospect I have ever seen since – on the river, on the sails of the ships, on the marshes, in the clouds, in the light, in the darkness, in the wind, in the woods, in the sea, in the streets (ch. 44).

Here too, the general searching for a person in all things calls to mind the longing of the mystic for contact with a divine being. Indeed, Estella is treated virtually as a celestial creature by Pip.

A similarly clear example of how a lost person may be identified with the objects of the natural world is found in Poe's 'Ligeia'. This story, which Poe described as his best, tells of a man who keeps his dead wife, Ligeia, alive in his imagination through objects. Her eyes haunt him before but particularly after he marries again:

...subsequently to the period when Ligeia's beauty passed into my spirit, there dwelling as in a shrine, I derived, from many existences in the material world, a sentiment such as I felt always aroused within me, by her large and luminous orbs. Yet not the more could I define that sentiment, or analyze, or even steadily view it. I recognized it, but let me repeat, sometimes in the survey of a rapidly growing vine – in the contemplation of a moth, a butterfly, a stream of running water. I have felt it in the ocean; in the falling of a meteor. I have felt it in the glances of unusually aged people. And there are one or two stars in heaven – (one especially, a star of the sixth magnitude, double and changeable, to be found near the large star in Lyra) in a telescopic scrutiny of which I have been made aware of the feeling. I have been filled with it by certain sounds from stringed instruments, and not unfrequently by passages from books (1975, p. 113).

Here once again, we need only substitute a divine being for Ligeia to recognize how similar this passage is to mystical confession. The longing for reunion, which can impel one to mysticism, drives the unnamed narrator to the verge of madness. At the end of the story, after losing his second wife, he has an hallucination of Ligeia rising from her death-bed.

A further stage in the movement towards mysticism may be identified as the point at which objects or ideas associated with the lost person are detached from that person. The German poet, Rainer Maria Rilke, frequently alludes in his poetry to his experience of separation in childhood: his parents divorced when he was nine and he was sent to a military school for five years. In the lyric *Abschied* ('Parting'), Rilke describes the process of detachment:

> How I have felt that thing that's called 'to part',
> And feel it still: a dark, invincible
> cruel something by which what was joined so well
> is once more shown, held out, and torn apart.
>
> In what defenceless gaze at that I've stood,
> which, as it, calling to me, let me go,
> stayed there, as though it were all womanhood,
> yet small and white and nothing more than, oh,
>
> a waving, now already unrelated
> to me, a slight, continuous wave, – scarce now
> explainable: perhaps a plum-tree bough
> some perching cuckoo's hastily vacated.

(1964, p. 37)

In Rilke's poetry, the attachment to objects 'unrelated to me... scarce now explainable' ('nicht mehr auf mich bezogen...kaum erklärbar mehr') as if to a lost person, can lead in the direction of mysticism. The semi-mystical contemplation of objects becomes an end in itself, detached from any grief which might have first aroused the need for this contemplation. In the *Duino Elegies*, Rilke returns to the theme of grief detached from its cause. In the passage beginning 'Preise dem Engel die Welt' (Praise this world to the Angel) in the Ninth Elegy, Rilke suggests that the product of grief becomes, through art, a thing in its own right, apart from the lost person who might have provoked this emotion:

> Show him how happy a thing can be, how guileless and ours;
> how even the moaning of grief purely determines on form,
> serves as a thing, or dies into a thing – to escape
> to a bliss beyond the fiddle (pp. 64–5).

The poetry of Wordsworth and Bialik offers further illustrations how an attachment to objects might derive from a broken bond with a person. As we saw in Chapter Four, both poets suffered the complete break-up of their families at about the age of seven, Wordsworth after the death of his mother, and Bialik, his father. Both were separated from the surviving parent, and their conditions for mourning were poor.

Among the many likely effects of their loss and separation was the heightening of the poets' response to the natural world, finding in it some of the attributes of parental love and care, and the paradisal emblem of the lost time before the break-up of their families. Nature is frequently depicted in their works as a mother or nurse, a source of food from which they derive spiritual nourishment, consolation and peace. Both poets describe the first perception of the language and bond of Nature in babyhood. In the first chapter of his semi-mythical autobiography, *Safiah* (Aftergrowth), published in 1923, Bialik compares this language to the love which silently radiates from a mother to her child, constituting his bond with external reality:

> There was no speech and no words – only a vision. Such utterance as there was came without words or even sounds. It was a mystic utterance, especially created, from which all sound had evaporated, yet which still remained. Nor did I hear it with my ears, but it entered my soul through another medium. In the same way a mother's tenderness and loving gaze penetrate the soul of her baby, asleep in the cradle, when she stands over him anxious and excited – and he knows nothing (1973, p. 17).

Wordsworth, too, connects the love of Nature with the love of the mother in babyhood:

> ...blest the Babe
> Nursed in his Mother's arms, who sinks to sleep
> Rocked on his Mother's breast; who with his soul
> Drinks in the feelings of his Mother's eye!...
> Along his infant veins are interfused
> The gravitation and the filial bond
> Of Nature that connect him with the world.

> (*The Prelude*, 1850 edn., II, 234–7, 242–4)

Separation from the mother or, in Wordsworth's case, her death, seems to have created or intensified in both poets the need for a mystic bond with the natural world. This bond, detached from the lost person, is so strong that even inanimate objects appear to have the breath of life. (We are reminded that Spinoza, father of the philosophy of pantheism, lost his mother at approximately the same age as Bialik and Wordsworth.[15]) To Bialik, again, this bond is expressed in a 'silent immanent language' in the poem *Ha-Brekha* ('The Pool'):

> ...a secret language of gods
> without sound, only shades of colours

made of magic, majestic pictures, hosts of visions.
In this language God reveals himself
to those he chooses,
he meditates in it, uses it, creator that he is,
to give body to his thoughts, to find
the secret of the unformed dream.
It is the language of images:
a blue strip of sky and its expanse,
the purity of small silver clouds and their dark mass,
the tremor of golden wheat, the pride
of the mighty cedar, the flap of the dove's white wing,
the sweep of an eagle...
the roar of a sea of flame, sunrise after sunset –
in this language, tongue of tongues,
the pool, too, formed me
her eternal mystery.

This language of Nature through which the divine presence communicates with his chosen ones is remarkably like that of the 'sense sublime' in Wordsworth's 'Tintern Abbey':

> And I have felt
> A presence that disturbs me with the joy
> Of elevated thoughts; a sense sublime
> Of something far more deeply interfused,
> Whose presence is the light of setting suns,
> And the round ocean and the living air,
> And the blue sky...

It may be that the impulse to pantheism (or panentheism), such as that in Wordsworth and Bialik, is particularly strong among certain individuals bereaved in childhood who persist in searching for and finding the lost person, or some abstract substitute, in Nature.

In Bialik's poetry, loss may underlie the search for an indeterminate being in objects, for example in the lyric *Ayekh?* ('Where Are You?'):

> And I still don't know who or what you are,
> though your name trembled on my lips,
> and at night you burned in my heart like a coal.
> I cried restlessly, I gnashed my pillow, my flesh
> longed for your memory. All day long, between
> letters of the Talmud, in a shaft of light,
> a bright cloud, in my prayers and my purest

thought, in my bitter suffering – I searched
only for you, only you,
you, you...

The detachment of the lost person from the objects sought is
more pronounced here that in Rilke's 'Parting': the poet confesses, 'I still don't know who or what you are' (*va-ani od lo yadati mi
va-ma at*). A similarly intense search for someone or something
unknown is described by the Chilean poet, Pablo Neruda, in the
poem *El Abandonado* ('The Abandoned One'). Here too, the poet is
uncertain of the object of his quest – 'I do not know who you are'
(*no sé quién eres*) – but seeks it everywhere. The speaker is the
abandoned one, 'born from death's rattle':

> I look for you, I look for your image among the medals
> that the grey sky models and abandons,
> I do not know who you are but I owe you so much
> that the earth is filled with my bitter treasure.
> What salt, what geography, what stone does not lift
> its secret banner from what it was shielding?
> What leaf on falling was not for me a long book
> of words addressed and loved by someone?
> Beneath what dark furniture did I not hide the sweetest
> buried sighs that sought signs
> and syllables that belonged to no one?

(1976, p. 225)

In his *Memoirs*, Neruda gives a biographical clue to one reading of
this poem and to many of his other works, for he, too, was an
abandoned one, 'born from death's rattle': 'My mother, Doña
Rosa Basoalto, died before I could have a memory of her, before I
knew it was she my eyes gazed upon. I was born on July 12, 1904,
and a month later, in August, wasted away by tuberculosis, my
mother was gone' (1977, pp. 7–8).

A further stage on the path from grief to mysticism is reached
when the bereaved, having detached the objects of his yearning
and searching from the lost person, identifies himself or even
becomes united with those objects. As we have seen, a feeling of
union with the lost person, of that person's continuing presence,
of identification with him or her, are part of normal grief.[16] The
manner in which inanimate objects may be incorporated into the
bereaved is shown in Tennyson's *In Memoriam*, begun after the
death of the poet's friend, Arthur Hallam, in 1833:[17]

Old Yew, which graspest at the stones
  That name the under-lying dead,
  Thy fibres net the dreamless head,
Thy roots are wrapt about the bones...

And gazing on thee, sullen tree,
  Sick for thy stubborn hardihood,
  I seem to fail from out my blood
And grow incorporate into thee.

Incorporation into natural objects might, of course, have mean-
ings other than identification with a lost person. Yet, the experience of incorporation, of union with objects, appears to be
especially frequent and intense among those bereaved or severely
deprived, particularly in childhood. Wordsworth, for example,
recalled his incorporative tendencies after his mother's death:

> I was often unable to think of external things as having external
> existence, and I communed with all that I saw as something not
> apart from, but inherent in, my own immaterial nature. Many
> times while going to school have I grasped at a wall or tree to
> recall myself from this abyss of idealism to the reality. At that
> time I was afraid of such processes (de Selincourt, IV, 1947, p.
> 463).

Similarly, Bialik writes in *Aftergrowth* that as a child he would
'enter' objects such as trees and stones, 'absorbing all they contained and giving nothing in return' (1939, p. 56).[18]

Comparable semi-mystical sensations of union with objects are
found regularly in the writings of others who suffered childhood
loss. In his 'Childhood Recollections', Byron describes one of the
effects of his father's desertion and death when he was three, as a
need to 'seek abroad the love denied at home'. This searching
might have impelled the poet to find love through union with the
natural world, for he writes in his semi-biographical poem, *Childe
Harold's Pilgrimage*:

> I live not in myself, but I become
> Portion of that around me...
> Are not the mountains, waves, and skies, a part
> Of me and of my soul, as I of them?
> Is not the love of these deep in my heart
> With a pure passion?

> (Canto III, lxxii, lxxv)

A parallel sense of union with nature is expressed in the writings of Forrest Reid, particularly his autobiographical memoir, *Apostate* (1926):

> There were hours when I could pass *into* nature, and feel the grass growing, and float with the clouds through the transparent air; when I could hear the low breathing of the earth, when the colour and smell of it were so close to me that I seemed to lose consciousness of any separate existence. Then, one single emotion animated all things, one heart beat throughout the universe, and the mother and all her children were united (1926, p. 208).

As in Wordsworth, Bialik and Byron, Reid's feeling of incorporation with nature might be related partly to the effects of childhood loss, for Reid lost his father at the age of five and the conditions for mourning which followed this loss were poor.

In a similar way, Jean-Paul Sartre's identification with objects as a young child might be linked with his father's death soon after his birth.[19] In *Words*, Sartre describes his identification with objects as a child: 'I was a dog: I yawned, the tears flowed, I could feel them flowing. I was a tree and the wind clung to my branches and made them stir vaguely. I was a fly; I climbed all the way up a window-pane, slid down, and started to climb again' (1977, p. 60). This was no mere childish game but, as in the case of Wordsworth, an involuntary and rather frightening condition. Though the germ of Sartre's genius might also be detected in this capacity for entering into the existence of animate and inanimate objects, he was at this time alarmed by being under a 'constant sentence of extinction' (p. 61).

A mystical experience of union described by Martin Buber in his book of dialogues, *Daniel* (1913), might, likewise, be connected with childhood loss:

> On a gloomy morning I walked upon the highway, saw a piece of mica lying, picked it up and looked at it for a long time; the day was no longer gloomy, so much light was caught in the stone. And suddenly as I raised my eyes from it, I realized that while I had looked I had not been conscious of 'object' and 'subject'; in my looking the mica and 'I' had been one; in my looking I had tasted unity (1964, p. 140).

Buber's seeking for unity, as we shall see in Chapter Six, is explicable in the light of his mother's disappearance when he was three, which Friedman (1981) described as 'the decisive experience of Martin Buber's life' (p. 15).

Here we may add that Hasidic mysticism, which deeply influenced Buber, has at its core the idea of union, *devekut*.[20] This was originally a kabbalistic concept, but the Ba'al Shem Tov ('Master of the Good Name [of God]'), founder of Hasidism in the eighteenth century, attached far greater importance to *devekut* than his predecessors, making it truly 'the ultimate goal of religious perfection' (Scholem, 1955, p. 123). Through the *mitzvot* (commandments), the daily acts of kindness and love, through concentration on prayer and study, on the holy letters of the Hebrew alphabet – so the Ba'al Shem taught – man can make contact with divine worlds, and attain *devekut*, union with God. The Ba'al Shem's extraordinary exphasis on *devekut* might be attributed in part to the effects of childhood loss. For, like Buber, the Ba'al Shem lost his parents as a young child. In common with other mystics, such as Sister Teresa and John of the Cross, his quest for union with God might be interpreted as a sublimated, unconscious attempt to be reunited with his lost parents.

From having sensations of union with objects, the bereaved might develop full-blown mystical experiences of 'entering' or being 'at one' with the so-called 'greater life' of the entire world or of the cosmos. The nineteenth-century Canadian psychiatrist, Richard Maurice Bucke, coined the term 'cosmic consciousness' to describe the illumination of a higher presence experienced by mystics. Bucke tells of his own moment of cosmic consciousness which took place in London, in 1872 when he was thirty-five. Returning home from an evening reading poetry with friends, he suddenly felt as though he were wrapped in a flame-coloured cloud. The next instant he realized that the light was within him. There followed an ineffable sense of exultation and illumination which he describes as follows in the third person:

> Among other things he did not come to believe, he saw and knew that the Cosmos is not dead matter but a living Presence, that the soul of man is immortal, that the universe is so built and ordered that without any peradventure all things work together for the good of each and all, that the foundation principle of the world is what we call love and that the happiness of every one is in the long run absolutely certain (1982, p. 8).

In later years, Bucke discovered that many others had had similar experiences, and he collected these in his study of *Cosmic Consciousness* (1902). However, he overlooked the fact that a considerable number of these mystics had suffered severe loss in childhood, and he failed to consider the possibility that their mystical experiences were signs of, or connected with, unresolved grief. Bucke himself was susceptible to 'cosmic consciousness' as a means of sublimating, or working through, the grief process: he had lost his mother at seven and his father soon after.

Some of Bucke's illustrations are almost transparently linked with loss. One of the most touching of these is that of the anonymous 'J.W.W.' who sent Bucke a description of the circumstances in which a moment of illumination had occurred. Here clearly, cosmic consciousness is bound up with the process of grief:

> ...my mother's last illness and death were, by immeasurable odds, the heaviest grief and pain I have ever known, or shall, probably, ever know. But it is also true that the memory of them is for all time my most precious and priceless possession.
>
> That period was the supreme moment of my life and its deepest experience. In ordinary life we live only on the surface of things, our attention distracted endlessly by the shallowest illusions and baubles.
>
> But a great bereavement strips the scales from our eyes and compels us, in the intense solitude of our own souls, to gaze into the unfathomable depths in which we float and to question their vast and solemn meanings. It comes upon us clothed in thick darkness and mystery, and pierces our hearts with unutterable agony and grief, but it may be that the darkest hours of its visitation, the supreme moment itself, may also prove a revelation to our souls of the Highest and bring us into the very presense of the Infinite Love and Tenderness (p. 276).

In most cases of 'cosmic consciousness', however, the precipitating loss or losses are not so clear. Poe's prose-poem 'Eureka' (1848), his fullest and most bizarre exposition of his theory of cosmic unity, was written during the anguished last period of his life, between the time of his wife's death in 1847 and his own death in 1849. Poe had lost both his parents by the age of three.[21] The death of his wife after a long illness almost certainly revived Poe's feelings of abandonment and terror unconsciously associated with his mother's death, as well as the grief which he had never satisfactorily resolved. In the following passage form 'Eureka', Poe writes of the unity of all things, describing Unity as a 'lost parent', a parent who, in contrast with his real parents, could be found and retrieved:

Each atom, forming one of a generally uniform globe of atoms, finds more atoms in the direction of the centre, of course, than in any other, and in that direction, therefore, is impelled – but is *not* thus impelled because the centre *is the point of its origin*. It is not to any *point* that the atoms are allied. It is not to any *locality*, either in the concrete or in the abstract, to which I suppose them bound. Nothing like *location* was conceived as their origin. Their source lies in the principle, Unity. *This* is their lost parent. *This* they seek always – immediately – in all directions – wherever it is even partially to be found...I am not so sure that I speak and see – I am not so sure that my heart beats and that my soul lives: – of the rising of to-morrow's sun – a probability that as yet lies in the Future – I do not pretend to be one thousandth part as sure – as I am of the irretrievably by-gone *Fact* that All Things and All Thoughts of Things, with their ineffable Multiplicity of Relation, sprang at once into being from the primordial and irrelative *One* (1984, pp. 1287–9).

Poe's semi-mystical perception of the unity of all things appears to derive in part from a terror-stricken effort to hold onto and control an abstraction as being more secure than a person. Unity, the 'lost parent', offers a haven of solace and hope which the actual lost parent can no longer supply. Pascal, who was a mystic as well as a philosopher, writes in his *Pensées* of the frightening sense of abandonment and isolation which loss might bring: he, like Poe, lost his mother by the time he was three.[22] He compares himself to a man who finds himself trapped on a grim desert island without means of escape. A similar feeling of abandonment is described by John of the Cross, as we have seen earlier in this chapter. To lose a parent in early childhood, as did Poe, Pascal and John of the Cross, need not lead to existential angst or to mystical inclinations. Yet, those who suffer childhood loss are more likely than others to feel abandoned and afraid and the need for emotional support, which mysticism, philosophy or art might provide.

Moving away from the lost person, searching for someone or something unknown, the searcher might eventually grow desperate to achieve union with, or at least insight into, a higher truth. The alternative to mystical union, as Horton (1973) has pointed out, may be reunion with the lost person through suicide. Mystical states or experiences of 'cosmic consciousness' which might be traced to loss are described by Bialik, Wordsworth and John Masefield. Their childhood memories of transcendence are of particular interest as each lost his mother at about the same age as

Bucke, between six and eight. As a result of loss, these memories appear to have taken on greater importance for the three poets than they would otherwise have done. It may be that through these visionary moments each asserted and strengthened the emotional foundations of his identity, to withstand the later effects of loss, such as depression and anger.

Thus, in *Aftergrowth*, Bialik writes of his abandonment by his parents and his 'adoption' by the divine presence. Under God's wing, he perceived a higher truth, the riddles and wonders of creation:

> Every stone and pebble, every splinter of wood was an inexplicable text, and in every ditch and hollow external secrets lurked. How can a spark be contained in a mute stone, and who puts the dumb shadows on the house walls? Who heaps up the fiery mountains in the skirts of heaven, and who holds the moon in the thickets of the forest? Whither stream the caravans of clouds, and whom does the wind in the field pursue? Why does my flesh sing in the morning, and what is the yearning in my heart at evening time? What is wrong with the waters of the spring that they weep quietly, and why does my heart leap at the sound? These wonders were all about me, caught me up, passed over my poor little head – and refuge or escape there was none. They widened my eyes and deepened my heart, until I could sense mysteries even in commonplace things and secrets everywhere (1973, p. 17).

Wordsworth, too, writes of the deepening of childhood insight, in *The Prelude*, the *Ode on Immortality* and 'Tintern Abbey'. In 'Tintern Abbey', the poet gives thanks to the 'beauteous forms' of Nature for the moments of transcendence,

> . . .that serene and blessed mood
> In which the affections gently lead us on
> Until, the breath of this corporeal frame
> And even the motion of our human blood
> Almost suspended, we are laid asleep
> In body, and become a living soul;
> While with an eye made quiet by the power
> Of harmony, and the deep power of joy,
> We see into the life of things.

As Bialik enters the mystery of creation and Wordsworth becomes a 'living soul', so also Masefield joins a 'greater life' in childhood:

I was sure that a greater life was near us: in dreams I sometimes seemed to enter a part of it, and woke with rapture and longing. Then, on one wonderful day, when I was a little more than five years old, as I stood looking north, over a clump of honeysuckle in flower, I entered that greater life; and that life entered into me with a delight that I can never forget. I found suddenly that I could imagine imaginary beings complete in every detail, with every faculty and possession, and that these imaginations did what I wished for my delight, with an incredible perfection, in a brightness not of this world (1952, p. 11).[23]

Such revelations might follow loss or be heightened by loss as a way of compensation, a manic defence against depression, a form of restitution towards the dead; or, by asserting the alleged harmony which underpins existence, they might act as a stay against anger and the horrifying apprehension of the random, chaotic nature of existence.

We have explored some of the parallels between the process of grief and the mystical process. In addition, we have considered a hypothetical evolution from grief-ridden yearning for union with a lost person to a sense of cosmic union with a higher being. Like grief, mysticism may serve as a vehicle for the expression of pathological as well as normative inclinations. Some degree of mystical faith, whether or not as part of an orthodox religious tradition, is probably sought or felt by most people at certain times in their lives. Whatever the truth of mysticism, there is no doubting the mystic's need for certainty, there is no doubting his subjective perception of being objective, or the religious and aesthetic power of his conviction. The strength of this conviction might be a gauge of his trauma. The need for therapeutic illusion is apparent in his 'knowing' rather than merely 'believing'. As with Picasso's definition of art, mysticism might act as 'a lie through which we learn the truth', Even Freud, a stern rationalist by training, was prepared to accept that the mystic is fortunate to be in touch with higher realms. In *Civilization and Its Discontents* (1930), he first dismisses mysticism as a defence, then, with characteristic irony mingled with admiration, he quotes from Schiller: 'Es freue sich/Wer da atmet im rosigten Licht' (let him rejoice/Who breathes up here in the roseate light.)

We may conclude this chapter with a story which vividly illustrates man's blind, paradoxical need for faith. This need emerges even, perhaps especially, in conditions which bespeak the totally random, meaningless, and barbaric side of his exist- ence. A group of rabbis imprisoned in Auschwitz decide to bring God to judgment. They make up a court and prosecute God, one by one accusing him of causing the horror around them. In the end, they reach a unanimous verdict: Guilty. Then they silently adjourn to say the evening prayers.

6

LOSS AND PHILOSOPHICAL IDEAS

'When a man's finger is caught in a door, all his being goes into that finger.'

Hasidic saying

I might have thrown poor words away
And been content to live.

W.B. Yeats, 'Words'

Philosophical systems are often stamped with the frailties, biases, and limitations of their creators, and whether or not these are brought on by traumas such as loss, they often appear to act as motives in the struggle for creative mastery. In this respect, philosophical literature is no different from poetry, fiction and drama deriving from loss. While there is some critical recognition of the importance of loss among certain philosophers, for example, Nelson (1981) on Pascal, Gedo (1978) on Nietzsche, Atwood (1983) on Sartre, Friedman (1981) on Buber, and Stern (1966) and Scharfstein (1981) on philosophers generally, there has been no attempt until now to examine the role of loss in philosophical literature in the context of a general thematic study of loss and creative literature.

Some of the most probing studies on philosophy and loss have been made upon the works of Descartes, and, as we have seen in Chapter Three, the Cartesian origins of modern philosophy are interpreted by a number of scholars to be a reflection of Descartes' experience of loss in infancy. As in the case of mystical ideas, the embrace of abstract concepts may replace that of the loving parent, and the search for Truth may transcend that for the lost person. This does not mean that all philosophy is ascribable to some lack or distortion in early family life, or that the subjective motives of the philosopher are necessarily as important as the objective truth of his thought. Yet, Scharfstein (1980) in particular has shown how many of the great philosophers suffered loss in childhood and that the development of their thinking often clearly represents an attempt to confront delayed grief and master it.

The purpose of this chapter is mainly to interpret a number of philosophical ideas in the light of recent work on loss: Spinoza's concept of Nature, the motifs of Uncertainty and Faith in Pascal, Childhood in Rousseau, Nietzsche and the Death of God, Sartre's notions of Being and Nothingness, Buber on Meeting and Dialogue. These themes are by no means treated comprehensively, but they appear to illustrate a progression in the conception of Man, from what Gilbert Ryle describes as the Cartesian 'ghost in the machine' to Buber's stress upon the vitality of human attachments. Especially inasmuch as philosophy deals primarily with unanswerable questions, the issues raised by a study of loss provide scope for fruitful analysis and interpretation.

The philosophy of Spinoza raises one such question: to what extent, if at all, was it a response to loss? For Spinoza lost his mother at the age of six (Hampshire, 1976). We have no biographical evidence as to the nature of his grief after the loss, and neither do we know if, or how, this loss inclined him to philosophy. Yet, in view of the research on childhood loss in recent years, it seems likely that Spinoza's loss was at least partly responsible for his attachment to Nature, which is central to his philosophy. According to Spinoza, Nature is God – not a transcendent deity distant from his creations, as was the accepted belief in the seventeenth century, but the necessary cause and being of the natural world: 'Besides God no substance can be nor can be conceived' (*Ethics*, Pt. I, *Prop.* 14). Spinoza's philosophy, indeed, his entire way of life, was founded on the belief that one can know, and love, God only through rational enquiry. His view of man as stated in the *Ethics* (Pt. III, *Prop.* 59 note) may be compared with that of a child of six who has lost his mother: a helplessly irrational, pathetically unstable and unreasonable creature, buffeted by contrary winds like waves in a sea. Feeling, to Spinoza, is our 'human bondage'; freedom lies in our capacity to think; happiness consists in our understanding of the causes of things. As was the case with Descartes, loss had provoked passions too strong to master and express, and Spinoza may have found succour in the world of the mind, in which discord could be mastered through reason, and comfort achieved by perceiving the underlying unity and harmony of all things.[1] The inner conflicts caused by bereavement and finding an outlet in philosophy might be alluded to obliquely in the section of the *Ethics* entitled 'Origin and Nature of Emotions':

Prop. 14. If the mind were once affected at the same time by two emotions, when afterwards it is affected by one of them it will also be affected by the other.

Prop. 15. Anything can accidentally be the cause of pleasure, pain, or desire.

Prop. 16. From the fact alone that we imagine anything which has something similar to an object which is wont to affect the mind with pleasure or pain, although that in which the thing is similar to the object be not the effecting cause of those emotions, nevertheless we shall hate or love it accordingly.

Prop. 17. If we imagine a thing which is wont to affect us with the emotion of sadness to have something similar to another thing which equally affects us with the emotion of pleasure, we will hate and love that thing at the same time.

Prop. 18. A man is affected with the same emotion of pleasure or pain from the image of a thing past or future as from the image of a thing present.

Prop. 19. He will be saddened who imagines that which he loves to be destroyed: if he imagines it to be preserved he is rejoiced.

In these propositions, Spinoza comes to a startlingly modern conclusion, anticipatory of Freud,[2] suggesting that he was deeply aware that the death of a loved one could provoke an ambivalent reaction. In applying this insight to Spinoza's loss of his mother, we may note the second part of *Proposition* 19, 'if he imagines [that which he loves] to be preserved he is rejoiced', as a possible motive underlying his philosophy. For by perceiving God as Nature, Spinoza identified all things, including himself, with God; by regarding the human mind as not totally destructible, but an eternal entity, part of God (*Ethics* Pt. v, *Prop.* 23), he was indirectly arguing that he was united with his dead mother through God, and could perceive her through rational thought. In this way, through the power of thought, Spinoza was holding onto her, understanding her, loving her, indeed, keeping her alive. His intoxication with Nature might thus be interpreted, on one level, as a form of self-therapy, offering protection and consolation in the wake of trauma. The importance of Spinoza's ideas to him was such that he devoted his life to them, never marrying, and enduring the pain of ostracism because of them.[3]

This interpretation of Spinoza's lifelong absorption in the study of Nature may be strengthened by analogy with Wordsworth and Darwin, among others. Onorato has suggested that in the case of

Wordsworth, the loss of his mother, when he was just a year or so older than Spinoza, inclined him to an unusually strong attachment to Nature: 'In Wordsworth's dependency on Nature...he denied his feelings about the mother's undependability' (1971, p. 240), a view corroborated by Brink (1974) and Wordsworth (1981). Similarly, Pickering (1974) has connected Darwin's devotion to the study of the natural world with the loss of his mother when he was eight. These analogies serve to illustrate not only the possible similarities in the responses to loss, but also, perhaps even more significantly, the enormous differences in these responses. To each thinker, Nature has a different meaning. Although the general concept of Nature might, in cases such as these, be identified with a lost parent, it is equally possible to be attached to Nature (in any number of forms) without losing one's mother, or to lose one's mother without becoming attached to Nature. Yet, as we have seen, the large body of literature on loss has established beyond reasonable doubt that, as in the case of Spinoza, a child's loss of his mother at six is not likely to leave him unscarred. The attachment to Nature is only one of many possible ways in which a bereaved individual might attempt to mitigate or resolve his grief.

Whereas in Spinoza's philosophy the anxiety, uncertainty, emptiness and misery deriving from loss may be inferred, in the philosophy of his older contemporary, Blaise Pascal, they are stated openly as being motivations which underlie his thought. 'I strive', wrote Pascal in his *Pensées* (1670), 'only to know my nothingness' (1973, p. 44). To Pascal, man's natural state is of sickness, corruption, wretchedness; he is defined in terms of 'dependence, longing for independence, need' (*ibid.*, p. 45); he is compared to a prisoner in chains, sentenced to death, watching his fellow-prisoners butchered one by one, awaiting his turn; his activities, at best, divert him from these stark realities, but can never overcome them. A feeling of abandonment amid the terrifying vastness of cosmic space pervades Pascal's writings and gives them at times an almost existential quality:

When I see the blindness and misery of man, when I gaze upon the whole silent world, and upon man without light, abandoned to himself, lost, as it were, in this corner of the universe, without knowing who has placed him there, for what purpose, or what will happen to him at death, and altogether incapable of knowledge, I become terrified, as would a man who had been carried off while asleep to some grim desert island and awoke without knowing where he was and without means of getting away (p. 105).[4]

In common with Spinoza, Pascal regarded his rather personal conception of reason as a means of salvation from human bondage, and he looked upon divine love as ultimately the only stay against a chaotic, hostile world. Like Spinoza, too, Pascal lost his mother as a child. In a detailed analysis of Pascal's thought and psychology, Nelson (1981) has found possible origins of Pascal's sense of abandonment and his need to overcome chronic insecurity through religious faith (and even mysticism) in the loss of his mother when he was three: '...like many another child whose parent dies, he may have felt betrayed – ('abandoned' in the religious vocabulary he would cultivate) by his mother in her death' (p. 64). To lose a parent as a child, as Pascal did, is course, no pre-requisite for existential *angst*, but those who suffer such loss are more likely than others to feel frightened and abandoned and the need for an emotional anchor, which philosophy or mysticism, among other things, might bring. The Hegelian view that the purpose of philosophy is to make men feel 'at home' in the universe may be particularly true of those who, like Pascal, suffer the disruption of the family home in childhood through bereavement.

Pascal, like Descartes, appears to have found a substitute for the mother in 'mother Church' (pp. 63–4), in which the warmth of divine love could overcome the cold of traumatic loss. In the *Pensées*, he writes of his wariness at forming attachments to others, and his dislike of others becoming attached to him. In one of the most pathetic of the *Pensées*, he concludes that he cannot be loved for his own beauty or for his intellectual attributes, as these can be lost. The despair at being loved for himself alone suggests the feelings of a small child who has lost his mother, has no proper substitutes and poor conditions for mourning:

> Where then is this Self, if it is neither in the body nor in the soul? And how can the body or the soul be loved, except for those qualities which do not constitute *me*, since they are perishable? For it is impossible and would be wrong to love the substance of someone's soul, abstractly, and whatever qualities it may contain. So we never love a person but only qualities (p. 47).

A childhood memory of his might be interpreted as a screen for the insecurity, the need to hold onto something, and the mistrust brought on by the mother's death: 'When I was a little boy I used to hug my book; and because it sometimes happened that I...while believing that I had hugged it, I was mistrustful' (p. 211).[5] The sense of superfluity described by Pascal also calls to mind the blow to self-esteem which a child may suffer as a result of a parent's death: 'I am aware that I might not have been, for my self consists in my thought. My self, therefore, which thinks, would not have been if my mother had been killed before I received life; so I am not a necessary being' (p. 70).

Pascal's awareness of the importance of childhood – 'Wisdom sends us to childhood' (p. 48) – was continued and greatly elaborated upon by Rousseau in the eighteenth century. Rousseau's crucial role in the development of modern thought cannot be exaggerated, for he above all changed Western thinking about childhood, and in this respect was a direct harbinger of Freud. As Coveney has observed in his study of the child in modern literature, 'About nothing did Rousseau *feel* more passionately than about childhood. His influence lies behind the whole progressive concentration of interest upon the child in the second half of the [eighteenth] century. He more than any created the climate in which Blake, Wordsworth, Lamb, Southey and Coleridge wrote' (1967, p. 41).

Rousseau's educational treatise, *Émile* (1762), though at times naive and misguided by today's perspective, expresses a revolutionary view of childhood which we have largely adopted. Children, according to Rousseau, should not be treated artificially, as miniature adults, but as individuals with an intrinsic nature and value of their own. 'Nature', he wrote, 'wants children to be children before they are men', and he entreated parents not to deprive their children of childhood. For in childhood, man is closest to the 'state of Nature', before the prison of society inhibits and corrupts him.

Like Spinoza, Rousseau saw man as enslaved, but, in contrast with Spinoza, he was convinced that reason was the cause of man's self-imprisonment, and not his means of attaining freedom. Whereas for Spinoza, Nature could be apprehended by rational thought, for Rousseau, Nature is deceived by reason and can be understood only through the 'inner voice' of conscience and intuition, and through emotions, which are good and trustworthy.

In his *Confessions* (1781), Rousseau offers many clues to the psychological underpinnings of his philosophy, and his account of his childhood in particular throws light upon his emphasis on childhood in his writings. The *Confessions* effectively mark the beginning of modern autobiography and self-revelation. We know no one prior to Rousseau so intimately and fully, and speculation regarding the personal origins of his philosophy is on surer ground than in the case of earlier philosophers such as Spinoza or Pascal.

The modern awareness of the possible importance of loss even in infancy is anticipated, in a modified form, by Rousseau. For his birth, he writes, 'cost my mother her life' (1977, p. 19) – nine days after he was born his mother died of puerperal fever. His father never got over this loss: 'He seemed to see her again in me, but could never forget that I had robbed him of her' (*ibid.*). A chronic, masochistic sense of guilt, which impelled him to write the *Confessions*, might have originated partly in this primeval, irrational feeling of self-blame for his mother's death, which his father never allowed him to forget. Among his earliest recollections were his father's groans: 'Give her back to me, console me for her, fill the void she has left in my heart!' (*ibid.*). In order to remain close to the mother, and hold onto her memory, father and son would spend whole nights devouring her novels.[6] Decades later, Rousseau writes, his father, now remarried, was still thinking of her, and he died with her name on his lips.

Among the consequences of this loss, Rousseau's lifelong need for mother-substitutes is one of the more obvious. Mlle Lambercier, with whom he boarded as a child, was 'one whom I loved as a mother, or perhaps even more dearly' (p. 32). The same was true of his attachments to Mlle Goton and Mlle Vulson, from whom Rousseau could never part without grief. Most important of these was Madame de Warens, who became his patroness and lover. He called her 'Maman', and returned her tender indulgence with filial deference. When she was absent he suffered terrible anxiety, and he likened their love to incest.

Other characteristics to which Rousseau confesses may also be understood more clearly in the light of his mother's death and its effect on him and his family, such as his need for expiation, his masochism in relation to women, his propensity for lying and theft, and his increasing suspiciousness of others as the years passed. Some of these traits, Rousseau surmises, had their origins in his early years. For example, he ascribes his masochism to the beatings administered by Mlle Lambercier, and his dishonesty to his cruel treatment by the engraver to whom he was apprenticed. He does not consider the possibility that he was inclined to these abnormalities or sins by his mother's death. It may well be that loss made Rousseau far more vulnerable than he would have been otherwise to the shocks and vagaries of existence, to maltreatment and exploitation, and to pathological inclinations later in life.

There is little doubt, at any rate, that Rousseau's views on childhood were largely determined by his own early experiences. His upbringing appears to have been fairly stable and happy for the first ten years after his mother died. He was brought up by his father and his aunts in Geneva. But then his father was forced to leave the town after a quarrel and he passed into the care of the pastor M. Lambercier. This arrangement did not work out and Rousseau was apprenticed to the engraver until he was sixteen. He was so miserable that he ran away and soon after met his future benefactress, Madame de Warens. Thus, until he was ten, Rousseau was raised mainly by a rather troubled father, inconsolably in mourning for his beloved wife, and after the age of ten he was in the care of others who, at best, misunderstood him and, at worst, undermined his basically good nature. No wonder that he came to reward children as essentially good but corrupted by the adult world as they grew older, and he looked on his early childhood, before his father left home, as a lost paradise, which it almost certainly was not, except in comparison with what followed. His fascination with childhood and education might be attributed, in no small measure, to the distortions in his own childhood, deriving mainly from the loss of his mother and, later, his father's disappearance.

If Rousseau was a precursor of Freud in stressing the importance of childhood, Nietzsche, a hundred years later, anticipated Freud in his recognition of the dynamics of the unconscious. Indeed, Jones wrote that Freud 'several times said of Nietzsche that he had a more penetrating knowledge of himself than any other man who ever lived or was ever likely to live' (1955, II, p. 385). Self-revelation is the acknowledged mainspring of Nietzsche's philosophy: in *Beyond Good and Evil* (1886) he alleged that every great philosophy is the confession of its author and a kind of involuntary memoir. In *From my Life*, a memoir written when he was thirteen, Nietzsche confessed that his character had been shaped by the loss of his father. This loss might, therefore, have been at the root of his genius (Gedo, 1978).[7]

Like Spinoza, whom he regarded as a blood-brother, Nietzsche was a renegade against the conventional beliefs and mores of his age, denying freedom of the will, teleology, the moral world-order, the unegoistic, and evil.[8] Even more than Pascal, he saw man as an unstable creature, helpless in the face of the vast chaotic emptiness of the universe. In *The Gay Science* (1882), he writes of a Diogenes-like madman who lights a lantern in the morning, and runs to the crowded market to look for God to provide direction and meaning for his existence:

> Whither are we moving now? Away from all suns? Are we not plunging continually? Backward, sideward, foreward, in all directions? Is there any up or down left? Are we not straying as through an infinite nothing? Do we not feel the breath of empty space? Has it not become colder? Is not night and more night coming on all the while? Must not lanterns be lit in the morning? (in Kaufmann, 1975, p. 95).

Whereas in Pascal's philosophy, man may defeat his impotence through faith in Nietzsche's philosophy, man may do this through the overcoming of the self, through the will to power. The madman has not overcome his need for faith amid the chaos of the universe; yet, to him God is dead. Presumably this denial of his deepest needs has contributed in driving him mad. The God who might offer solace in the wake of loss is anthropomorphized to the point of being mortal and, indeed, capable of being murdered, leaving mankind in utter despair:

> Whither is God? I shall tell you. *We have killed him* – you and I. All of us are his murderers...Do we not hear anything yet of the noise of the gravediggers who are burying God? Do we not smell anything yet of God's decomposition? Gods too decompose. God is dead. God remains dead. And we have killed him (*ibid.*).

Nietzsche's rejection of traditional faith is a key to the psychology which underlies his philosophy. By the time he entered Bonn University in 1864, Nietzsche had completely abandoned Christianity. Hollingdale (1973) has plausibly argued that Nietzsche's denial of God's existence was linked with the death of his father. For Nietzsche's father was a Lutheran pastor and, after his death, Nietzsche was raised by his mother and maiden aunts in a stifling atmosphere of Lutheran piety. To the Lutheran, as Hollingdale observes, immortality is a fact and, therefore, Nietzsche's rejection of Lutheranism was a form of parricide:

> ...when survival after death is believed in so firmly that it is taken simply for a fact, so that the dead are not really dead at all, denial of this belief may, if your father is dead, become a

sort of parricide. If you deny immortality, you deny that the dead are still living: and if you have previously believed in immortality with the intensity of faith demonstrated by the Nietzsche who wrote *From my Life*, the affect attending such a denial may be that you have killed him (p. 47).[9]

This unconscious guilt at being a parricide might have been exacerbated by a natural feeling of self-blame after the death, for as we have seen, bereaved children not infrequently hold themselves to be responsible for the loss. Anger at the father for dying might also have been expressed in Nietzsche's vehement condemnation of the Christian beliefs which his father embodied. In addition, Nietzsche's physical and psychological torments, culminating in madness during the last eleven years of his life, might be linked with his 'parricidal' rejection of the faith into which he had been born. Illness, as Hayman has indicated, was both Nietzsche's punishment for his loss and his ultimate escape: 'One of the reasons his case history is important is that with his headaches, his vomiting and his madness, he was, more directly than any other thinker, living out the consequences of losing faith in a system of belief which is now generally discredited' (1981, p. 11).

The exaggerated image of masculinity in Nietzsche's writings might be interpreted as a sign of his need to compensate for the lost father. This god-like superman has to be created by man himself, now that he has murdered God:

How shall we, the murderers of all murderers, comfort ourselves? What was holiest and most powerful of all that the world has yet owned has bled to death under our knives. Who will wipe this blood off us? What water is there for us to clean ourselves? What festivals of atonement, what sacred games should we have to invent? Is not the greatness of this deed too great for us? Must not we ourselves become gods simply to seem worthy of it? (in Kaufmann, 1975, pp. 95–6).

As well as expressing an overwhelming sense of guilt, this passage, with its pose of superiority – 'Must not we ourselves become gods...' – might also betray the anxious fear of failure and rejection, and of low self-esteem felt by a lonely, inturned man, partly as a result of a severe childhood loss, and the absence of a father to offer love, guidance, and a model of emulation.

Nietzsche's view that all great philosophical systems are the veiled confessions of their authors is borne out further in the writings of Sartre (who, incidentally, was much indebted to Nietzsche and regarded him as a forerunner of Existentialism). In his autobiography, *Words* (1964), Sartre reveals many of the personal sources of his philosophy. He was separated from his mother as an infant while his father was dying and sent away to be nursed by a farmer's wife; and rather unnatural conditions followed his father's death, when he and his mother moved in with his maternal grandparents. The existential dilemma which he described in his writings was first experienced as a child. When he returned to his mother after several months with the wet-nurse, he found 'a stranger' (1977, p. 13). As he grew up in his grandfather's house, he felt increasingly his own inauthenticity, his nothingness, as if he had no identity of his own, but was merely living up to the rather idealized image of him cultivated by the adults around him (he was an only child): 'I was an imposter' (p. 53); 'I was malleable as clay' (pp. 55–6); 'I was *nothing*' (p. 58). Even after his mother remarried, 'I remained an abstraction...I had no soul' (p. 56).[10] His lack of stable character, of a sense of purpose and meaning in life was largely the result of being fatherless, he confesses with grudging irony, despite his earlier insistence that he was fortunate to have lost his father:[11]

> A father would have ballasted me with a few lasting prejudices; creating my principles from his moods, my knowledge from his ignorance, my pride from his rancour, and my laws from his manias, he would have dwelt in me; this respectable tenant would have given me self-respect. I would have based my right to live on this respect. My begetter would have decided on my future: destined from birth to be an engineer, I should have been reassured for life. But if Jean-Baptiste Sartre had ever known my destination, he had gone off with its secret; all my mother remembered was that he had said: 'My son will not join the Navy.' Lacking more precise information, no one, beginning with myself, knew what the hell I had come on earth to do (p. 56).

In Sartre's philosophy, the question is applied to humanity as a whole: what has man come on earth to do? His novel *Nausea* (1938) states his position plainly and forcefully through the character of Antoine Roquentin: 'I hadn't any right to exist. I had appeared by chance, I existed like a stone, a plant, a microbe' (1975, p. 124); '...there's nothing, nothing, absolutely no reason for existing' (p. 162); '...we hadn't the slightest reason for being there' (p. 184). Like Pascal, Sartre saw man as a creature abandoned on earth, alone, ignorant of the purpose of his existence, plunging himself into activities to divert himself from his loneliness and the futility of his life. But while Pascal found succour through faith, Sartre regarded man as having no destiny other than the one which he forges for himself. To Sartre, the individual is constantly threatened by being engulfed with alien consciousnesses. There is little possiblity of empathetic understanding among human beings. The central preoccupation of Sartre's philosophy, the dialectic of being and nothingness, is, in the view of Atwood, a mirror and symbol of Sartre's own struggle for self-definition and self-formation, achieved finally through his writings:

> ...his image of interpersonal life replicates the situation in his family during his childhood, wherein he constantly felt absorbed into roles with which he could not truly identify. His treatment of social relationships does not include the possibility of being empathetically understood in such a manner that one's sense of self is mirrored and enhanced rather than ensnared and degraded (1983, p. 161).

The concept of an 'I-Thou' relationship, of mutually enhancing meeting and dialogue, is absent in the philosophy of Sartre. To Sartre, life consists of competing subjectivities struggling to rid each other of freedom and to reduce each other to objects. Buber's differentiation between I-Thou and I-It, which he states more emphatically than his predecessors, including Hegel, is apparently meaningless to Sartre. To Buber, there are absolute values which guide each person and which cannot be derived from what he or she is. Buber cannot accept, as Sartre can, Nietzsche's declaration that 'God is dead'. Through man's affirmation of his fellow man, he affirms not just himself but also 'the eternal Thou'.

Buber's relationship to objects is fundamentally opposed to that of Sartre. In the climactic scene in *Nausea*, Antoine Roquentin contemplates the root of a chestnut tree in a public park. At this moment, he has a revelation into the nature of existence: 'To exist is simply *to be there*; what exists appears, lets itself be *encountered*, but you can never *deduce* it' (p. 188). The encounter with the tree involves the possession and becoming of the root: 'I *was* the root of the chestnut tree' (*ibid.*). The philosopher's contemplation of the tree in Buber's *Ich und Du* (I and Thou, 1923), in contrast, allows the possibility of an 'I-Thou' relationship between the human being and the object: '...it can also happen, if will and

121

grace are joined, that as I contemplate the tree I am drawn into a relation, and the tree ceases to be an It' (1970, p. 58).[12]

Buber's emphasis on the vital importance of relationships as a source of man's purpose and dignity is identical with that of psychologists such as Klein, Fairbairn, Winnicott, and Bowlby, who have modified the Freudian view of man as a creature of drives and instincts. Winnicott's concept of 'transitional objects' (1971), whereby an infant becomes attached to objects as temporary substitutes for a care-giver, usually the mother, is anticipated in *I and Thou*, where Buber writes of the baby's explorations of its world:[13]

> Let anyone call this animalic: that does not help our comprehension. For precisely these glances will eventually, after many trials, come to rest upon a red wallpaper arabesque and not leave it until the soul of red has opened up to them. Precisely this motion will gain its sensuous form and definiteness in contact with a shaggy toy bear and eventually apprehend lovingly and unforgettably a complete body (pp. 77–8).

We are reminded here of Nietzsche's contention that the sick man, being more aware of what he lacks than the healthy man of what he possesses, is better qualified to write about health. Buber's biographer, Maurice Friedman (1981), has emphasized that Buber's insight into the nature of meeting and dialogue is inseparable from the childhood traumas which underlie it. When Buber was three, his mother 'disappeared without leaving a trace' (p. 4). He saw her only once afterwards, many years later (p. 11). This loss had an incalculable impact on Buber's life and thought. It was 'the decisive experience of Martin Buber's life, the one without which neither his early seeking for unity nor his later focus on dialogue and on the meeting with the "eternal Thou" is understandable' (p. 15). The abandoned child was raised by his grandparents who, he recalled, never discussed with him the circumstances of the loss or his feelings, and whom he was frankly afraid to ask. In an autobiographical fragment, Buber describes his first apprehension that his mother would not return as the possible origin of his philosophy of meeting and dialogue (1973, pp. 18–19). The absence of an 'I-Thou' relationship in his parents' marriage might have been a cause of the break-up, for, as Buber writes in *I and Thou*: 'Marriage can never be renewed except by that which is always the source of all true marriage: that two human beings reveal the You to one another' (p. 95).

Like Sartre, Buber's early family life was severely disrupted and he was raised by grandparents. The personal testimonies of both leave little doubt that their experiences of loss deeply affected the nature of their thinking. Yet, whereas Sartre saw man as irrevocably alienated from man and from the universe, Buber emphasized the possibility of encounter. Insofar as these opposing views derive from loss, they show, again, the impossibility of predicting how loss might determine a person's character, thinking, and behaviour.

An interpretation of philosophical ideas as possible consequences of loss neither explains these ideas nor excludes other interpretations. As in the case of mystical concepts, philosophy has a transcendent, universal significance beyond the personal tragedies which might have provoked or affected them; and the same may be true of charisma, as we shall see in the next chapter.

7

LOSS AND CHARISMA

Mr. Skimpole (of Ada Clare): We will not call such a lovely young creature as that, who is a joy to all mankind, an orphan. She is the child of the universe.
Mr. Jarndyce: The universe makes rather an indifferent parent, I am afraid.

Charles Dickens, Bleak House (ch. 6)

'...when my mommy wasn't dead I didn't need so many people – I needed just one.' Wendy (quoted by Bowlby, 1980, p. 280)

In common with mysticism and philosophy, charisma may sometimes be understood as a displaced or transcendent form of yearning and searching impelled by grievous loss. The possible origins of charisma are illumined in Martin Buber's *I and Thou* in the passage describing an infant longing for relation and reaching out to the cosmic:

> The innateness of the longing for relation is apparent even in the earliest and dimmest stage. Before any particulars can be perceived, dull glances push into the unclear space toward the indefinite; and at times when there is obviously no desire for nourishment, soft projections of the hands reach, aimlessly to all appearances, into the empty air towards the indefinite (1970, p. 77).

The yearning for the cosmic may thus begin with the infant's bond with its mother and its normal creative desire to explore the world around it. The baby's seemingly aimless 'charismatic' appeal – for what baby is not charismatic? – has an almost mystical quality. If the baby has mastery over its caregivers, if its needs are responded to and satisfied, this appeal will presumably remain in moderation and be directed mainly on to loved ones. If unsatisfied, it may expand promiscuously into an all-consuming and often-distorted search for compensation, or an overblown drive for the mastery which the infant should have had but did not. In adult life, the charismatic may continue to reach 'towards the indefinite', to merge with a greater being; or he may seek unity with society or humanity at large, through the mastery of a medium such as literature, music, film, religion, or politics.

The concepts of incorporation with the lost person and of the 'new identity' created through the grief process (Parkes, 1986), which we have discussed in previous chapters, may thus be applied also to the charismatic. For the charismatic often appears to create a 'new identity', a semi-mythic persona, out of a character split and distorted by unresolved childhood griefs, and to incorporate this persona into a wider social or political entity. In this way, the charismatic may master grief, by transforming it into a creative motivation. Charismatic 'appeal' may be understood in both senses of the word: as a powerful aesthetic attraction to the public, and as a cry for help artfully disguised or transcended. The response to charismatic appeal might involve not merely a reaction to an aesthetic phenomenon but also, at the same time, a simple human reply to the appeal for help.

The word 'charisma' is susceptible to many interpretations as its meaning is vague (Wilson, 1975), and an assessment of the word in the light of research on loss is overdue. Originally used in a theological context, in the sense of 'a free gift or favour specially vouchsafed by God; a grace, a talent' (*OED*), it was popularized by the German sociologist Max Weber (1864–1920) in a more general sociological as well as religious meaning and applied 'to a certain quality of an individual personality by virtue of which he is set apart from ordinary men and treated as endowed with supernatural, super-human, or at least specifically exceptional powers or qualities' (1947, III, p. 329).[1] Among salient elements which contribute to charisma are physical attraction, talent, a cause, and success. In Weber's view, charisma is a quality of groups, not just of individuals, and the essence of charisma lies in the interconnection of the personal and the public need. Weber suggests that charisma might stem from suffering or conflict, but neither he nor later sociologists consider the possible role of grief as a motivational force in charisma.[2] Similarly, the concept of charisma has until now been almost totally absent from the literature on grief.

The life and career of Winston Churchill give an unusually well-documented portrait of charismatic leadership which is almost certainly bound up with loss or deprivation in childhood and whose personal creative aim was to master the effects of loss. Storr's interpretation of Churchill (1973), though not concerned specifically with charisma, is relevant to the argument here.

125

Throughout his life, Churchill went through bouts of depression, or the 'Black Dog' as he called it, which were at times so severe that he was driven to thoughts of suicide. Churchill was inclined to depression, among other reasons, as a result of serious neglect in infancy and childhood. His mother, Jennie, though warm, vivacious and highly intelligent, was preoccupied by a ceaseless whirl of social activities and had relatively little time for him. His father, Lord Randolph Churchill, had his political career—he rose to the position of Chancellor of the Exchequer—which, likewise, left him with little time for his son whom he seems to have disliked. An important element in the relationship, or the lack of one, between father and son was that Randolph suffered from syphilis. He died from this disease when Winston was twenty, and it is significant that Winston discovered the true nature of his father's illness only a few weeks before the latter's death. It may be that his father kept him at a distance for reasons having to do with his disease. At any rate, Churchill was virtually abandoned by his parents and was raised by a nanny. His son Randolph wrote of him: 'The neglect and lack of interest in him shown by his parents were remarkable even by the standards of late Victorian and Edwardian days' (1966, I, p. 43).

As a result, writes Storr, Churchill apparently failed to develop a firm inner source of self-esteem and was, therefore, exceptionally prone to depression. Deprivation fueled his compulsive ambition and his dependence upon external sources of self-esteem, such as success in political life. It also made him liable to compensatory fantasies of being special and of having a heroic mission. The stimulus of war was the strongest antidote against depression, and Churchill was never happier than in wartime. The horror of war counted less to him than the chivalry, the glory and the exhilaration of the struggle. On the eve of the 1914–18 war, he confessed to his wife his happiness as an abnormality: 'Everything tends towards catastrophe and collapse. I am interested, geared up and happy. Is it not horrible to be built like that?' (Gilbert, III, p. 80). As for the Second World War, he said that 1940 and 1941 were the best years of his life. He felt that Destiny had chosen him for this hour and that his past life had been but a preparation for the trial of standing alone against Germany (ibid., VI, p. 317). It is almost impossible to distinguish between Churchill's undoubted courage and his craving for stimulus to overcome the Black Dog which led him on many occasions in a number of wars to risk his life unnecessarily. He enjoyed the sounds and sights of war and wanted to be where the action was: 'I love the bangs', he said during the London Blitz.

In battling the potential sources of weakness in him, Churchill built up formidable inner strength and courage. His charismatic appeal in 1940 derived largely from his ability to make use of external stimulus in order to overcome despair. In 1940, with Britain on the verge of defeat, Churchill drew upon his psychological resources to inspire the nation with the will to overcome collective despair, to fight and survive. Until the summer of 1940, there were still influential members of the British government, such as Lord Halifax, who were ready to negotiate a peace settlement with Hitler; and when Hitler made his peace offer to Britain on 19 July 1940, a leader less pugnacious and determined and less capable of inspiring the nation than Churchill – Halifax was the second choice for Prime Minister – might have lost heart and succumbed. At this moment of impending doom, Churchill was fully identified with Britain and with the free world. The key to Churchill's impact in 1940, writes Storr, lay in the interconnection of his inner battles against depression and the enemy which threatened Britain: 'In 1940, any political leader might have tried to rally Britain with brave words, although his heart was full of despair. But only a man who had known and faced despair within himself could carry conviction at such a moment' (p. 206). His aggressive defiance is immortalized in lines such as those spoken in the House of Commons on 4 June 1940:

> We shall not flag or fail. We shall fight in France, we shall fight on the seas and oceans, we shall fight with growing confidence and growing strength in the air, we shall defend our island, whatever the cost may be, we shall fight on the beaches, we shall fight on the landing grounds, we shall fight in the fields and in the streets, we shall fight in the hills; we shall never surrender.

This belligerent style was often a liability in war as in peace, and in the 1930s had been highly unpopular as it was then out of fashion. Yet in 1940, for once, Churchill's aggressiveness could be given full rein against a legitimate demonic target. The intensity of this hostility, in Storr's view, was related to Churchill's emotional deprivations in childhood and to the depression which subsequently plagued him:

> The emotionally deprived child who later becomes prey to depression has enormous difficulty in the disposal of his hostility. He resents those who have deprived him, but he

cannot afford to show this resentment, since he needs the very people he resents; and any hostility he does manifest results in still further deprivation of the approval and affection he so much requires. In periods of depression, this hostility becomes turned against the self, with the result that the depressive under-values himself or even alleges that he is worthless. 'I have achieved a great deal to achieve nothing in the end.'

It is this difficulty in disposing of hostility which drives some depressives to seek for opponents in the external world. It is a great relief to find an enemy on whom it is justifiable to lavish wrath...when he was finally confronted by an enemy whom he felt to be wholly evil, it was a release which gave him enormous vitality. Hitler was such an enemy; and it is probable that Churchill was never happier than when he was fully engaged in bringing about Hitler's destruction (pp. 231–2).

Storr anticipates the criticism that any argument of this kind applied to such a great man as Churchill may easily be dismissed as futile and impertinent. He emphasizes that although Churchill has become a universal symbol of defiant bravery, he was also a human being. To draw attention to Churchill's humanity, to his flaws as well as to his inordinate strengths, in no way detracts from his achievements. His charismatic power appears to have been born out of a mixture of these weaknesses and strengths.

Just as good and evil sometimes counterpart one another, so also Churchill and Hitler, in the eyes of some historians (e.g. Manchester, 1983), were mirror images of each other; and the nature of their charismatic appeal has certain elements in common. Although Churchill in the 1930s stood virtually alone in Parliament in warning of the dangers of Hitler and Nazism, he also, up to a point, admired Hitler: he expressed the hope that if Britain were defeated in war as Germany had been in 1918, she too would have a revivalist leader of Hitler's stature. Both Churchill and Hitler have been described (Storr, 1973; Carr, 1978) as men who, to a marked degree, went against their own natures. Both were driven by the conviction of being chosen by Destiny and were fully identified with their respective countries. Sharing the belief that man's nobility is best expressed in war, both were jubilant at the outbreak of war and, in battle, showed exceptional bravery under fire. Artists by temperament – both painted – they were guided by instinct rather than by reason. Both were inherently unstable: Lloyd George once compared Churchill to an apparently sane chauffeur who drives with great skill for several months, then suddenly without warning takes the car over a cliff. Under the pressure of war, Churchill, too, showed, signs of despotism and megalomania, though he was curbed from his more extreme impulses by his war cabinet and his generals. Like Hitler, Churchill depended for his appeal on oratory, and in conversation they both tended to soliloquize and to dominate their listeners. Both were deeply troubled by distortions in family background, suffering hostility at the hands of their fathers and greatly idealizing their mothers, and thus they were led to seek sources of self-esteem in public life. Both needed an enemy: Hitler found his in the Jews, Churchill, in Hitler.

Yet, whereas Churchill was a saviour of the free world, Hitler was a cold-blooded tyrant, the murderer of millions of innocent civilians, the very incarnation of evil. An exploration of Hitler's charismatic appeal in Germany of the 1930s involves seeing Hitler as a human being, warped but human still, and it is not easy to regard Hitler as anything other than inhuman. In fact, though, just as Churchill's greatness is not diminished by a consideration of his weaknesses, so also Hitler's crimes can in no way be condoned or glossed over by examining the possible family roots of his charismatic power and the political path which he chose.

Wilson has described Hitler as the last political leader to succeed through unrestrained appeal to the primitive, romantic, and atavistic passions of men, through the 'rhetoric of charisma' which,

> employs an earthy vocabulary of body imagery and basic biological elements. In these terms the in-group is reassured of itself and its boundaries, and its being as a 'natural' entity. It is no accident that Hitler's ideological repertoire drew so heavily on race, blood, ruralism, primary native virtue, pre-Christian religious imagery, folk values, and semi-mystical atavism (1975, p. 105).

In Bullock's view (1986), no political leader has ever shown greater understanding of the irrational and emotional factors in politics, or exploited them more masterfully. Hitler's instinct for the theatrical (Chaplin once described him as 'the greatest actor of us all'), his fanatically sincere oratory, his use of his hands and eyes (for which he received professional training), hypnotized his audiences and brought about their complete identification with him.

Hitler's magnetism, like that of Churchill, lay chiefly in his oratory. In the course of his speeches, he would undergo an immense transformation, from a nervous, insecure, indecisive man, into his opposite: hard, brutal, all-powerful, capable of mass-murder, heedless of conscience and guilt – *der Führer*.[3] This transformation, which had an unmistakeable sexual element, appears to have expressed his audiences' own secret desire to be transformed after the 1914–18 debacle and the 1929 Wall Street crash, and to be omnipotent and victorious. The power of his oratory created an almost mystical bond between him and his audiences. The public need for transformation and decisive leadership to which Hitler ministered propelled him to the chancellorship in 1933.

Nevertheless, as in the case of Churchill, there was also a corresponding private need which gave Hitler's speeches the stamp of fanatical conviction. Thus Carr (1978) has interpreted Hitler's semi-mystical union with Germany as a possible renewal of the symbiosis between Hitler and his mother who had died of cancer when he was eighteen, in 1907. The bond between mother and son was unusually intense and protective as she had lost three children before his birth and was fearful of losing him too.[4] The attachment of mother and son was heightened further by the father's tyrannical behaviour at home and by the age difference between father and mother, she being twenty-three years younger than he. Hitler's family doctor, Eduard Bloch, recalled that his mother's death was a crushing blow to Hitler: 'In all my career I never saw anyone so prostrate with grief as Adolf Hitler' (in Toland, 1976, p. 36).

Hitler's grief-stricken bond with his lost mother might well have been displaced on to Germany, and Langer (1972) has called attention to the fact that in Hitler's writings and speeches Germany is almost invariably identified with the 'faithful mother'. Fromm (1977) argues, however, that Hitler's attachment to his mother was cold and destructive and that his deepest motivation was not to save mother- Germany but to destroy her. At any rate, it may be that Germany's defeat in 1918 revived the terrible grief which he had felt on losing his mother. At this time, while recovering in hospital from a mustard gas attack which had temporarily blinded him, Hitler allegedly heard visionary voices summoning him to liberate Germany and lead her to greatness whereupon his sight returned and he vowed to enter politics (Toland, 1976).

The work of Bion (1961), himself a veteran of the First World

War, on groups and leaders gives insight into the close links between Hitler's personal experiences and his charismatic appeal in Germany of the 1920s and 1930s. The First World War had caused loss of life on a scale unprecedented in history. In Germany, hardly a family did not have a father, a son, or a close relative killed or maimed. Among Bion's various types of groups with different motives, one is particularly applicable to Germany: the basic assumption and oneness group which seeks a sense of well-being and unity. In such a group, the followers idolize the leader in order to overcome their fear of desertion. In a society wracked with bereavement and the humiliation of defeat as Germany was after 1918, the need for well-being and unity could become especially pressing, and could point the way to a dictatorship. For such a group, the natural leader might be one who has himself experienced severe loss and has developed inner defences by which to overcome the effects of grief. Hitler was such a leader.

Hitler was no ordinary politician but the founder of a new religion. He was worshipped by millions virtually as a deity, as Germany's Messiah. Other modern messiahs have used their charismatic powers for good rather than evil ends. One of these was the Indian religious leader, Jiddu Krishnamurti. It is rare, if not unique, for a relatively impartial and detailed biography to be written about such a man, but Lutyens' biography (1975, 1983) is exceptional as the author is a sophisticated former adherent who still retains a critical admiration for the man and his gifts. Among other things, Lutyens makes clear the possible links between Krishnamurti's charisma and his experience of childhood loss.

Krishnamurti's story begins with the creation of the Theosophical Society in America in 1875. The moving spirit of the society was the notorious Russian, Madame Blavatsky, worshipped by her followers as a seer and miracle worker. The society set out to create a so-called Universal Brotherhood of Humanity, without distinction of race, creed, sex, caste, or colour. The breaking down of barriers between peoples was to be a dominant theme in Krishnamurti's teachings even after he broke with the theosophists. The society moved to India in 1882 and from there it rapidly became an international movement. Many of its early members were idealistic British Indiaphiles, notably the social reformer Annie Besant who converted to Hinduism, and included clergymen, artists and political leaders as well as a number of wealthy and well-connected, if somewhat eccentric, aristocrats. By the turn of the century, the society numbered over ten thousand.

The central aim of the society since the time of Madame Blavatsky, who had died in 1891, was to prepare humanity for the Lord Maitreya, the World Teacher, who would bring a vital message in a time of dire need. According to the theosophists, the World Teacher had appeared in two previous incarnations, as Sri Krishna in the fourth century B.C.E., and as Jesus. In 1909, at the international headquarters of the society in Adyar near Madras, the third incarnation of the World Teacher was 'discovered' – Krishnamurti.

Krishnamurti was born in 1895, the son of Jiddu Narianiah, an Indian civil servant, and his wife, Sanjeevamma. He was the eighth of eleven children, of whom six survived childhood. In 1905, when he was 9½, his mother died, and this tragedy had a decisive impact upon his inner life. Narianiah had great difficulty in raising his children and his situation worsened when he retired two years later on half salary. As a longstanding member of the Theosophical Society, he appealed to its president, Annie Besant (who was looked upon in his household as something of a saint), for a job at Adyar which would provide accommodation for him and his family. His appeal was eventually answered and in early 1909 he moved with his children to Adyar where he worked as a secretarial assistant. The family lived in an overcrowded, dilapidated cottage without sanitation.

The boy who was to become the elegant Messiah was at this time dirty and undernourished, his ribs showed through his skin and he had a persistent cough; his face was vacant of expression and he was thought to be dull-witted. He was so weak physically that his father declared more than once that he was bound to die.

The 'discovery' of Krishnamurti was made later in 1909 by C.L. Leadbeater, a former clergyman with a tainted reputation who for many years had worked closely with Annie Besant. Leadbeater was bathing in the Adyar river near the Theosophical Society estate when he saw among a crowd of boys a boy with 'the most wonderful aura he had ever seen...a most extraordinary aura' (1975, p. 21). (In later years, Krishnamurti, who apparently had no memory of this momentous event in his life, would speak of 'the boy' as if he were some other creature belonging to a distant world and wonder in amazement why he had been picked out.) Later, after discovering the boy's identity, Leadbeater resolved to train him as the human incarnation of the World Teacher and began to investigate his past lives.[5] He removed Krishnamurti (and his brother Nitya) from school and arranged private tuition for him. In 1910 the father was persuaded to transfer guardianship of his sons to Annie Besant and the following year the 'Order of the Star in the East' was founded with the purpose of preparing the world for Krishnamurti's messianic 'coming'. These sudden, extraordinary changes in his life seem not to have affected Krishnamurti adversely. One of his tutors, E.A. Wodehouse, brother of the writer, recalled his exceptional qualities:

> We were no blind devotees, prepared to see in him nothing but perfection. We were older people, educationalists, and with some experience of youth. Had there been a trace in him of conceit or affectation, or any posing as the 'holy child', or of priggish self-consciousness, we would undoubtedly have given an adverse verdict (Lutyens, 1975, p. 45).

Yet, Krishnamurti's power went far beyond that of most popular charismatics as it was believed, especially by his early followers, to be a genuine gift of God. From the age of fourteen until he was thirty-four, Krishnamurti was revered and groomed by them as the Messiah. As the years passed, however, Krishnamurti became increasingly disenchanted with this role and in 1929 he publicly renounced it, broke up the 'Order of the Star in the East', and launched out on his own as an independent religious teacher. Ironically, as a spiritual leader whose message was that one should not seek leaders but find the truth within oneself, Krishnamurti gained far more influence than he ever had as the Messiah. By the time of his death in 1986, he was one of the best-known and loved religious figures both in Western and Eastern countries.

Though he believed that one should live in the present and lose the memory of the past in the process of spiritual elevation, Krishnamurti did not diminish the impact on him of his mother's death, which was a massive blow, all the more so as conditions for mourning were poor. In a memoir written when he was eighteen, Krishnamurti states that his happiest childhood memories were of himself and his mother together and that her death was catastrophic: 'My mother's death in 1905 deprived my brothers and myself of the one who loved and cared for us most, and my father was too much occupied to pay much attention to us...there was really nobody to look after us' (in Lutyens, 1975, p. 5). Lady Emily Lutyens, his disciple and closest confidante during his years with the theosophists (and mother of his biographer), whom he addressed as 'my holy mother', recalled his longing to be reunited with his dead mother. Her wish to compensate him for his loss illumines the mystery of his appeal, for no doubt many others responded to him, perhaps unconsciously, for similar reasons:

> His mother having died when he was very young, he was always yearning to be back in her arms. He had seen a picture in the *Daily Mirror* one day of a small boy seated on a bench in the park and dreaming that he was sitting on his mother's lap. He cut out this picture and told me that he felt he was that little boy...I longed to compensate him for his loss (p. 82).[6]

From an early age, Krishnamurti was inclined to 'spiritual' experiences owing to unresolved grief. In common with many others who have illusions or hallucinations of the lost person, he had visions of his dead mother (p. 5), which apparently signified his denial of her death and his yearning to be reunited with her. In Hindu society, and, in general, in the pre-modern world, such 'visions' were more likely to be regarded as evidence of contact with higher Beings than as signs of grief. Also, five of his eleven siblings died in childhood or in early adult life. He was deeply affected by some of these losses, and his sense of being 'chosen' and 'protected' by the higher Beings might have derived in part from his having survived. In the year before his mother's death, he lost his eldest sister and discovered that he, like his mother, could occasionally 'see' the dead girl.

For much of his adult life, Krishnamurti was periodically afflicted with immense unexplained physical pain during which he would behave like a small child in need of its mother and would address the women around him as 'Amma' or 'Mother'. Lutyens was present on a number of these occasions in the 1920s and recalled that 'He had behaved to me at times as if I were his mother and he a child of about four' (1983, p. 69n). Furthermore, she wrote, 'It seemed that only when he became a child again was he able to relax and thereby obtain some relief from the pain, which was with him all day now as a dull ache as well as intensely in the evenings. But he could not become a child without a "mother" to look after the body' (1975, p. 184). At one point, he had recurrent visions of his dead mother, as he had in childhood (*ibid.*, pp. 165–6). As part of this 'process', as he called it, he would have hallucinations of union not only with his mother but also with the entire world, and this may be regarded as the basis of his mystical-charismatic identity. In 1922 he had an hallucination which might be taken to foreshadow his later role as an international spiritual teacher, for it shows how deep was his need and his impulse to identify himself with all animate and inanimate things:[7]

There was a man mending the road; that man was myself; the pickaxe he held was myself; the very stone which he was breaking up was a part of me; the tender blade of grass was my very being, and the tree beside the man was myself. I almost could feel and think like the roadmender, and I could feel the wind passing through the tree, and the little ant on the blade of grass I could feel. The birds, the dust, and the very noise were a part of me. Just then there was a car passing by at some distance; I was the driver, the engine, and the tyres; as the car went further away from me, I was going away from myself. I was in everything, or rather everything was in me, inanimate and animate, the mountain, the worm, and all breathing things (p. 158).

Krishnamurti's desire to 'belong to the world' might thus have been a direct result of his mother's death as he no longer belonged to a secure family. The need for reunion with the mother – a yearning 'to be back in her arms' which could not be satisfied – evolved into a need which could be satisfied – to be one with the Public, with the whole world and with the higher ideal or Beings, which he called his 'Beloved'. He eventually felt that he had attained unity with his 'Beloved', which he described as 'the open skies, the flower, every human being' and which could be found 'in every animal, in every blade of grass, in every person that is suffering, in every individual' (p. 250). In one of his most Christ-like pronouncements, he declared:

I belong to all people, to all who really love, to all who are suffering. And if you would walk, you must walk with me. If you would understand you must look through my mind. If you would feel, you must look through my heart. And because I really love, I want you to love (p. 233).

His break with the Theosophical Society in 1929 was accompanied by a new sense of union and self-overcoming. It is of great psychological interest that this spiritual turning point involved the conviction that 'henceforth there will be no separation':

If I say, and I will say, that I am one with the Beloved, it is because I feel and know it. I have found what I longed for, I have become united, so that henceforth there will be no separation, because my thoughts, my desires, my longings – those of the individual self – have been destroyed...I have been united with my Beloved, and my Beloved and I will wander together the face of the earth (p. 250).

A remarkably similar sensation of belonging to the universe is described by Marilyn Monroe (1974) in a passage telling of her first intimations of her charismatic appeal and of her later screen persona:

I paid no attention to the whistles and whoops. In fact, I didn't hear them. I was full of a strange feeling, as if I were two people. One of them was Norma Jean from the orphanage who belonged to nobody. The other was someone whose name I didn't know. But I knew where she belonged. She belonged to the ocean and the sky and the whole world (p. 25).

Belonging to nobody, she too belonged to everyone and everything, for the Public was her only home: 'I belonged to the Public and to the world, not because I was talented or even beautiful but because I had never belonged to anything or anyone else. The Public was the only family, the only Prince Charming and the only home I ever dreamed of' (p. 124). This admission was literally true as she had been raised on public funds virtually from birth: born Norma Jean Mortensen in Los Angeles in 1926, she never knew her father and hardly saw her mother who was an institutionalized schizophrenic. Until her first marriage at sixteen, she lived with a succession of families (nine in all, she claimed), and for about two years (1935–7), after her mother was confined to an asylum, she lived in a Los Angeles orphanage.[8] Bowlby, in his classic study for the World Health Organization (1953), reached conclusions which, while not applicable to all foster children, are certainly true of Marilyn Monroe:

Neither foster-homes nor institutions can provide children with the security and affection which they need; for the child they always have a make-shift quality...However devoted foster-parents may be, they have not the same sense of absolute obligation to a child which all but the worst parents possess. When other interests and duties call, a foster-child takes second place. A child is therefore right to distrust them – from his point of view there is no one like his own parents (1965, pp. 80–1, 137).

Her charismatic appeal seems to have emanated from the aura of public availability which surrounded her and which she cultivated. Her orphanhood, wrote Arthur Miller, 'heightened her charged presence' (1987, p. 306), and she wrote of herself:

> As I grew older I knew I was different from other children because there were no kisses or promises in my life. I often felt lonely and wanted to die. I would try to cheer myself up with daydreams. I never dreamed of anyone loving me as I saw other children loved. That was too big a stretch for my imagination. I compromised by dreaming of my attracting someone's attention (besides God), of having people look at me and say my name (1974, p. 16).

This attraction succeeded beyond her dreams, and the language of charisma is frequently used of her: she is 'worshipped' by her 'devotees' who are 'enchanted' by her 'spell' or 'aura' as by a 'goddess'. Billy Wilder, who directed her in 'Some Like It Hot', once made a wry comment which might be applied to charismatics generally: 'The question really is whether Marilyn is a real person or one of the greatest synthetic products ever invented.' She described herself as a 'superstructure without a foundation'. Her luscious persona belonging 'to the ocean and the sky and the whole world' was largely her own creation, the blend of sexual allure, wit and pathos the product of much calculation and art. She spent hours each day in front of mirrors with lipsticks, powders and mascara. 'There's not a single movement', she said, 'not a single inflection in a line that I haven't learned by myself, working it over a thousand times' (Lembourn, 1979, pp. 16–17). She spoke of 'the face that I've made', a face and an image which she did not believe to be naturally beautiful but which she virtually willed into being. She transcended her roles, using them as showcases for moments of child-like wistful radiance, innocence and freshness. She was tragic and suggestive of unfathomable disturbance yet sweetened this image with physical beauty, self-mockery and the honey of sex. Her roles are memorable not for themselves as much as for her screen persona, and the fascination of her persona does not lie in the acting, fine as it often is, but in the hints of the real, vulnerable creature behind the mask.

Her marriages were a continuation of early patterns of attachment, suspicion and betrayal, with the difference that she could – and did – terminate each relationship. Each of her three husbands, and other men with whom she was involved, were considerably older than she. She sought in marriage the father whom she never had. As a child, she had fantasied that Clark Gable was her father. Later, she came to admire Abraham Lincoln and said that she thought of Lincoln as her father. Arthur Miller was 'Papa' to her. And her need for a father showed itself in many other ways. For example, in her first appearance on stage, at the New York Actors' Studio in 1956, she chose the part of Anna Christie in Eugene O'Neill's play and acted the opening scene in which Anna, a prostitute who has never known her father, is about to meet him for the first time. Her lifelong search for a father was part of the mystery of her appeal, but contrary to the impression projected on screen, there was often a deadening of feeling in her attachments to men. Grief, anxiety, anger – the emotional detritus of childhood – conspired to prevent her from loving. She recalled that already as a schoolgirl surrounded by admiring men, she had wanted to feel but could not: '. . . with all my lipstick and mascara and precocious curves, I was as unsensual as a fossil. . . I would have liked to want something as much as they did. I wanted nothing' (1974, pp. 26–7). As a grown woman, she came to see that her promiscuity had not led to the deepening of her attachments but, on the contrary, had numbed her like a drug: 'I sometimes felt I was hooked on sex, the way an alcoholic is on liquor or a junkie on dope. My body turned all these people on, like turning on an electric light, and there was so rarely anything human in it' (Weatherby, 1977, p. 146). Friends and acquaintances were often struck by the air of insulation which surrounded her. She sometimes gave the impression of being a somnambulist or of being hidden behind a great wall of cotton. Arthur Schlesinger described the 'terrible unreality' of talking with her, 'as if talking with someone under water'.

Belonging to the public, she found in the end the same fragmentation and the absence of consistent love that she had known as a child. In conversation, she would often describe herself using disturbing images of being cut to pieces, eaten up or disappearing. For example, she said, 'I sometimes feel as if I'm too exposed, I've given myself away, the whole of me, every part, and there's nothing left that's private, just me alone' (Weatherby, p. 127). She even intimated that the escape into make-believe was analogous to suicide: '. . . sometimes it seems you escape altogether and people never let you come back' (p. 150). Only up to a point did her gifts enable her to transcend and master her childhood griefs; beyond that, they pointed the way to her tragic death. In one of her recurrent nightmares, she would run naked through a cemetery looking frantically for a way out. She dreamed of herself as a wilful Icarus bent on self-destruction: 'I dream of breaking out through the bars and soaring up, up, up. . . Sometimes at night I dream I become free and fly upward toward the sun and into it, so my wings burn off and I fall through the universe' (Lembourn, p. 56).

The charisma of John Lennon, too, was based partly on an appeal for help, and he once said that his song 'Help' was an actual cry for help in the trough of depression: 'Now I may be very positive – yes, yes – but I also go through deep depressions where I would like to jump out the window. It becomes easier to deal with as I get older' (1981, p. 112). These depressions were caused at least partly by repeated losses in childhood, and the concomitant feelings of abandonment and isolation, of being emotionally crippled, of pain and insecurity, of a distorted self-image, are explored repeatedly in Lennon's songs: '. . . creating is a result of pain. . . I have to put it somewhere and I write songs' (1980, p. 94). He believed that all creative people like himself are motivated by an appalling need for love and said that 'If I had the capabilities of being something other than I am, I would' (p. 11).

Lennon's early childhood was unsettled to the point that until he was five it was not certain who would raise him. His parents were both musical, happy-go-lucky, and unstable, and their marriage was doomed from the start. The father, a waiter at sea, had married while on leave in Liverpool. He was rarely home and at the time of Lennon's birth in 1940, no one knew his where-abouts. The mother, despite her affection for her son, was disin-clined or unable to care for him properly, especially when she became involved with another man. After an incident in which the father absconded with him to Blackpool and he was asked to choose between his father and mother, he hardly saw either parent, though his mother lived only a short distance away. Still, he was always conscious of her existence and, as he put it 'my feelings never died off for her' (Davies, 1978, p. 26). In the song 'Mother', he starkly laments his loss, 'you had me but I never had you' and in another song addressed to her, 'Julia', he writes; 'Half of what I say is meaningless/But I say it just to reach you, Julia.' Her sudden death in a car accident in 1958 was an enormous blow, and he described himself as being in a blind rage for about two years afterwards.

Nevertheless, conditions for Lennon after his parents' separa-tion were fairly good, and the strength which he derived from substitute mothering enabled him in later life to confront his trauma and try to master it:

There were five women who were my family. Five strong, intelligent women. Five sisters. One happened to be my mother. My mother was the youngest. She just couldn't deal with life. She had a husband who ran away to sea and the war was on and she couldn't cope with me, and when I was four and a half, I ended up living with her elder sister. Now, those women were fantastic (1981, p. 110).

In retrospect, he felt that not having parents was a gift as well as an overwhelming trauma: 'I was free from the parents' stranglehold. That was the gift I got for not having parents. I cried a lot about not having them and it was torture, but it also gave me an awareness early' (*ibid.*). Scars left from childhood were deeply etched into Lennon's character. Shy, self-doubting and dependent, he hid his feelings from others and immersed himself in an intense fantasy life. At times, he would have moments of 'cosmic consciousness' not unlike those of mystics:

I was always seeing things in a hallucinatory way. It was scary as a child, because there was nobody to relate to...Surrealism to me is reality. Psychic vision to me is reality. Even as a child...I would find myself seeing hallucinatory images of my face changing and becoming cosmic and complete (*ibid.*).

In the song 'Yer Blues', he amplifies on this sense of belonging to the universe, not having belonged to a secure family:

My mother was of the sky.
My father was of the earth.
But I am of the universe
And you know what it's worth.

The enormous number of styles and faces with which he experimented testify to the insecurity of his self-image, and his songs reflect this variety: in some he affirms a vision of universal harmony and love, but in others he emerges as vulgar, violent, and cruel. Acutely conscious of being cut off from the world, Lennon was often aggrieved by his own egocentricity and aggressive ambition. Age, success, a happy marriage and fatherhood mellowed him, but as a schoolboy and in his adolescence he had been delinquent, in his young manhood he came close to being an alcoholic and a drug addict, in his early married life he was at times unbearable, and he knew it: 'I am a violent man who has learned not to be violent and regrets his violence' (p. 114).

Having been 'abandoned' by his father and having also lost his step-father when he was twelve, Lennon had a notorious need for and hatred of parental authority. In the absence of a strong father, he developed an unusually tough, aggressive 'macho' image with which to identify himself. Throughout much of his life, he was regularly attracted to parent-figures, such as the Maharishi, and he rejected them all in the end. (His song 'God' includes an entire litany of failed gods.) His anti-authoritarianism was an important facet of his appeal to the young during the 1960s and 1970s. For him as for other charismatics, independence and originality were bound up with unresolved grief, depression and hostility towards parental authority: 'Daddy doesn't heal us', he said. 'You have to do it yourself' (1981, p. 144).

It may be that his collaboration with Paul McCartney was determined by shared experiences of loss, especially as many of their songs tell openly of the effects of loss and separation and of the need for love. McCartney had shown relatively little interest in music before his mother died of cancer in 1956 when he became obsessed by the guitar (Davies, p. 44). According to his brother, Michael McCartney, after the death of Lennon's mother 'John and Paul had a bond that went beyond even the music' (Coleman, 1984, p. 91).

In Lennon's charismatic appeal, as in that of the others whom we have considered here, two qualities stand out in relation to our interpretation of loss and creativity: the combination of weakness and strength, and the creation of a 'new identity' to counteract the effects of loss. The weakness of the charismatic springs from early family loss or deprivation, leading to low self-esteem, depression and the blockage of feeling, while the strength arises from the positive conditions following the loss coupled with natural gifts and a creative outlet. In the struggle to overcome or to master his weaknesses, the successful charismatic enhances his worth in his own eyes and in the eyes of his society or nation or the entire world. Not having belonged to a secure home, he may find or create a home within an abstract entity such as the Public or the Universe. In the process of doing so, he may split off the new, magnetic being from the wounded, unwanted self. In Churchill, Storr emphasizes, *'we have a picture of a man who was, to a marked extent, forcing himself to go against his own inner nature'* (p. 212); and the same is generally true of all the charismatics whom we have discussed. The new self, like the work of art which it creates or which is created by it, is a superstructure with a poor or nonexistent foundation, for it belongs not to a secure family but 'to the ocean and the sky and the whole world'.

141

8

GRIEF AND PATHOLOGY

'I am but mad north-north-west; when the wind is southerly I know a hawk from a handsaw.'

Hamlet, II, ii, 359–60

Much that has been said in previous chapters concerns the creative uses of pathology resulting from grief. Pathology, writes Freud, 'by making things larger and coarser, can draw our attention to normal conditions which would otherwise have escaped us' (1933, p. 58). However, pathology is never isolated from the normal; it is the exaggeration and distortion of the normal. The act of creation in response to pathological grief may be seen as an attempt to reduce the extent of distortion and exaggeration by making the pathology visible, less frightening and more controllable. Mental illness may be held in check through creativity, as Storr writes: 'Manic-depressive psychopathology may spur a man to create: but manic-depressive illness stops him from doing so, and the same is true of schizophrenia' (1972, p. 213), therefore the creative act is itself a sign of health and courage, for 'it tends to protect the individual against mental breakdown' (p. 31).

As we have seen, temporary disorder is normal after a loss: numbness, denial, yearning and searching, depression, are some of the recognized features of mourning which pass with time. In pathological grief, in contrast, the temporary becomes chronic, often in distorted form, and this delayed grief may assume harmful dominance in the character of the bereaved. Parkes has likened normal and pathological grief to physical injury which may or may not be accompanied by complications:

On the whole, grief resembles a physical injury more closely than any other type of illness. The loss may be spoken of as a 'blow'. As in the case of a physical injury, the 'wound' gradually heals; at least, it usually does. But occasionally complications set in, healing is delayed, or a further injury reopens a

142

healing wound. In such cases abnormal forms arise, which may even be complicated by the onset of other types of illness. Sometimes it seems that the outcome may be fatal (1986, p. 25).[1]

The following circumstances illustrate how the elements of normal grief might evolve into psychopathology: the withdrawal which frequently results from a severe loss is an indication of mental illness; depression after a loss might become a pathological illness, and the denial of depression might, in turn, be expressed in the form of mania; anger might incline the bereaved to sadism, and guilt might give rise to masochistic feelings; loss, in addition, may cause or contribute to anxiety, obsessions, compulsions, phobias, hypochrondria, and hysteria or hallucinations or delusions; the sense of injustice or persecution caused by particularly cruel losses might, in some cases, turn the bereaved in the direction of paranoia. And so on. Aetiology, as Parkes points out, is the bugbear of psychiatry, but the statistical evidence is, perhaps, less important here than common sense: grief makes one exceptionally vulnerable to mental illness.

This vulnerability is especially great in infancy and childhood; and the world-view given in Jonathan Swift's *Gulliver's Travels* (1726) might be understood in the light of an infant's response to loss (Greenacre, 1955). At the age of one, Swift, who had lost his father before birth, was kidnapped by his nurse and spirited to England. After his return to Ireland and his mother at the age of four or five, he led an institutional life at school and university until he reached manhood. *Gulliver's Travels* suggests how a baby separated from its mother might perceive things, for Gulliver's world has no scale of time or space, no predictability or control. Like Swift, Gulliver is 'kidnapped', three times, by a dog, a kite, and a monkey. Like the kidnapped baby Swift had been, Gulliver is totally dependent on strangers such as the nurse in Brobdingnag. Terror of disaster threatens him constantly. Gulliver's preoccupation with bodily functions may also have an infantile side. The changes in size, too, bring to mind the fact that a baby has little sense of the relative size of objects and persons; a person who approaches will seem to be expanding, and one who moves away will appear to be shrinking. Physical exaggeration of this sort may signify emotional distortion resulting from early loss or separation, as in Nerval's *Aurélia* or Plath's 'The Colossus'.

Among salient characteristics of grief, the intensity and frequency of guilt appear most clearly to distinguish the normal from the pathological (Parkes, 1986). Nathaniel Hawthorne's story 'Alice Doane's Appeal' (1835) is a haunting evocation of guilt after a death. Set in early nineteenth-century America, it tells of a young man named Leonard Doane who is taunted by Walter Brome, a stranger attracted to Leonard's sister, Alice. In his fury Leonard murders Walter. As the dead man lies at his feet, Leonard in an anguish of guilt recalls his father's death when he was a child:

> Methought I stood a weeping infant by my father's hearth; by the cold and blood-stained hearth where he lay dead. I heard the childish wail of Alice, and my own cry arose with hers, as we beheld the features of our parent, fierce with the strife and distorted with the pain, in which his spirit had passed away. As I gazed, a cold wind whistled by, and waved my father's hair. Immediately, I stood again by the lonesome road, no more a sinless child, but a man of blood, whose tears were falling fast over the face of his dead enemy. But the delusion was not wholly gone; that face still wore a likeness of my father; and because my soul shrank from the fixed glare of the eyes, I bore the body to the lake (1982, p. 211).

Leonard's guilt over the murder is clearly linked to his childhood guilt at having 'murdered' his father, as Walter's features now resemble those of the father in death.

Poe's story 'The Black Cat' tells of an even less rational act of violence and consequent guilt. The narrator is tormented by his own inability to understand why he has suddenly conceived a murderous hatred of a black cat, Pluto, whom he loves and who loves him and has done him no harm. Finally, he hangs the cat:

> One morning, in cool blood, I slipped a noose about its neck and hung it to the limb of a tree; – hung it with the tears streaming from my eyes, and with the bitterest remorse at my heart; – hung it *because* I knew that it loved me, and *because* I felt it had given me no reason of offence; – hung it *because* I knew that in so doing I was committing a sin – a deadly sin that would so jeopardize my immortal soul as to place it – if such a thing were possible – even beyond the reach of the infinite mercy of the Most Merciful and Most Terrible God (1975, pp. 322–3).[2]

This sadism and guilt make better sense when interpreted in the context of pathological responses to loss. In normal circumstances, an infant will express sadistic rage at being frustrated, and in psychoanalytic theory this rage can cause fear of destroying the mother and guilt at doing so in the imagination (Klein, 1948). However, most infants have the reassurance, based on consistent and loving care, that their violent impulses do not eradicate the love object, for their love is more powerful than their hate. Infants whose mothers have died, as Poe's did before he was three, may unconsciously blame themselves, and create their own sadistic fantasies. Guilt after loss is common among rational adults but infants and children are particularly susceptible to self-blame if, as in the case of Poe, their conditions for grieving after the loss are poor. 'Poe had no subject but himself', writes Symons (1978, p. 240), and the otherwise incomprehensible sadism and guilt in 'The Black Cat' may be linked with Poe's allegedly pathological response to his mother's death.

Like Poe, Tolstoy explored areas of psychopathology in his art to which he was inclined by loss, and his art, too, may have averted some of the worst effects of this loss. 'The Kreutzer Sonata', like 'The Black Cat', ends with the narrator's murder of his wife, a deed which is as outrageous and senseless to him as it is to the murderer in Poe's story. Pozonyshev, the narrator, is afflicted throughout his married life by pathological jealousy of his wife. Selfish and egocentric, he perversely identifies himself with his first-born son, whom the mother is unable to breast-feed. Suspicious that his wife purposefully withholds her milk, he is aroused to insane rage at the thought that she will withhold herself from him. So overwhelming is his rage and jealousy towards her that he ruins his marriage. Dependent upon his wife almost as a baby is upon its mother, Pozonyshev regards his children as rivals for the mother's love. Later, he imagines that she has taken a lover. His fury with her grows until one day he seizes a knife and stabs her to death. His remorse is immediate and he is horrified by his criminal deed.

Tolstoy attempts to explain Pozonyshev's psychology in general sociological terms, but the story is far more compelling as a personal confession, for, as Troyat writes, 'apart from the murder, the entire story might be autobiographical' (1968, p. 477). Pozonyshev's infantile jealousy and egocenticity, his identification with his infant son, and his murderous rage at his wife for imagined neglect are explicable, again, in the context of delayed and distorted grief. In Troyat's view, Tolstoy never recovered from his mother's death when he was two, and he quotes diary entries from Tolstoy's old age describing the mother as 'my highest image of love', 'an ideal of saintliness for me'

(p. 14). In this respect, Levin in *Anna Karenina* is clearly an autobiographical creation inasmuch as he, too, has virtually no memory of his mother and elevates her to an ideal of saintliness: 'He scarcely remembered his mother. The thought of her was sacred to him, and in his imagination his future wife was to be a repetition of that exquisite and holy ideal of womanhood which his mother had been' (Pt. 1, ch. 27). Levin's idealized attachment to the Shcherbatsky girls, and to Kitty in particular, is openly portrayed by Tolstoy as a consequence of loss:

> He could not remember his mother, and his only sister was older than himself so that in the Shcherbatskys' house he encountered for the first time the home life of a cultured, honourable family of the old aristocracy, of which he had been deprived by the death of his own father and mother. All the members of the family, in particular the feminine half, appeared to him as though wrapped in some mysterious, poetic veil, and he not only saw no defects in them but imagined behind that poetic veil the loftiest sentiments and every possible perfection...for Levin all the girls in the world were divided into two classes: one class included all the girls in the world except Kitty, and they had all the human weaknesses and were very ordinary girls; while Kitty was in a class by herself, without the least imperfection and above the rest of humanity (chs. 6, 10).

Such extreme idealization deriving from loss may serve, as we have seen, to counterbalance extremes of unconscious hatred and guilt also provoked by the loss. It is found with unusual frequency and intensity among writers who, like Tolstoy, lost their mothers early on, such as Dante, Keats, Poe, Bialik, and Nerval. Bialik, in *The Scroll of Fire*, tells of an orphan stranded on a desert island who, at the climax of the poem, addresses an unnamed madonna-like woman standing at the top of a cliff:

> All my life my soul cried out to you in a thousand voices, and in tens of thousands of ways, crooked and invisible, fled from you to you...Even as a baby in the black of night, I saw your beauty and coveted your hidden light...With the sorrow of a mother the golden light of your eye rested on me...at night like a weaned child on his mother's lap I made my love known and I waited.[3]

Similarly, Nerval, in his dream fantasy 'Sylvie' (1853), writes of climbing the poet's ivory tower to find a glowing image of love:

'Love, however, of vague forms, of blue and rosy hues, of metaphysical phantoms! Seen at close quarters, the real woman revolted our ingenuous souls. She had to be a queen or goddess; above all, she had to be unapproachable' (1958, pp. 30–1). To the poet bereaved of his mother in infancy or childhood, the 'real woman' may be revolting and rage-inducing as she is linked with the unbearable pain of separation.

Another feature of normal grief which may become similarly exaggerated and prolonged is the numbing of feeling, which appears in the writings of Coleridge and Keats as a possible sign of delayed mourning. Each suffered the loss of his father at age eight, each was sent to boarding school and separated from the surviving family, each describes a sense of numbness which might, among other things, be linked to childhood loss. In his 'Letter to – – [Asra]', which evolved into the 'Dejection Ode', Coleridge confesses to his bride-to-be, Sara (= Asra) Hutchinson, that his greatest and most persistent torment was a numb grief:

A Grief without a pang, void, dark and drear,
A stifling, drowsy unimpassion'd Grief
That finds no natural outlet, no relief
In word, or sigh, or tear —
This, Sara! Well thou know'st
Is that sore Evil, which I dread the most,
And oft'nest suffer!

This confession is followed by a memory of the London boarding school where Coleridge was sent after his father's death. His grief apparently found 'no natural outlet' at this time, he had no one to confide in, and so it remained to be intermingled with later, unresolved griefs.

Keats was similarly vulnerable to a numb grief as a result of childhood loss.[4] He wrote that he had never known unalloyed happiness for long: 'the death or sickness of some one has always spoilt my hours' (Gittings, 1970, p. 263). He was especially troubled by separations from his mother and by her early death, and he confided in his friend Joseph Severn that his great misfortune had been that from infancy he had no mother (Gittings, 1971, p. 47). The numbness of which he complained in his writings might, as in Coleridge's case, be linked with childhood loss, family disruption, and poor conditions for mourning: 'I sometimes feel not the influence of a Passion or Affection during a whole week' (Gittings, 1970, p. 38). Keats was strongly aware that as a result of 'the early loss of our parents' he had become exceptionally attached to his brothers George and Tom (p. 99). Shortly before George left for America, Keats wrote of his 'unpleasant numbness' (p. 97), and the aching deathly numbness in 'Ode to a Nightingale', written after Tom's death from tuberculosis (Keats nursed him during his final illness) may be connected with this tragic loss:

My heart aches, and a drowsy numbness pains
  My sense, as though from hemlock I had drunk,
Or emptied some dull opiate to the drains
  One minute past, and Lethe-wards had sunk...

Such absence of feeling may signify the denial of loss, and in marriage this expression of grief may be poisonous. In the poem 'Home Burial', Robert Frost records the impact of the unexpected death from cholera of his firstborn son, Elliott, in 1900. This crushed the parents, especially Frost who, according to Thompson 'blamed himself, and said he had been guilty of neglect which amounted to murder' (1966, p. 258). The heart of the poem is an acrid exchange between a husband and wife many years after their infant son has died. The wife's anger – 'You *couldn't* care!' – is a function of her grief as she recalls her husband's seemingly callous behaviour after burying the child with his own hands:

You could sit there with the stains on your shoes
Of the fresh earth from your own baby's grave
And talk about your everyday concerns.

In the same way, the yearning and searching which subside in the normal grief process become chronic in pathological grief. The searcher, clinging to the hope of finding the lost person may do so by prosthetic means, as in the case of William Cowper and his mother's portrait or J.M. Barrie's mother and her lost son's christening robe. 'Finding' the object takes the place of finding the lost person. Cowper's mother died when he was six and he was left with neither a clear recollection nor a portrait of her. Over fifty years later, in 1790, a relative sent him a picture of his mother. In a letter written at the time, Cowper exulted over the picture: 'I had rather possess it than the richest jewel in the British crown, for I loved her with an affection that her death, 52 years since has not in the least abated' (*Letters*, III, p. 347–8). His poem 'On the Receipt of My Mother's Picture out of Norfolk' was composed on this occasion. After the death, he was encouraged to believe that his mother would come back: 'What ardently I wished, I long believed'. Now he had an object on which to direct his yearning, for he could imagine that the picture was the mother in fact:

Fancy shall weave a charm for my relief, –
Shall steep me in Elysian reverie,
A momentary dream, that thou art she.[5]

A more extreme and obviously pathological case of 'finding' a lost person through an inanimate object is described by Barrie in his autobiographical memoir *Margaret Ogilvy* (1923). Here, too, the object – a christening robe – arouses deep attachment and fantasies of restoration. Margaret Ogilvy, Barrie's mother, lost her eldest son in an accident when he was thirteen. For many months afterwards, Barrie recalled, she was ill. She became deeply attached to the robe in which the boy was christened, though, as Barrie later discovered, hundreds of children, including himself, had been christened in it. His mother would treat it 'as if it were itself a child', lending it and receiving it, enacting over and over a fantasy of the son's return. Her obsessional use of this object indicates a failure to relinquish the lost child and a continuation of yearning and searching for him:

It was carried carefully from house to house, as if it were itself a child; my mother made much of it, smoothed it out, petted it, smiled to it before putting it into the arms of those to whom it was being lent...And when it was brought back to her she took it in her arms as softly as if it might be asleep, and unconsciously pressed it to her breast; there was never anything in the house that spoke to her quite so eloquently as that little white robe; it was the one of her children that always remained a baby (pp. 6–7).

Another element of grief which might, in an exaggerated form, be symptomatic of delayed grief is a sensation of triumph or euphoria – perhaps that a burden has been lifted or a rival or inhibitor eliminated – in which the pain of grief is denied. In Jean-Paul Sartre's account of his father's death (1964), there is an unmistakable note of triumph which seems not to have been a temporary phenomenon as in normal grief. Sartre's pronouncement on fathers, delivered, not without irony, as universal truth, portrays the author as a fortunate Aeneas released from his crushing burden, his father Anchises:

Jean-Baptiste's death was the great event of my life: it returned my mother to her chains and it gave me my freedom.

The rule is that there are no good fathers; it is not the men who are at fault but the paternal bond which is rotten. There is nothing better than to produce children, but what a sin to *have* some! If he had lived, my father would have lain down on me and crushed me. Fortunately, he died young; among the Aeneases each carrying his Anchises on his shoulders, I cross from one bank to the other, alone, detesting those invisible fathers who ride piggy-back on their sons throughout their lives; I left behind me a dead young man who did not have time to be my father and who could, today, be my son. Was it a good or a bad thing? I do not know; but I am happy to subscribe to the judgement of an eminent psychoanalyst: I have no Super-Ego.

Dying is not everything: you have to die in time. Later on, I felt guilty; a sensitive orphan blames himself: his parents offended by the sight of him, have retired to their flats in the sky. But I was delighted: my unhappy condition imposed respect and established my importance (1977, pp. 14–15).

Sartre professes to have been delighted by his father's death, though this delight is directly contradicted later in his own memoir (p. 56).[6] While loss of a parent is a tragedy for the vast majority, 'for a minority it is a change for the better' (Bowlby, 1980, p. 212). Yet even in the passage just quoted, Sartre's uncertainty whether his loss was, in fact, a change for the better is also apparent. He admits that he blamed himself later on (despite his claim not to have a super-ego), and he entertains doubt as to whether the death was 'a good or a bad thing'. In denouncing the paternal bond as rotten, he protests too much. His triumphal assertion, 'Fortunately, he died young', might be interpreted as a defence, against grief and against the suspicion that he would have been better off if his father had lived.

Depression provoked by loss might, similarly, grow and continue beyond normal bounds, and its mastery is often an aim in creativity (Storr, 1972). This again appears to be especially true of artists bereaved in childhood:

To me was sent the dark time, I know well,
For it has always been with me since birth.

And like all things which make a counterfeit
Of their own nature, so I make my fate
More black by feelings full of pain and grief.

Michelangelo, Sonnet XLI, (1961, p. 67)

Study me then, you who shall lovers be
At the next world, that is, at the next spring:
   For I am every dead thing,
    In whom love wrought new alchemy.
     For his art did express
A quintessence even from nothingness,
From dull privations, and lean emptiness
He ruined me, and I am re-begot
Of absence, darkness, death: things which are not.

> John Donne, 'A Nocturnal upon S. Lucy's Day,
> being the shortest day'

When the low heavy sky weighs like a lid
Upon the spirit aching for the light
And all the wide horizon's line is hid
By a black day sadder than any light...

And hearses, without drum or instrument,
File slowly through my soul; crushed, sorrowful,
Weeps Hope, and Grief, fierce and omnipotent,
Plants his black banner on my drooping skull.

> Baudelaire, 'Spleen', tr. John Squire
> (1958, pp. 63–5)

Identification with the dead is yet another characteristic of normal grief which might be magnified in chronic form; an illustration of this is found in the poetry of John Clare. Clare, born in Northamptonshire in 1793, had a twin-sister, Elizabeth, who died a month after birth. Of this loss, Storey writes:

> Clare was to mourn the loss of his twin-sister on more than one occasion and he always seemed to be searching for her. She was the first person he was to lose from life. Because of this, and his physical illness as a child, he was over-mothered. His life was to be one of several dualities. He was to be a man always in love with two women (1982, p. 41).

The son of a farm-labourer, Clare worked on a farm from about the age of twelve, attending school in the evenings. At sixteen, he fell deeply in love with Mary Joyce, daughter of a well-to-do farmer who apparently forbade her to meet her lover. Clare never forgot this first love and in his periods of insanity, long after Mary's death in 1838, he used to hold conversations with her, under the delusion that she still lived and was his wife and had his children. In fact, she had never married.

'The poignancy and perfection of many of Clare's best poems', writes Grigson, 'comes out of that incomplete merger, that almost simultaneous feeling that Mary was with him and his realization that she was absent' (1949, p. 15). Clare's chronic grief for Mary hauntingly suggests a deeper level of unconscious grief for his lost sister, for at times he writes of Mary almost as if she were a part of him, his twin:

Thy beauty made youth's life divine
Till my soul grew a part of thine
Mary, I mourn no pleasures gone –
The past hath made us both as one

Child Harold ('Lovely Mary, when we parted')

Mary, thy name loved long still keeps me free
Till my lost life becomes a part of thee

Ibid. (Song)

The extremity of Clare's response to rejection and loss in early manhood points to a vulnerability on his part owing, perhaps, to the loss of his twin. In his darkest moments of despair, Clare would often think of her;[7] and the sonnet beginnning 'Bessy – I call thee by that earthly name' ends with an admission of the poet's sorrow, and a hint of guilt at having survived:

Ah, had we gone together, had I been
Strange with the world as thou thy mother's love,
What years of sorrow I had not seen!
Fullness of joy that leaves no hearts to bleed
Had then with thine been purchased cheap indeed.

Such grief-ridden 'madness' as that of Clare can act as a force in creativity which, in turn, may keep madness in check without being consumed by it. We may conclude this chapter by considering the life and writings of Rimbaud, who describes a conscious welcoming of psychological turmoil, a purposeful disordering of the senses, in order to reach a transcendent, visionary state, that of the *voyant*. In the act of becoming a *voyant*, the poet must be ready to sacrifice himself, his sanity, Rimbaud writes in his 'Lettre du Voyant' of 15 May 1871 to Paul Demeney:

The Poet makes himself a *voyant* through a long, immense and reasoned *deranging* of *all his senses*. All the forms of love, of suffering, of madness; he tries to find himself, he exhausts in himself all the poisons, to keep only their quintessences. Unutterable torture in which he needs all his faith, all his superhuman strength, in which he becomes among all men the great invalid, the great criminal, the great accursed one, – and the supreme Savant! – For he arrives at the *unknown*! Since he has cultivated his soul, already rich, more than anyone else! He arrives at the unknown, and although, crazed, he would end up by losing the understanding of his visions, he has seen them! Let him die in his leaping through unheard-of and unnameable things: other horrible workers will come; they will begin on the horizons where the other collapsed (Rimbaud, 1973, pp. 7–8).

Rimbaud placed the self-controlled deranging of his senses at the heart of his aesthetic theory. His madness, though, was less than mad but more than feigned: his theory arose from his own innate susceptibility to psychological disorder and served as a means of dealing with it, justifying and elevating it. Starkie (1973) ascribes the poet's 'curse of instability' partly to the loss of his father when he was six. Rimbaud's parents were incompatible: his earliest memory was of them quarrelling and hurling a valuable silver bowl on to the floor; and 'there is no doubt that the memory of the discord between his parents left a lasting mark on Arthur's sensitive nature' (p. 31). Perhaps equally true is that Rimbaud's sensitivity was a mark of this discord. At any rate, the parents' separation was final, and Rimbaud never saw his father again.

Rimbaud's mother was a parvenu peasant of limited intelligence, stubborn, narrow-minded, and fanatically religious. She was a strict disciplinarian. The loss of her husband – she pretended to be a widow for the sake of appearances – made her bitter and anxious. Though she also possessed many good qualities, sympathy and generosity among them, she was not demonstrative, and Rimbaud had little warmth and love as a child: 'This early loneliness and lack of affection warped Arthur's personality, making him feel different from other boys, solitary and set aside' (p. 32). She allowed her children to believe that their father was a satanic creature and 'always made [them] feel that they had inherited all their bad qualities from their father' (p. 172).

Rimbaud's family life with the father's absence and his mother's over-dominance, provided the classic environment for the making of a homosexual son (Bieber *et al.*, 1962). The two greatest passions of his life were not for women but for his schoolteacher,

Georges Izambard, and for the poet Paul Verlaine. The poet, wrote Rimbaud, tries to experience 'all the forms of love, of suffering, of madness' in order to find himself, poisoning himself in the act of making himself a God-like instrument of creation. These deranged forms of love were experienced in his 'marriage' to Verlaine, and in the poetry which came out of their stormy liason he gave oblique expression to the effects of losing his father. Verlaine was ten years older than Rimbaud, an established poet, a husband and father, and on one level he served Rimbaud as a father-figure, though the younger poet was a far more forceful personality than he. Captivated by the wild and daring Rimbaud, Verlaine abandoned his family and 'eloped' with Rimbaud to Beligium and England. Though at first they were happy, Rimbaud came to loathe Verlaine's weakness of character and threatened to leave him, whereupon Verlaine, drunk and furious, shot him in the wrist. Rimbaud returned to his mother's farm to recover, and at this time, in mid-1873, wrote his astonishing prose-poem, *A Season in Hell*. He was eighteen.

The chapter on 'The Infernal Bridegroom and the Foolish Virgin' alludes to the broken homosexual marriage, whose tensions in some ways mirrored those leading to his father's desertion some twelve years previously. In the character of the Bridegroom, Rimbaud depicts himself as seen through the eyes of Verlaine, the Foolish Virgin (Starkie, p. 187); and the emotion which, more than any other, dominates the Foolish Virgin is the terror of being abandoned:

> ...after a poignant caress, he [the Bridegroom] would say: 'How odd this will s/em to you, when I am no longer here, this which you have gone through. When you no longer have my arms upon your neck, nor my heart to rest on, nor these lips on your eyes. Because I shall have to go away, very far, one day. Then I must help others: it is my duty. Though it will hardly be pleasing...dear soul...' At once I could foresee myself, with him gone, in the clutch of vertigo, plunged into the most frightful darkness: death. I made him promise that he would not cast me off. He made it twenty times, this promise of a lover. It was as frivolous as my saying to him: 'I understand you' (Rimbaud, 1973, p. 73).

Such wilful derangement of the senses as that depicted in Rimbaud's poetry may act as a means of confronting and mastering psychological disorder stemming from loss. As we have seen, loss may incline one to numerous, unpredictable disturbances, in which the effects of grief are exaggerated and distorted; and loss in infancy and childhood makes one particularly vulnerable to mental illness later on. Yet, by means of creativity, the bereaved may learn to see themselves more dispassionately, with greater control and self-esteem, and, in so doing, stave off the worst effects of grief. The artist can, to some extent, manipulate his 'madness', for like Hamlet he is 'but mad north-north-west' – the act of creation implies a certain distance from the madness. Insofar as creativity derives from loss, the quality of the art reflects the artist's success in mastering it, and in this way he may achieve a measure of symbolic repair (Brink, 1977). For the artist must need to be healed though his art; otherwise, he will never create the remedy. Some, however, fail to heal themselves; they are the subject of the next, and final, chapter, on loss and suicide.

9

LOSS AND SUICIDE

Clinical studies (e.g. Greer *et al.*, 1966; Koller & Castanos, 1968; Murphy *et al.*, 1979) have shown consistently the links between loss and suicide. While each suicide has its own varied, unpredictable dynamics (Stengel, 1983), loss is directly or indirectly one of the chief causes. A large number of suicides either lost a close relative or friend prior to the act, or suffered severe loss in childhood or adolescence, and elements of grief, such as depression, anger, guilt, the loss of self-esteem, the wish to rejoin the lost person, may incline the bereaved to suicide. Childhood loss makes the bereaved especially vulnerable to suicidal thinking later in life: 'of all the sequelae attributed to early childhood loss the evidence with regard to suicidal behaviour is among the strongest' (Adam, 1973, p. 278). These findings are borne out and illumined in creative literature; and among writers explored in earlier chapters a number who suffered loss in childhood – Cowper, Wordsworth, Nerval, Poe, and Reid among them – attempted suicide; others, such as Donne, Keats, Tolstoy, Nietzsche, Bialik, and Frost, seriously contemplated suicide.

The identification of the bereaved with the lost person may be a key factor in suicide deriving from loss (Freud, 1917). For if the dead is excessively hated, not least for dying, this identification might cause pathological self-hatred leading to suicide. Poe often hinted at suicide and tried to kill himself at least once and his story 'William Wilson' (1839), which Symons describes as 'an instructive essay in self-revelation' (1978, p. 215) – illustrates how a hated object of identification may drive one to suicide. The narrator at critical moments finds himself unexpectedly confronted with William Wilson. Wilson infuriatingly acts on him as a whispering alter-ego, a hated conscience. Finally, the narrator, crazed with hate and guilt, fights Wilson in a duel. In the act of mortally wounding his opponent, he comes face to face with his murderous self-hatred:

> Not a thread in all his raiment – not a line in all the marked and singular lineaments of his face which was not, even in the most absolute identity, *mine own*!

It was Wilson; but he spoke no longer in a whisper, and I could have fancied that I myself was speaking while he said: *'You have conquered, and I yield. Yet henceforward art thou also dead – dead to the World, to Heaven and to Home! In me didst thou exist – and, in my death, see by this image, which is thine own, how utterly thou hast murdered thyself'* (1975, p. 178).

In O'Neill's *Mourning Becomes Electra* (1931), similarly, Orin Mannon, shortly before his suicide, is described as having taken on the appearance of his dead father: 'He carries himself woodenly erect now like a soldier. His movements and attitudes have the statue-like quality that was so marked in his father. He now wears a close-cropped beard in addition to his mustache, and this accentuates his resemblance to his father.'[1]

Bialik, in the poem *Bet Olam* (Graveyard, 1901), links the impulse to self-murder with identification, not with a lost person but, in a semi-mystical fashion, with objects:[2] trees tempt the poet to take his own life and, in the process, become a part of them:

Instead of dying a thousand deaths each day, die just once quickly, rest in peace and silence. We'll bend over you and divide you up. Worms will eat one half, we'll have the rest for sap. Life grows forever out of all things – you'll blossom in a flower or grow in a tree. You'll live in everything, wherever you are – come beneath us, come to our roots, O flesh and blood!

Bialik was prone to dark depression and suicidal feelings as a result of loss, and already as a child after his father's death, he contemplated taking his own life (Ravnitzky, 1946, p. 182). In a letter to a friend in 1907, he wrote of his death-wish: 'Sometimes I feel like committing suicide – and I am too idle to do this good thing' (Lachower, ed., 1938, II, p. 46).

Wordsworth, who, as we have seen, suffered total family break-up at about the same age as Bialik, also came close to taking his own life. The following incident apparently took place after he passed into the care of grandparents at Penrith (Moorman, 1957): 'I was of a stiff, moody, and violent temper; so much so that I remember going once into the attics of my grandfather's house at Penrith...with an intention of destroying myself with one of the foils which I knew was kept there. I took the foil in hand, but my hand failed' (Owen & Smyser, eds., 1974, III, p. 372).

Like anger, depression stemming from loss may provoke suicidal thinking, and Keats warns in 'Ode on Melancholy':

No, no! go not to Lethe, neither twist
  Wolf's-bane, tight-rooted, for its poisonous wine...

Keats' many childhood losses might be reflected in his 'horrid Melancholy', as he called it, and in a letter to Fanny Brawne, he was frank about his inclination to self-murder: 'I hate the world: it batters too much the wings of my self-will, and would I could take a sweet poison from your lips to send me out of it' (Gittings, ed., 1970, p. 271). The temptation to suicide is described in 'Ode to a Nightingale':

Darkling I listen; and, for many a time
  I have been half in love with easeful Death,
Called him soft names in many a musèd rhyme,
  To take into the air my quiet breath;
Now more than ever seems it rich to die,
  To cease upon the midnight with no pain,
    While thou art pouring forth thy soul abroad
      In such an ecstasy!

The works of Joseph Conrad, too, bear out the link between childhood loss and severe depression leading to suicidal thoughts (Meyer, 1967). As a young man, Conrad tried unsuccessfully to kill himself, and his account of the suicide of Martin Decoud in *Nostromo* is revealing of the psychology of the suicide. Decoud, stranded on an island for ten days, suffers immense melancholy and, among other things, begins to have 'doubt of his own individuality' and of the reality of his actions:

Not a living being, not a speck of distant sail, appeared within the range of his vision; and, as if to escape from this solitude, he absorbed himself in his melancholy... the solitude appeared like a great void, and the silence of the gulf like a tense, thin cord to which he hung suspended by both hands, without fear, without surprise, without any sort of emotion whatever (ch. 10).

Little in what we are told of Decoud would lead to the prediction of suicide, for he is, in fact, depicted as having much to live for, being a patriot and in love. As in Poe's 'The Black Cat' and Tolstoy's 'The Kreutzer Sonata', the reader senses a level of emotion in excess of the facts, which Leavis (1973) for one has found in the life of the author. The loss of parents in childhood and poor conditions for mourning (as in Conrad's own experience) might bring on a reaction such as that of Decoud.

The conviction of being outcast is depicted also by Cowper in his last poem, 'The Castaway', in the image of a man washed headlong from a ship and, before drowning, of his horror at being abandoned:

Of friends, of hope, of all bereft,
His floating home for ever left.[3]

An almost identical image appears in Robert Frost's poem, 'Despair', written under the impact of the poet's loss of mother and son, when he was sorely tempted to drown himself (Thompson, 1966):

I am like a dead diver after all's
Done, still held fast in the weeds' snare below,
Where in the gloom his limbs begin to glow
Swaying at his moorings as the roiled bottom falls.
There was a moment when with vainest calls
He drank the water, saying, 'Oh let me go –
God let me go!'

In some cases, the works may anticipate the form of suicide:

. . . there is a line
You must not cross nor ever trust beyond it
Spry cordage of your bodies to caresses
Too lichen-faithful from too wide a breast.
The bottom of the sea is cruel.

Hart Crane, 'Voyages'

We launch out now over the precipice. Beneath us lie the lights of the herring fleet. The cliffs vanish. Rippling small, rippling grey, innumerable waves spread beneath us. I touch nothing. I see nothing. We may sink and settle on the waves. The sea will drum in my ears. The white petals will be darkened with sea water. They will float for a moment and then sink. Rolling me over the waves will shoulder me under. Everything falls in a tremendous shower, dissolving me (Virginia Woolf, *The Waves*, p. 177).

Tolstoy is another who describes a chronic sense of abandonment leading to suicidal thoughts. In 'A Confession' (1882), written after a crisis which brought him to the verge of suicide, Tolstoy – in a manner strikingly reminiscent of Levin in Anna Karenina[4] – compares himself to a fledgling whose mother has gone: 'I cry because I know that a mother has borne me within her, has hatched me, warmed me, fed me, and loved me. Where is she – that mother? If I have been deserted, who has deserted me?' (1940, p. 63). At this time, Tolstoy was so terrified that he would kill himself that he hid his rope and stopped carrying a gun. His feeling of utter forsakenness is to be taken literally: not having a memory or even a portrait of his mother, he could not say for sure who had borne him, loved him, and abandoned him at the age of two. In the process of passing through the crisis, Tolstoy underwent a religious conversion in which his searching became directed towards God: 'I cannot hide from myself that someone bore me, loving me. Who was that someone? Again 'God'? He knows and sees my searching, my despair, and my struggle' (*ibid.*).

Others who endured severe childhood loss and later attempted or committed suicide are: Thomas Chatterton, Goethe, Maxim Gorky, Sergei Esenin, Mayakovsky, John Berryman, and Sylvia Plath. Plath lost her father at the age of eight after a four-year illness. She remembered her father, an American academic born in Germany, as a difficult man, stern and disciplined. His death and the poor conditions for mourning provoked extreme grief reactions which were never resolved: 'He was an autocrat,' Plath told a friend. 'I adored and despised him, and I probably wished many times that he were dead. When he obliged me and died, I imagined that I had killed him' (Steiner, 1974, p. 21). Her mother hid her grief and did not encourage discussion about the loss. In Plath's autobiographical novel, *The Bell Jar* (1963), the heroine, shortly before taking an overdose of sleeping tablets, visits her father's grave. She weeps uncontrollably and realizes that she has never wept for her father before, that her grief has remained unexpressed since childhood.

Sylvia Plath's marriage to the poet Ted Hughes in 1956 was apparently undermined by her suppressed grief for her father. At first, she felt that he 'fills that huge, sad hole I felt in having no father' (1975, p. 289), but after seven years together they separated, in October 1962. We have seen in Chapter Two how a loss may trigger off an intense period of creativity, and the break-up of her marriage did indeed precipitate the most creative period of Plath's life. During the month of October alone, she wrote some twenty-five poems, including a few, such as 'Daddy' and 'Lady Lazarus', which she knew were 'the best poems of my life' (p. 468). Alvarez, who knew Plath towards the end of her life, has suggested that the separation revived her grief for her father, and this led directly to her suicide several months later:

> I suspect that finding herself alone again now, whatever her pretence of indifference, all the anguish she had experienced at her father's death was reactivated: despite herself, she felt abandoned, injured, enraged and bereaved as purely and defencelessly as she had as a child twenty years before. As a result, the pain that had buit up steadily inside her all that time came flooding out (1971, p. 36).

Anger owing to unexpressed grief was a chief driving force in Plath's creativity. In her journals she wrote: 'I have a violence in me that is as hot as death blood' (McCullough and Hughes, eds., 1982, p. 237). That this anger could reach homicidal proportions in fantasy is suggested in the poem 'Daddy':

> If I've killed one man, I've killed two...
> Daddy, I have had to kill you.

Yet the very act of creation could ease the rage that was its motive and cause: 'Fury jams the gullet and spreads poison, but, as soon as I start to write, dissipates, flows out into the figure of the letters...' (p. 256).

The struggle to master grief creatively, even if unsuccessful, is itself a tribute to human courage and resilience in adverse conditions. The artist afflicted by the effects of childhood loss or separation may thus become a symbol of collective tragedy, an identity of which Plath for one was well aware in poems such as 'Lady Lazarus':[5]

> Ash, ash –
> You poke and stir.
> Flesh, bone, there is nothing there –

But something does remain: the testimony of poetry, such as that found in Mayakovsky's pocket after his suicide in 1930, which possesses the transcendent mastery of art, the merger of personal and universal loss:[6]

> Past one o'clock. You must have gone to bed.
> The Milky Way streams silver through the night.
> I'm in no hurry; with lightning telegrams
> I have no cause to wake or trouble you.
> And, as they say, the incident is closed.

161

Love's boat has smashed against the daily grind.
Now you and I are quits. Why bother then
to balance mutual sorrows, pains, and hurts.
Behold what quiet settles on the world.
Night wraps the sky in tribute from the stars.
In hours like these, one rises to address
The ages, history, and all creation.

Notes

Chapter 1. Creativity and the Survivor

1. On the potential value of this concept in literary analysis, see Trilling's essay on 'Freud and Literature' in *The Liberal Imagination* (1970). Trilling's observation in this essay that anything that we learn about the artist may be legitimate and enriching in understanding the work is also relevant here. More recent discussions of issues pertaining to psychoanalysis and biography are those of Lichtenberg (1978), Wolf (1983) and Young-Bruehl (1985).
2. A similarly analogy made by Parkes (1986, p. 25) is quoted below, pp. 142–3. The link between psychopathology and physiopathology is made by Dickens in *Dombey and Son*: Paul Dombey's physical weakness and almost geriatrically morose constitution are implicitly attributed to the loss of his mother at birth, a loss which shadows his life like a devastating illness, and whose effects appear to bring about his untimely death.
3. On Plath's self-image as a survivor as a result of childhood loss, see Alvarez (1971); also see ch. 9 below. Compare Anne Sexton's 'For Mr. Death Who Stands With His Door Open':

   > Next Mr. Death, you held out the bait
   > during my first decline, as they say,
   > telling that suicide baby to celebrate
   > her own going in her own puppet play.
   > I went out popping pills and crying adieu
   > in my own death camp with my own little Jew.

4. See Appelfeld's semi-biographical novel, *The Age of Wonders* (1983, p. 160). A parallel illustration of bereavement in more normal circumstances which is compared with an amputated or paralyzed limb occurs in Proust's *Remembrance of Things Past* (1981, III, p. 534). On this phenomenon, see Parkes (1986).
5. Here are some example of children's denial of, or disbelief at, loss:

   > 'How many are you then,' said I,
   > 'If they two are in Heaven?'
   > The little maiden did reply,
   > 'O master! we are seven.'
   >
   > 'But they are dead: those two are dead!
   > Their spirits are in Heaven!'
   > 'Twas throwing words away; for still
   > The little maid would have her will,
   > And say, 'Nay, we are seven!'
   >
   > Wordsworth, 'We are Seven'

The servant comes to tell the children
Their mother has died. They hear it said,
And yet with one voice say the brothers:
It is not true, she is not dead.
Rückert, *Kindertotenlieder* in Plank, 1978, p. 610.

(This passage, from *Anna Karenina*, describes nine-year-old Seriozha, Anna's son, who is told falsely that his mother is dead after she elopes with Count Vronsky.)

One of his favourite occupations was to keep a look-out for his mother during his walks. He did not believe in death generally, and in her death in particular, in spite of what Lydia Ivanovna had told him and his father had confirmed, and it was just because of that, and after he had been told she was dead, that he had begun looking for her when he was having his walk. Every comely, graceful woman with dark hair was his mother. At the sight of every such woman his heart would swell with tenderness until his breath failed him and the tears came into his eyes (Pt. 5, ch. 27).

(This passage, from Somerset Maugham's autobiographical novel, *Of Human Bondage* [1915], tells of nine-year-old Philip Carey who goes into his mother's bedroom where she died a week before.)

Philip opened a large cupboard filled with dresses and, stepping in, took as many of them as he could in his arms and buried his face in them. They smelt of the scent his mother used. Then he pulled open the drawers, filled with his mother's things, and looked at them: there were lavender bags among the linen; and their scent was fresh and pleasant. The strangeness of the room left it, and it seemed to him that his mother had just gone out for a walk. She would be in presently and would come upstairs to have nursery tea with him. And he seemed to feel her kiss on his lips.
It was not true that he would never see her again. It was not true simply because it was impossible (1973, pp. 12–13).

(Freud tells the following anecdote in *The Interpretation of Dreams*.) 'I was astonished to hear a highly intelligent boy of ten remark after the sudden death of his father: "I know father's dead, but what I can't understand is why he doesn't come home to supper."' (SE, IV, p. 254n).
Among other well-known illustrations of a child's inability to accept the fact of a parent's death, see Tolstoy's *Childhood, Boyhood and Youth*, ch. 27, and Gorky's *My Childhood*, ch. 1. In the latter, the child's most vivid memory of his father's burial is not the father, but the frogs trapped in the grave as it was being filled.
6. Imagery of the mother's hair recurs in Celan's harrowing *Todesfuge*, in which the Holocaust is symbolically alluded to in the repeated phrase, *dein aschenes Haar Sulamith*.
7. On this phenomenon in creative literature, see ch. 5 below.
8. In Japanese prison camps, too, the apathy of depression was responsible for a large number of deaths. See Nardini (1952).

Chapter 2. Loss and Creativity

1. See below, p. 55.
2. The impact on Bloom of his son's death may be compared with that on Tobias after the loss of his son in Edward Albee's *A Delicate Balance*:

Agnes: We *could* have had another son; we could have tried. But no . . .
those months – or was it a year –?
Tobias: No more of this!
Agnes: . . . I think it was a year, when you spilled yourself on my belly, sir?
Please? Please, Tobias? No, you wouldn't even say it out: 'I don't want
another child, another loss.'

(1967, p. 137)

Illustrations of similar tragedies appear also in the novels *The Lover*, by
A.B. Yehoshua, and *A Perfect Peace*, by Amos Oz: both depict couples whose
marriage is blighted by the loss of a child.

3. The reference here is to Keats' 'Ode to a Nightingale': 'for many a time/ I
have been half in love with easeful Death.' A mother's attachment to a dead
child at the expence of a living child, as in *Long Day's Journey Into Night*, is
treated also by J.M. Barrie in his autobigraphical work, *Margaret Ogilvy*. See
p. 149 below. A dream of O'Neill's is notable as an expression of the
incompleteness felt by a child as a result of a sibling's death:

It was a dream of my childhood – when I had to dream that I was not
alone. There was me and one other in this dream. I dreamed it often – and
during the day sometimes this other seemed to be within me and then I
was a happy little boy. But this *other* in my dream, this other I never quite
saw. It was a presence felt that made me complete. (Sheaffer, 1968, p. 67).

On loss and dreams, see ch. 3 below. For fuller discussion of the role of
loss in O'Neill's creativity, see Hamilton (1976, 1979).

4. On Hardy's poems of 1912–13, see, for example, Gittings (1978) and
Millgate (1982); on Agnon's stories of 1908–11, see Band (1968) and Aber-
bach (1984); on Lawrence's works of 1910–12, see Kermode (1973) and
Moore (1974). Most of these works contain bibliographies for further study.

5. 'The Voice' is quoted in full above, p. 8. Hardy's letters, too, reflect his
searching for his lost wife. A month after she died, Hardy wrote to Edmund
Gosse:

What you say on the incredibility of this event I feel even now – it seeming
sometimes for a moment that it cannot have happened, & that I shall see
her coming in from the garden with a little trowel in her hand, after
pottering among the plants as she used to do (Purdy & Millgate, eds.,
1984, p. 242).

6. Agnon (1888?–1970) is the most distinguished modern Hebrew writer.
While describing the lost world of the east European Jews with great insight
and charm, Agnon is also a sophisticated modernist, strongly influenced
by Freud and Kafka. Born in the Galician town of Buczacz (then in the
Austro-Hungarian empire), Agnon came to Palestine in 1908 and lived there
until 1912. After spending the war years in Germany and marrying in 1920,
he returned to Palestine in 1924. He lived in Jerusalem with his family until
his death. He is the author of five novels, of which *The Bridal Canopy* (1931),
A Simple Story (1934) and *A Guest for the Night* (1939) have been translated
into English. Other works of Agnon's in translation include the novella *In
the Heart of Seas* (1934), *Two Tales* (1966) and *Twenty-One Stories* (1970). Agnon
was awarded the Nobel Prize for Literature in 1966.

7. Biographical information about Agnon is taken mostly from Band.

8. See Aberbach (1984, p. 84).

9. There are three versions of 'Agunot', but the 1908 version is quoted here as it

most directly reflects Agnon's impending bereavement. The later drafts tone down considerably the impassioned expressions of grief.

10. Compare this with the attachment to the dead mother's novels in Rousseau's *Confessions*. After his mother's death, Rousseau relates, he and his father would read her novels voraciously, day and night: '. . . we could never leave off till the end of the book. Sometimes my father would say with shame as we heard the morning larks: "Come, let us go to bed. I am more of a child than you are"' (1977, p. 20). (Further discussion of Rousseau appears in ch. 6 below.) On the subject of books and loss, in Dickens' *David Copperfield* (1849–50), likewise, David becomes exceptionally attached to his dead father's books after his mother's death, when he comes under the pernicious care of the Murdstones: 'They were my only comfort, and I was as true to them as they were to me, and read them over and over I don't know how many times more' (ch. 10).

11. Lawrence's sister, Mrs Emily King, has said that during the many days that Lawrence spent by his mother's beside when she was dying he had a notebook with him and constantly wrote in it (in notes to *Collected Poems*, 1972, p. 1047).

12. For a psychoanalytic interpretation of Lawrence, see Weiss (1962).

13. Intense idealization of the dead woman appears elsewhere in Lawrence's works of this period, for example the poems 'The Virgin Mother' and 'On That Day'.

14. On detachment after loss as a possible cause or accompaniment of mystical withdrawal, see ch. 5 below.

15. A parallel example of grief revived by seemingly innocuous objects appears in Mallarmé's poem, *Plainte d'Automne* (Autumn Lament).

16. A brief summary of illustrations of conflict with the mother, or mother-figure, in Lawrence's fiction is given by Aberbach (1983).

Chapter 3. Loss and Dreams

1. These biographical details are discussed, with sources, later in this chapter.

2. Klein's account (1940) of idealization as a defence against depressive 'pining', hatred of the lost person for 'disappearing', and irrational fears that the lost person will retaliate, is relevant here.

3. A summary of the scholarship on this question is given by Carey (1971, p. 413).

4. 'Seeing' or 'feeling' the presence of a lost person as part of the grief process is analogous to certain mystical phenomena. See ch. 5 below.

5. Nerval's doctor, Émile Blanche, a compassionate, intelligent man, encouraged Nerval to 'write out' his dreams and fantasies in the hope that by doing so he would be released from them. The influence of Émile Blanche may be detected in Nerval's statement of his aims in *Aurélia*: 'a writer's duty is to analyze with sincerity what he feels in grave moments of life' (1958, p. 121). He is not merely a patient in need of help, but virtually a scientist, attempting to 'analyze' his experiences and dreams. In this respect, Nerval could be compared with Anna O. and Émile Blanche with Josef Breuer. On Nerval and other French writers in whom loss and maternal deprivation are prominent, see Segal (1988).

6. A further analogy between parental loss and the destruction of an entire world is implicit in the legends of J.R.R. Tolkien, some of which were based

on his 'Atlantis-complex', a recurrent nightmare of disaster which haunted him for much of his life. In 1964, at the age of seventy, he wrote:

> This legend or myth or dim memory of some ancient history has always troubled me. In sleep I had the dreadful dream of the ineluctable Wave, either coming out of the quiet sea, or coming in towering over the green islands. It still occurs occasionally, though now exorcized by writing about it. It always ends by surrender, and I awake gasping out of deep water (1981, p. 347).

This dream appears to have been a crucial element in the evolution of Tolkein's art: it was the kernel of one of his earliest legends, on 'The Downfall of Númenor' which, Tolkien wrote, 'lies immediately behind *The Lord of the Rings*' (p. 189). The downfall of Tolkien's Atlantis came with the death of his mother when he was twelve (his father had died when he was a small child), and this loss, writes his biographer Humphrey Carpenter, changed him, making him vulnerable to profound despair, the feeling that his world was built on shaky foundations: 'More precisely, and more closely related to his mother's death, when he was in this mood [of despair] he had a deep sense of impending loss. Nothing was safe. Nothing would last. No battle would be won forever' (1977, p. 31). Tolkien's art assuaged this chronic sense of insecurity by 'exorcizing' the nightmare and by creating an enduring world of make-believe. If the sunk Atlantis may signify family breakdown in Tolkien, it certainly bears that meaning as a symbol of a parallel disaster in the life of his friend and colleague at Oxford, C.S. Lewis. In his autobiography, *Surprised by Joy* (1955), Lewis writes of the emotional upheaval resulting from his mother's death when he was nine as equivalent to the sinking of Atlantis:

> With my mother's death all settled happiness, all that was tranquil and reliable, disappeared from my life. There was to be much fun, many pleasures, many stabs of Joy; but no more of the old security. It was sea and islands now; the great continent had sunk like Atlantis (p. 23).

7. In Sylvia Plath's poem 'The Colossus', similarly, the lost father is depicted as a colossus with whom the poetess struggles to come to terms.
8. A comparable feeling of triumph as a result of a parent's death is described by Jean-Paul Sartre in *Words*. See ch. 6, note 11 below, and ch. 8 below.
9. For a summary of details of visits to Roznau, and sources, see Krüll (1986, p. 262, n. 52).
10. A 'screen memory' of Freud's dating from his earliest childhood might also be interpreted as having relevence in interpreting his alleged incestuous feelings towards his mother (Jones, 1953). See below, pp. 77–8.
11. In *The Interpretation of Dreams*, this dream is stated to have occurred on the night before the funeral, but in the letter to Fliess of 2 November 1896 (eight days after the funeral), on the night of the funeral.
12. Freud's insights in *The Interpretation of Dreams* into Shakespeare's loss of his father and the writing of *Hamlet*, which occured around the same time, were in all probability affected by the loss of his own father. For a recent discussion of the role of grief in the writing of *Hamlet*, see Oremland (1983).
13. On this issue, see Robert (1976).
14. An observation by Freud of his grandson is quoted and discussed below, pp. 90–1.

Chapter 4. Loss and Childhood Memories

1. For a general discussion of screen memories of writers, with bibliography, see Aberbach (1983).
2. See ch. 2 n. 10 above.
3. See above, p. 55.
4. See below, p. 122.
5. On the role of loss in Bialik's life and art, see Aberbach (1988).
6. See p. 56 ff. and ch. 3 n. 6 above.
7. See below, p. 157.
8. Some critics, including F.W. Bateson (1971), believe that the woman to whom 'Nutting' is addressed is Dorothy, Wordsworth's sister. Wordsworth regarded his sister as a mother-surrogate, and in *The Vale of Esthwaite*, composed at the time of his reunion with her after a ten year separation dating from the death of their mother, he explains his love for Dorothy as a displaced love for his mother: 'I fondly view/ All, all that Heav'n has claimed, in you.'

Chapter 5. Grief and Mysticism

1. A notable exception is Bennett and Nancy Simon's insightful and convincing interpretation (1972) of a case of mystical illumination experienced by Bertrand Russell as being linked with the loss of his mother at age two. This experience had a profound influence upon Russell's later philosophy; and other examples of philosophers whose ideas were affected or determined by loss are discussed in ch. 6 below.
2. Storr's views on art as a form of reparation appear to have been influenced by Fairbairn (1937–8, 1938–9). On literature as a means of symbolic repair, see Brink (1977).
3. See, for example, Milton's sonnet on his dead wife, pp. 50–1 above.
4. A good illustration of this phenomenon is found in *Great Expectations* and is quoted above, pp. 51–2.
5. This observation anticipates Freud's conclusion in *Inhibitions, Symptoms and Anxiety* (1926) that 'missing someone who is loved and longed for [is] the key to anxiety' (pp. 137–8). The evolution of Freud's ideas on loss is discussed in ch. 3 above.
6. Comparable examples of a 'transitional object' or 'substitute object' taking the place of a lost person are described by William Cowper and J.M. Barrie. See below, pp. 148–9.
7. On *devekut* and Hasidism, see below, p. 104.
8. Further examples of mystical union in the literature of world religions are given by Parrinder (1976), and literary illustrations of this phenomenon appear below, pp. 101 ff.
9. Literary portrayals of the sensation of identification with a lost person are given in ch. 1 above and in ch. 5 below, *et passim*.
10. This idea is developed by Horton (1974). The use of 'transitional objects' may be seen in the child observation of Freud's, pp. 90–1 above.
11. The attainment of a 'new identity' after a loss is discussed with reference to Walt Whitman and other writers in ch. 2 above.
12. The effects of loss on these writers have been noted by biographers. Gerin (1971, p. 4) points out that Emily Brontë was profoundly and lastingly hurt

by her mother's death when she was three. Dickens as a child was separated from his family when his father was sent to a debtors prison. His portrayal of women, according to one study (Slater, 1983), was largely determined by his sense of spiritual abandonment by his mother during this period, particularly her enthusiasm for him to continue working in the blacking factory after his father's release from prison. Poe lost his father at one and his mother before he was three. On some of the effects of these losses on Poe and his creative life, as well as comparable phenomena among other creative artists, see Terr (1987). Further discussion on Poe appears in chs. 5, 8, and 9 below.

13. This and the next two quotations vividly illustrate yearning and searching for a lost person. For other examples of this phase of grief, see ch. 1 above, *et passim*.
14. On Pip's response to his sister's death, see above, pp. 51–2.
15. For a discussion of the possible influence of Spinoza's childhood loss of his mother on the evolution of his philosophy, see below, pp. 111–13.
16. Literary illustrations of identification of the bereaved with the lost person may be found in the poetry of Donne, and are quoted in ch. 1 above, and in Eugene O'Neill's *Mourning Becomes Electra*. On the latter, see below, p. 157.
17. On *In Memoriam*, see above, pp. 25–6.
18 Other illustrations of incorporation in Bialik's writings are given by Aberbach (1982).
19. The role of loss in Sartre's life and thought is discussed further in chs. 6 and 8 below.
20. On *devekut* and its counterparts in other religions, see ch. 5 above.
21. See ch. 5, note 12 above and below, pp. 144–5.
22. For a discussion of the possible effects of childhood loss on Pascal's philosophy, see below, pp. 113–15.
23. On Masefield's early life, see Babington Smith (1978). Masefield occasionally hints at the effects on him of his mother's death when he was six, which was followed by his father's derangement and the complete break-up of his family. See, for example, his *Letters to Reyna* (1983, p. 380) and his poem entitled 'C.L.M.'

Chapter 6. Loss and Philosophical Ideas

1. Spinoza's attempts to understand the unity and harmony which allegedly underlie existence may be compared with those of mystics; and, indeed, Spinoza's philosophy is often regarded as mystical or semi-mystical. It may be significant, too, that Spinoza lost at least two siblings as well as his stepmother in his youth, although we know virtually nothing of them.
2. In a letter of 28 June 1931, Freud wrote: 'I readily admit my dependence on Spinoza's doctrine' (quoted by Hessing, 1977, p. 227). On this influence, see the articles by Hessing and Bernard (*ibid.*) and Silbermann (1973).
3. Spinoza's public declarations of his heresy against orthodox Jewish tradition in Amsterdam began shortly after his father's death in 1654, when he was twenty-two. It may be that this loss triggered off the process leading to his excommunication. The death might have freed Spinoza to declare his heresy now that he was no longer bound by his father's authority, but his rebellion might also have been a means of defending himself against depression and of expressing anger at the father for dying. His feeling of abandonment, of being outcast, to which he might have been prone as a result of his mother's

death, might have been reinforced by the death of the father. What was the use of a faith which could not protect him against such calamities? His heresy might thus have been a means of externalizing an inner state of excommunication, which had less to do with religious or social issues than with traumatic upheaval within the family.

4. Similar passages expressing the terrifying chaos of abandonment appear in a number of other writers discussed elsewhere in this book, including John of the Cross, Tolstoy, and Nietzsche, all of whom suffered loss in childhood. Compare these with Camus, in *The Myth of Sisyphus* (1942), who describes chaos and the consequent search for unity and meaning as the only certainty:

> And here are trees and I know their gnarled surface, water and I feel its taste. These scents of grass and stars at night, certain evenings when the heart relaxes – how shall I negate this world whose power and strength I feel? Yet all the knowledge on earth will give me nothing to assure me that the world is mine. You describe it to me and you teach me to classify it. You enumerate its laws and in my thirst for knowledge I admit that they are true. You take apart its mechanism and my hope increases. At the final stage you teach me that this wondrous and multi-coloured universe can be reduced to the atom and that the atom itself can be reduced to the electron. All this is good and I wait for you to continue. But you tell me of an invisible planetary system in which electrons gravitate around a nucleus. You explain this world to me with an image...I realize then that you have been reduced to poetry: I shall never know...What I know, what is certain, what I cannot deny, what I cannot reject – this is what counts. I can negate everything of that part of me that lives on vague nostalgias, except this desire for unity, this longing to solve, this need for clarity and cohesion. I can refute everything in the world surrounding me that offends or enraptures me, except this chaos, this sovereign chance and this divine equivalence which springs from anarchy. I don't know whether this world has a meaning that transcends it. But I know that I do not know that meaning and that it is impossible for me just now to know it (1979, pp. 24–5, 51).

5. Attachments to books connected with a lost person are described in Dickens' *David Copperfield*, Rousseau's *Confessions*, and Agnon's 'The Sister'. See ch. 2 n. 10 above.

6. See n. 5 above.

7. Another important loss in Nietzsche's early life was the death of his younger brother, Joseph, several months after the father's death (Gedo, 1978).

8. See the letter to Overbeck of 30 July 1881 (in Kaufmann, 1975, p. 140).

9. Nietzsche's 'parricidal' nature might have been expressed also in his tendency of putting older men, such as Schopenhauer or Wagner, on a pedestal, then knocking them off; and in particular, he loved Wagner 'more than he had ever loved anyone since his father' (Hayman, 1981, p. 108).

10. The remarriage of Sartre's mother was a severe blow, for he was displaced by his stepfather and, having lost his privileged position in his mother's life, turned into 'a prince of the second rank' (de Beauvoir, 1984, p. 350). Sartre said of his stepfather: '...he was perpetually the person I wrote against. All my life. The fact of writing was against him' (*ibid.*, p. 144).

11. 'Fortunately, he died young; among the Aeneases each carrying his Anchises on his shoulders, I cross from one bank to the other, alone, detesting those invisible fathers who ride piggy-back on their sons throughout their

lives...' (1977, p. 15). See below, p. 150. For a comparable example of a feeling of triumph after a loss in the memoirs of Jung, see above, pp. 62–3.

12. At one point in his life, however, Buber went through a 'mystical' phase and had experiences which could be described as mystical, such as becoming one with objects. See ch. 5 above.

13. Similarities between the thought of Buber and of Winnicott are discussed by Ticho (1974).

Chapter 7. Loss and Charisma

1. A translated selection of Weber's writings on charisma has been edited by Eisenstadt (1968). A survey of the use of the word is given by Wilson (1975).
2. For a critical review of the literature on charisma, see Theobald (1977).
3. Compare with Churchill's oratorical style: 'He would open a speech with a sluggish large tempo, apparently unsure of himself; then he would pull out his organ's Grand Swell and the Vox Humana, and the essence of his prose would be revealed; a bold, ponderous, rolling, pealing, easy rhythm, broken by vivid stalking strokes' (Manchester, 1983, p. 30).
4. On this and other factors, both social and personal, in Hitler's development, see Langer (1972), Waite (1977), and Aberbach (1985).
5. Leadbeater 'reconstructed' thirty of Krishnamurti's alleged lives, going back to 22,662 B.C.E. (Lutyens, 1975, pp. 23–4).
6. Far more important to him as a mother-substitute, however, was Annie Besant, whom he also addressed as 'my holy mother'. From his first letter to her, it is touchingly clear that he loved her as a surrogate-mother: 'My dear mother, Will you let me call you mother when I write to you? I have no other mother now to love, and I feel as if you were our mother because you have been so kind to us' (ibid., p. 31).
7. For other illustrations of this phenomenon, see ch. 5 above.
8. Detailed accounts of Marilyn Monroe's childhood are given by Zolotow (1961) and Guiles (1969).

Chapter 8. Grief and Pathology

1. Compare this with Bowlby's analogy between the effects of childhood loss and rheumatic fever (1980, p. 22). See above, p. 4.
2. Poe was himself apparently capable of a sudden, irrational act of sadism such as that of the narrator of 'The Black Cat': 'On one occasion he wantonly killed a pet fawn belonging to his foster-mother, the first Mrs. Allan, something for which he very likely later felt remorse' (Mabbott, ed., 1978, p. 848).
3. Further illustrations of extreme idealization alternating with extreme anger in Bialik's poetry are given by Aberbach (1988).
4. On loss as a motive and theme in Keats, see Hamilton (1969) and Baudry (1986). A more recent literary expression of the absence of feeling as a result of loss, in Edward Albee's play *The American Dream*, is so remarkable that it deserves to be quoted in full:

> *Young Man*: My mother died the night that I was born, and I never knew my father; I doubt my mother did. But, I wasn't alone, because lying with me...in the placenta...there was someone else...my brother...my twin.
> *Grandma*: Oh, my child.
> *Young Man*: We were identical twins...he and I...not fraternal...

identical; we were derived from the same ovum; and in *this*, in that we were twins not from separate ova but from the same one, we had a kinship such as you cannot imagine. We...we felt each other breathe...his heartbeats thundered in my temples...mine in his...our stomachs ached and we cried for feeding at the same time...are you old enough to understand?

Grandma: I think so, child; I think I'm nearly old enough.

Young man: I hope so. But we were separated when we were still very young, my brother, my twin and I...inasmuch as you can separate one being. We were torn apart...thrown to opposite ends of the continent. I don't know what became of my brother...to the rest of myself...except that, from time to time, in the years that have passed, I have suffered losses...that I can't explain. A fall from grace...a departure of innocence...loss...loss. How can I put it to you? All right; like this: Once...it was as if all at once my heart...became numb...almost as though I...almost as though...just like that...it had been wrenched from my body...and from that time I have been unable to love. Once...I was asleep at the time...I awoke, and my eyes were burning. And since that time I have been unable to see anything, *anything*, with pity, with affection...with anything but...cool disinterest. And my groin...even there ...since one time... one specific agony...since then I have not been able to *love* anyone with my body. And even my hands...I cannot touch another person and feel love. And there is more...there are more losses, but it all comes down to this: I no longer have the capacity to feel anything. I have no emotions. I have been drained, torn asunder...disembowelled. I have, now, only my person...my body, my face. I use what I have...I let people love me...I accept the syntax around me, for while I know I cannot relate...I know I must be related *to*. I let people love me...I let people touch me...I let them draw pleasure from my groin...from my presence...from the fact of me...but, that is all it comes to. As I told you, I am incomplete...I can feel nothing. I can feel nothing. And so...here I am...as you see me. I am...but this...what you see. And it will always be thus.

Grandma: Oh, my child; my child.

(1961, pp. 77–9)

5. On Cowper's experience of loss and his creativity, see Brink (1977).
6. See above, p. 120.
7. See Storey (1982, p. 164). In addition, Clare was deeply moved by the deaths of children, and several of his poems are concerned with this theme: 'To an Infant Sister', 'On An Infant Killed by Lightning', 'Stanzas on a Child', and 'The Dying Child'. On creativity and the loss of siblings, see Pollock (1978) and Farrell (1987).

Chapter 9. Loss and Suicide

1. This illustration of identification with the lost person is given by Krupp (1965). Further examples appear in ch. 5 above, *inter alia*.
2. Other examples of incorporation with objects in Bialik are given by Aberbach (1982). Also, see ch. 5 above.
3. Alvarez (1971), calling attention to the link between Cowper's loss of his mother and his inclination to suicide, writes of 'The Castaway' that 'Cowper

himself had been prematurely thrown out of his loving home as a child and set adrift in a hostile world' (p. 208).

4. 'And Levin, a happy father and husband, in perfect health, was several times so near suicide that he had to hide a rope lest he be tempted to hang himself, and would not go out with a gun for a fear of shooting himself' (Pt. 8, ch. 9).

5. See above, p. 4.

6. Tr. George Reavey (Barnstone, ed., 1970, p. 411).

Bibliography

Aberbach, D. (1981). 'On Re-reading Bialik: Paradoxes of a "National Poet".' *Encounter*, 56, VI, pp. 41–8.

—— (1981). 'Mind Readings' (on literature and psychology). *Times Higher Education Supplement*, 9.9.81.

—— (1982). 'Loss and Separation in Bialik and Wordsworth.' *Prooftexts* 2, II, pp. 197–208.

—— (1983). 'Screen Memories of Writers.' *International Review of Psycho-Analysis*, 10, I, pp. 47–62.

—— (1984). *At the Handles of the Lock: Themes in the Fiction of S.J. Agnon*. The Littman Library, Oxford University Press.

—— (1984). 'Loss and Dreams.' *International Review of Psycho-Analysis*, 11, IV, pp. 383–98.

—— (1985). 'Hitler's Politics and Psychopathology.' *Encounter*, 65, III, pp. 74–7.

—— (1987). 'Grief and Mysticism.' *International Review of Psycho-Analysis*, 14, IV, pp. 509–29.

—— (1988). *Bialik*. Jewish Thinkers series. London; Peter Halban and Weidenfeld & Nicolson; New York; Grove Press.

—— (1989). 'Creativity and the Survivor: The Struggle for Mastery.' *International Review of Psycho-Analysis*, 16, III, pp. 273–86.

Abramson, G. (1979). *Modern Hebrew Drama*. New York: St Martin's Press.

Adam, K.S. (1973). 'Childhood Parental Loss, Suicidal Ideation and Suicidal Behaviour.' In Anthony & Koupernik, eds., pp. 275–97.

Agee, J. (1980; orig. 1957). *A Death in the Family*. London: Quartet Books.

Agnon, S.J. (1908). 'Agunot' (Hebrew). *Ha-Omer* 2, I, pp. 53–65.

—— (1909). 'The Well of Miriam' (Hebrew). *Ha-Poel ha-Tza'ir* 2, 14–18 (21 May, 3 June, 17 June, 1 July).

—— (1947). *In the Heart of the Seas*. Tr. I.M. Lask. New York: Schocken Books.

—— (1953–62). *Collected Works* (Hebrew). 8 vols. Tel Aviv: Schocken.

—— (1966). *Two Tales*. Tr. W. Lever. New York: Schocken Books.

—— (1967; orig. 1931). *The Bridal Canopy*. Tr. I.M. Lask. New York: Schocken Books.

—— (1968; orig. 1939). *A Guest for the Night*. Tr. M. Louvish. New York: Schocken Books.

—— (1970). *Twenty-One Stories*. N. Glatzer, ed. New York: Schocken Books.

Albee, E. (1967). *A Delicate Balance*. New York: Atheneum.

—— (1961), *The American Dream*. New York: Coward-McCann, Inc.

Alvarez, A. (1971). *The Savage God: A Study of Suicide*. London: Penguin Books.

Anthony, E.J., and Koupernik, C., eds. (1973). *The Child in his Family: The Impact of Disease and Death*. New York and London: John Wiley.

Anthony, S. (1973). *The Discovery of Death in Childhood and After*. London: Penguin Educational.

Appelfeld, A. (1983; orig. 1978). *The Age of Wonders (Tor ha-Pla'ot)*. Tr. D. Bilu. New York, Washington Square Press.

Arieti, S. (1976). *Creativity: The Magic Synthesis*. New York: Basic Books.

Arthur, B. and Kemme, M.L. (1964). 'Bereavement in Childhood.' *Journal of Child Psychology and Psychiatry*, V, pp. 37–49.

Atlas, J. (1977). *Delmore Schwartz: The Life of an American Poet*. New York: Farrar, Straus & Giroux.

Atwood, G. (1983). 'The Pursuit of Being in the Life and Thought of Jean-Paul Sartre.' *Psychoanalytic Review*, 70, II, pp. 143–62.

Babington Smith, C. (1978). *John Masefield: A Life*. Oxford University Press.

Balint, M. (1968). *The Basic Fault: Therapeutic Aspects of Regression*. London: Tavistock Publications.

Band, A. (1968). *Nostalgia and Nightmare: a Study in the Fiction of S.Y. Agnon*. Berkeley and Los Angeles; University of California Press.

Barnstone, W., ed. (1970). *Modern European Poetry*. New York: Bantam Books.

Barrie, J.M. (1923). *Margaret Ogilvy*. London: Hodder and Stoughton.

Bateson, F.W. (1971). *Wordsworth: a Re-Interpretation*. London: Longman.

Bateson, G., ed. (1961). *Perceval's Narrative: A Patient's Account of His Psychosis*. Stanford University Press.

Baudelaire, C. (1955; orig. 1857). *The Flowers of Evil: a Selection*. M. & J. Mathews, eds. New York: New Directions.

Baudry, F. (1986). 'A Dream, a Sonnet, and a Ballad: The Path to Keats' "La Belle Dame Sans Merci".' *Psychoanalytic Quarterly*, LV, pp. 69–98.

The Beatles' Lyrics (1980). New York: Dell Publishing Co.

de Beauvoir, S. (1984; orig. 1981). *Adieux: A Farewell to Sartre*. London: André Deutsch & Weidenfeld.

Bellow, S. (1982). *The Dean's December*. London: Penguin Books.

Bergmann, M.S., and Jucovy, M.E., eds. (1982). *Generations of the Holocaust*. New York: Basic Books.

Bettelheim, B. (1979). *Surviving and Other Essays*. London: Thames & Hudson.

Bialik, C.N. (1935). *Speeches* (Hebrew). 2 vols. F. Lachower, ed. Tel Aviv: Dvir.

—— (1939; orig. 1903–1923). *Aftergrowth and other Stories*. Tr. I.M. Lask. Philadelphia: Jewish Publication Society.

—— (1971). *Posthumous Works* (Hebrew). M. Ungerfeld, ed. Tel Aviv: Dvir.

—— (1973; orig. 1923). *Safiah* (Aftergrowth), from ch. 1. Tr. D. Patterson. *The Jewish Quarterly*, 20, IV, pp. 17–18.

The Holy Bible, Revised Standard Edition (1973). London: Collins.

Bieber, I., *et al.* (1962). *Homosexuality: A Psychoanalytic Study*. New York: Basic Books.

Bilik, D.S. (1981). *Immigrant-Survivors: Post-Holocaust Consciousness in Recent Jewish American Fiction*. Middleton, Connecticut: Wesleyan University Press.

Bion, W. (1961). *Experiences in Groups*. London: Tavistock Publications.

Black, S.A. (1975). *Whitman's Journeys into Chaos: a Psychoanalytic Study of the Creative Process*. Princeton University Press.

Bornstein, B. (1983). 'Virginia Woolf: Grief and the Need for Cohesion in *To the Lighthouse*.' *Psychoanalytic Inquiry*, 3, III, pp. 357–70.

Borowski, T. (1976; orig. 1959). *This way for the Gas, Ladies and Gentleman*. Tr. B. Vedder. London: Jonathan Cape.

Booth, W.C. (1961). *The Rhetoric of Fiction*. Chicago and London: University of Chicago Press.

Bowlby, J. (1965; orig. 1953). *Child Care and the Growth of Love*. London: Pelican Books.

—— (1969). *Attachment and Loss. Vol. 1: Attachment*. London: The Hogarth Press and The Institute of Psycho-Analysis.

—— (1973). *Attachment and Loss. Vol. 2: Separation: Anxiety and Anger*. London: The Hogarth Press and The Institute of Psycho-Analysis.

—— (1980). *Attachment and Loss. Vol. 3: Loss: Sadness and Depression*. London: The Hogarth Press and The Institute of Psycho-Analysis.

Brennan, G. (1973). *St. John of the Cross: His Life and Poetry*. Cambridge University Press.

Brink, A. (1974). 'On the Psychological Sources of Creative Imagination'. *Queen's Quarterly: A Canadian Review*, 81, I, pp. 1–19.

—— (1977). *Loss and Symbolic Repair: A Psychological Study of Some English Poets*. Hamilton, Ontario: The Cromlech Press.

—— (1982). *Creativity As Repair: Bipolarity and its Closure*. Hamilton, Ontario: The Cromlech Press.

Brontë, E. (1976; orig. 1847). *Wuthering Heights*. London: Pan Books.

Buber, M. (1964; orig. 1913). *Daniel: Dialogues of Realization*. Tr. M. Friedman. New York, Chicago, San Francisco: Holt, Rinehart and Winston.

—— (1970). *I and Thou* (Ich and Du). Tr. W. Kaufmann. Edinburgh: T. & T. Clark.

—— (1973). *Meetings*. M. Friedman, ed. La Salle, Illinois: Court Publishing Co.

Bucke, R.M. (1982; orig. 1902). *Cosmic Consciousness: A Study in the Evolution of the Human Mind*. Secaucus, New Jersey: Citadel Press.

Bullock, A. (1986; orig. 1952). *Hitler: a Study in Tyranny*. London: Penguin Books.

Bunch, J. (1972). 'Recent Bereavement in Relation to Suicide.' *Journal of Psychosomatic Research*, XVI, pp. 361–6.

Byron Poetical Works (1979; orig. 1904). F. Page & J. Jump, eds. Oxford University Press.

Camus, A. (1979; orig. 1942). *The Myth of Sisyphus*. Tr. J. O'Brien. London: Penguin Books.

Carpenter, H. (1977). *J.R.R. Tolkein: a Biography*. London: Allen and Unwin.

Carr, W. (1978). *Hitler: A Study in Personality and Politics*. London: Edward Arnold.

Celan, P. (1980). *Selected Poems*. Tr. M. Hamburger. London: Carcanet.

Churchill, R.S. (1966). *Winston S. Churchill, Vol. 1: Youth 1874–1900*. London: Heinemann.

The Poems of John Clare (1935). 2 vols. J.W. Tibble, ed. London: J.M. Dent & Sons Ltd.; New York: E.P. Dutton & Co. Inc.

The Later Poems of John Clare (1984), 2 vols., E. Robinson, D. Powell, eds. Oxford: Clarendon Press.

The Cloud of Unknowing (14th century)(1978; orig. 1961). Tr. C. Walters. London: Penguin Books.

Cocteau, J. (1933; orig. 1930). *Opium: The Diary of an Addict*. Tr. E. Boyd. London: Allen and Unwin.

Coleman, R. (1984). *John Winston Lennon. Vol. I 1940–1966*. London: Sidgwick & Jackson.

Coleridge, S.T. (1975; orig. 1963). *Poems*. J. Beer, ed. Everyman's Library. London: Dent; New York: Dutton.

Connely, W. (1934). *Sir Richard Steele*. London: Jonathan Cape.

Conrad, J. (1972; orig. 1904). *Nostromo*. London: Dent.

Coveney, P. (1967; orig. 1957). *The Image of Childhood*. London: Penguin Books.

The Letters and Prose Writings of William Cowper (1979–84). 4 vols. J. King & C. Ryskamp, eds. Oxford: Clarendon Press.

The Poetical Works of William Cowper (1963). 4th edn. H.S. Milford, ed. Oxford University Press.

Dante Alighieri (1973; written *c.* 1315). *The Divine Comedy: Hell*. Tr. D.L. Sayers. London: Penguin Classics.

——— (1975; written *c.* 1315). *The Divine Comedy: Purgatory*. Tr. D.L. Sayers. London: Penguin Classics.

——— (1980; written *c.* 1290). *La Vita Nuova*. Tr. B. Reynolds. London: Penguin Classics.

Davies, H. (1979; orig. 1968). *The Beatles: The Authorized Biography*. London: Granada Publishing Limited.

Dawidowicz, L. (1983; orig. 1975). *The War against the Jews 1933–45*. London: Penguin Books.

De Quincey, T. (1966). *Confessions of an English Opium Eater and Other Writings*. New York: Signet Classics.

Descartes, R. (1970; 1st edn. 1911). *The Philosophical Works of Descartes*, 2 vols. Tr. E.S. Haldane and G.R.T. Ross. Cambridge University Press.

Des Pres, T. (1976). *The Survivor*. Oxford University Press.

Deutsch, H. (1937). 'Absence of Grief.' *Psychoanalytic Quarterly*, VI, pp. 12–22.

Dickens, C. (1962; orig. 1849–50). *David Copperfield*. New York: Signet Classics.

—— (1957; orig. 1861). *Great Expectations*. London: Dent.

—— (1974; orig. 1846–8). *Dombey and Son*. New York: Signet Classics.

—— (1976; orig. 1853). *Bleak House*. London: Pan Classics.

John Donne: The Complete English Poems (1975; orig. 1971). A.J. Smith, ed. London: Penguin Educational.

Dostoyevsky, F. (1978; orig. 1880). *The Brothers Karamazov*. Tr. D. Magarshack. London: Penguin Classics.

Dyer, A.R. (1986). 'Descartes: Notes on the Origins of Scientific Thinking.' *The Annual of Psychoanalysis*, XIV, pp. 163–76.

Eisenbud, J. (1978). 'Descartes and Shaw: Some Spatial Aspects of Object Loss.' *International Review of Psycho-Analysis*, V, pp. 285–96.

Eliot, T.S. (1951). *Selected Essays*. London: Faber.

—— (1973). *Collected Poems and Plays*. London: Faber.

Ellmann, R. (1982; orig. 1959). *James Joyce*. Oxford University Press.

Fairbairn, W.R.D. (1937–8). 'Prolegomena to a Psychology of Art.' *British Journal of Psychology*, XXVIII, pp. 288–303.

—— (1938–9). 'The Ultimate Basis of Aesthetic Experience.' *British Journal of Psychology*, XXIX, pp. 167–81.

—— (1952). *Psychoanalytic Studies of the Personality*. London: Tavistock Publications.

Farrell, D. (1987). 'The Forgotten Childhood of Hermann Hesse.' *The Annual of Psychoanalysis*, XV, pp. 247–68.

Feuer, L. (1963). 'The Dreams of Descartes.' *American Imago*, XX, pp. 3–26.

Flaubert, G. (1961; orig. 1877). *Three Tales*. Tr. R. Baldick. London: Penguin Books.

Frankl, V. (1973). *Psychotherapy and Existentialism*. London: Pelican Books.

Fraser, M. (1976). *The Death of Narcissus*. London: Secker & Warburg.

Freud, A., and Burlingham, D. (1974). *Infants without Families and Reports on the Hampstead Nurseries 1939–1945*. London: The Hogarth Press.

Freud, S., and Breuer, J. (1895). *Studies on Hysteria.* SE, II.*

Freud, S. (1896). 'The Aetiology of Hysteria.' SE, III, pp. 189–221.

—— (1899). 'Screen Memories.' SE, III, pp. 303–22.

—— (1900). *The Interpretation of Dreams.* SE, IV–V.

—— (1901). *The Psychopathology of Everyday Life.* SE, VI.

—— (1917). 'Mourning and Melancholia.' SE, XIV, pp. 243–58.

—— (1920). *Beyond the Pleasure Principle.* SE, XVIII, pp. 7–64.

—— (1923). *The Ego and the Id.* SE, XIX, pp. 12–66.

—— (1926). *Inhibitions, Symptoms, and Anxiety.* SE, XX, pp. 87–172.

—— (1930). *Civilization and Its Discontents.* SE, XXI, pp. 59–145.

—— (1933). *New Introductory Lectures on Psychoanalysis.* SE, XXII, pp. 7–182.

—— (1954). *The Origins of Psycho-Analysis: Letters to Wilhelm Fliess, Drafts and Notes: 1887–1902.* M. Bonaparte, *et al* eds. Trs. E. Mosbacher, J. Strachey. London: Imago.

—— (1960). *Letters.* E.L. Freud, ed. Tr. T. & J. Stern. London: The Hogarth Press.

Friedman, M. (1981). *Martin Buber's Life and Work.* Vol. I. New York: E.P. Dutton.

Fromm, E. (1977; orig. 1973). *The Anatomy of Human Destructiveness.* London: Penguin Books.

Frost, R. (1973). *Selected Poems.* I. Hamilton, ed. London: Penguin Books.

Fruman, N. (1971). *Coleridge, the Damaged Archangel.* New York: George Braziller.

Furman, E. (1974). *A Child's Parent Dies: Studies in Childhood Bereavement.* New Haven and London: Yale University Press.

Furst, S.S., *et al.* (1976). *Mysticism: Spiritual Quest or Psychic Disorder?* IX, pub. no. 97. New York: Group for the Advancement of Psychiatry, Committee of Psychiatry and Religion.

Gay, M.J., and Tonge, W.L. (1967). 'The Late Effects of Loss of Parents in Childhood.' *British Journal of Psychiatry*, CXIII, pp. 753–9.

Gedo, J.E. (1978). 'Nietzsche and the Psychology of Genius.' *American Imago*, XXXV, 1–2, pp. 77–91.

Gerin, W. (1971). *Emily Brontë: a Biography.* Oxford: Clarendon Press.

Gershon, K. (1966). *Selected Poems.* London: Gollancz.

Gilbert, M. (1971) *Winston S. Churchill, Vol. 3: 1914–16.* London: Heinemann.

---

* The abbreviation SE denotes the Standard Edition of *The Complete Psychological Works of Sigmund Freud*, translated by J. Strachey and published in 24 volumes by The Hogarth Press Ltd., London, and distributed in America by W.W. Norton, New York.

—— (1983). *Winston S. Churchill, Vol. 6: Finest Hour 1939–41*. London: Heinemann.

Gittings, R., ed. (1970). *Letters of John Keats*. Oxford University Press.

—— (1971). *John Keats*. London: Pelican Books.

Goodenough, E.R. (1965). *The Psychology of Religious Experiences*. New York: Basic Books.

Gosse, E. (1976; orig. 1907). *Father and Son*. London: Penguin Modern Classics.

Greenacre, P. (1955). 'The Mutual Adventures of Jonathan Swift and Lemuel Gulliver: A Study in Pathology.' In *Emotional Growth*, vol. II. New York: International Universities Press, 1975.

—— (1957). 'The Childhood of the Artist.' *Psychoanalytic Study of the Child*, XII, pp. 47–72.

Greenberg, U.Z. (1968; orig. 1951). *The Streets of the River* (Hebrew). Jerusalem and Tel Aviv: Schocken.

Greer, S., *et al.* (1966). 'Aetiological Factors in Attempted Suicides.' *British Medical Journal*, II, pp. 1352–5.

Griggs, E.L. (1966). *Collected Letters of Samuel Taylor Coleridge. Vol 1: 1785–1800*. Oxford University Press.

Grigson, G. (1949). *Poems of John Clare's Madness*. London: Routledge & Kegan Paul.

Guiles, F. (1980; orig. 1969). *Norma Jean: The Life of Marilyn Monroe*. London: Granada.

Hamilton, J.W. (1969). 'Object Loss, Dreaming and Creativity: The Poetry of John Keats.' *Psychoanalytic Study of the Child*, XXIV, pp. 488–531.

—— (1976). 'Early Trauma, Dreaming and Creativity: The Work of Eugene O'Neill.' *International Review of Psycho-Analysis*, III, pp. 341–64.

—— (1979). 'Transitional Phenomena and the Early Writings of Eugene O'Neill.' *International Review of Psycho-Analysis*, VI, pp. 49–60.

Hampshire, S. (1976; orig. 1951). *Spinoza*. London: Pelican Books.

The Complete Poems of Thomas Hardy (1976). J. Gibson, ed. London: Macmillan.

Hawthorne, N. (1982). *Tales and Sketches*. Ohio State University Press.

Hayman, R. (1981). *Nietzsche: a Critical Life*. London: Quartet Books.

Heinicke, C.M., and Westheimer, I. (1966). *Brief Separations*. London: Longman; New York: International Universities Press.

Hessing, S. (1977). *Speculum Spinozanum 1677–1977*. London: Routledge & Kegan Paul.

Hollingdale, R.J. (1973). *Nietzsche*. London and Boston: Routledge & Kegan Paul.

Horton, P.C. (1973). 'The Mystical Experience as a Suicide Preventive.' *American Journal of Psychiatry*, CXXX, pp. 294–6.

—— (1974). 'The Mystical Experience: Substance of an Illusion.'

Journal of the American Psychoanalytic Association, XX, pp. 364–80.

Howe, I., Wisse, R.R., Shmeruk, C. eds. (1987). *The Penguin Book of Modern Yiddish Verse.*

John of the Cross (1973; orig. late 16th century). *The Dark Night of the Soul.* Tr. B. Zimmerman. Cambridge: Clarke.

Jones, E. (1949). *Hamlet and Oedipus.* London: Hogarth.

———— (1953–7). *Sigmund Freud: Life and Works.* 3 vols. London: The Hogarth Press.

Joyce, J. (1973; orig. 1922). *Ulysses.* London: Penguin Books.

Jung, C.G. (1919; orig. 1913). *Psychology of the Unconscious.* Tr. B.M. Hinkle. London: Kegan Paul, Trench, Trubner & Co. Revised as *Symbols of Transformation* (1956) in *The Collected Works of C.G. Jung,* vol. V, tr. R.F.C. Hull, London: Routledge & Kegan Paul.

———— (1935). Lecture III of The Tavistock Lectures, in *The Symbolic Life,* vol. XVIII of *The Collected Works of C.G. Jung.*

———— (1974; orig. 1961). *Memories, Dreams, Reflections.* London: Collins, The Fontana Library.

Kaufmann, W., ed. (1975). *The Portable Nietzsche.* New York: Viking.

Keats, J. (1964; orig. 1904). G. Bullett, ed. Everyman's Library. London: Dent; New York: Dutton.

Kermode, F. (1973). *Lawrence.* Modern Masters series. Bungay, Suffolk: Fontana/Collins.

Klein, M. (1948). *Contributions to Psycho-Analysis 1921–1945.* London: The Hogarth Press.

Kline, P. (1972). *Fact and Fantasy in Freudian Theory.* Edinburgh: T. & T. Constable.

Koestler, A. (1964). *The Act of Creation.* London: Hutchinson.

Koller, K.M., and Castanos, J.N. (1968). 'The Influence of Parental Deprivation in Attempted Suicide.' *Medical Journal of Australia,* I, pp. 396–9.

Kovner, A. (& Sachs, N.)(1971). *Selected Poems.* Tr. S. Kaufman, N. Orchan. London: Penguin Modern European Poets.

Kral, V.A. (1951). 'Psychiatric Observations under Severe Chronic Stress'. *American Journal of Psychiatry,* CVIII, pp. 185–92.

Krüll, M. (1986; orig. 1979). *Freud and His Father.* Tr. A.J. Pomerans. London: Hutchinson.

Krupp, G.R. (1965). 'Identification as a Defence against Anxiety in Coping with Loss'. *International Journal of Psychoanalysis,* XLVI, pp. 303–14.

Krystal, H., and Niederland, W. (1971). *Psychic Traumatization: After-Effects in Individuals and Communities.* Boston: Little, Brown.

Kübler-Ross, E. (1975; orig. 1969). *On Death and Dying.* New York: Macmillan.

Lachower, F., ed. (1937–9). *Letters of Chaim Nachman Bialik* (Hebrew). 5

vols. Tel Aviv: Dvir.

Laing, R.D. (1959). *The Divided Self*. London: Tavistock Publications.

Langer, L.L. (1975). *The Holocaust and the Literary Imagination*. New Haven and London: Yale University Press.

Langer, W. (1972). *The Mind of Adolf Hitler*. New York: Basic Books.

Lawrence, D.H. (1972; orig. 1964). *Collected Poems*. 2 vols. V. de Sola Pinto, W. Roberts, eds. London: Heinemann.

—— (1974; orig. 1913). *Sons and Lovers*. London: Penguin Books.

—— (1979–). *Letters*. 7 vols. J.T. Boulton *et al.*, eds. Cambridge University Press.

Leavis, F.R. (1973). *The Great Tradition*. London: Chatto and Windus.

Lembourn, H.J. (1979). *Forty Days with Marilyn*. London: Hutchinson.

Lennon, J. (1980, orig. 1971). *Lennon Remembers: The Rolling Stone Interviews*, with J. Wenner. London: Penguin Books.

—— (1981). Interview by D. Sheff with Lennon and Yoko Ono. *Playboy*, 28, I, pp. 75–144.

Levi, P. (1979; orig. 1947, 1963). *If This is a Man/ The Truce*. Tr. S. Woolf. London: Penguin Modern Classics.

Lewis, C.S. (1978; orig. 1955). *Surprised by Joy*. Glasgow, Fontana Books:

—— (1974; orig. 1961). *A Grief Observed*. London: Faber.

Lichtenberg, J. (1978). 'Psychoanalysis and Biography.' *The Annual of Psychoanalysis*, VI, pp. 397–427.

Lifton, R.J. (1967). *Death in Life: The Survivors of Hiroshima*. London: Weidenfeld & Nicholson.

Lindemann, E. (1944). 'Symptomatology and Management of Acute Grief.' *American Journal of Psychiatry*, CI, p. 141–9.

Lindop, G. (1981). *The Opium-Eater: A Life of Thomas De Quincey*. London: Dent.

Lutyens, M., ed. (1970). *The Penguin Krishnamurti Reader*.

—— (1975). *Krishnamurti: The Years of Awakening*. New York: Farrar, Straus and Giroux.

—— (1983). *Krishnamurti: The Years of Fulfilment*. London: John Murray.

Mabbott, T.O., ed. (1978). *Collected Works of Edgar Allan Poe, Tales and Sketches 1843–1849*, vol. III. Cambridge, Massachusetts: The Belknap Press of Harvard University Press.

Maddison, D., and Viola, A. (1968). 'The Health of Widows in the Year Following Bereavement.' *Journal of Psychosomatic Research*, XII, pp. 297–306.

Mallarmé, S. (1977). *The Poems*. Tr. K. Bosley. London: Penguin Books.

Manchester, W. (1983). *The Last Lion: Winston Spencer Churchill, Vol I: 1874–1932*. London: Michael Joseph

Marris, P. (1958). *Widows and their Families*. London: Routledge & Kegan Paul.

———— (1974). *Loss and Change*. London: Routledge & Kegan Paul.

Martin, R.B. (1980). *Tennyson: The Unquiet Heart*. Oxford University Press and Faber.

Masefield, J. (1923). *The Collected Poems of John Masefield*. London: Heinemann.

———— (1952). *So Long to Learn*. London: Heinemann.

———— (1983). *Letters to Reyna*. W. Buchan, ed. London: Buchan & Enright.

Maugham, S. (1973; orig. 1915). *Of Human Bondage*. The Collected Edition, vol. II. London: Heinemann.

McCullough, F., and Hughes, T., eds. (1982). *The Journals of Sylvia Plath*. New York: Dial Press.

Meyer, B.C. (1967). *Joseph Conrad: A Psychoanalytic Biography*. Oxford University Press.

The Sonnets of Michelangelo (1961). Tr. E. Jennings. London: The Folio Society.

Miller, A. (1987). *Timebends: A Life*. London: Methuen.

Millgate, M. (1982). *Thomas Hardy: a Biography*. Oxford University Press.

Milton, J. (1971). *Complete Shorter Poems*. J. Carey, ed. London: Longman.

———— (1971). *Paradise Lost*. A Fowler, ed. London: Longman.

Mintz, A. (1984). *Hurban: Response to Catastrophe in Hebrew Literature*. New York: Columbia University Press.

Monroe, M. (1974). *My Story*. Written by Ben Hecht. London: W.H. Allen.

Moore, H.T., ed. (1974). *The Priest of Love: a Life of D.H. Lawrence*. London: Heinemann.

Moorman, M. (1957, 1965) *William Wordsworth: A Biography*. 2 vols. Oxford University Press.

Muensterberger, W. (1962). 'The Creative Process: its Relation to Object Loss and Fetishism.' In Muensterberger & Axelrad, eds., *The Psychoanalytical Study of Society*, II, New York: International Universities Press.

Murphy, G.E., *et al.* (1979). 'Suicide and Alcoholism: Interpersonal Loss Confirmed as a Predictor.' *Archive of General Psychiatry*, 36, I, pp. 65–9.

Nardini, J.E. (1952). 'Survival Factors in American Prisoners of War of the Japanese.' *American Journal of Psychiatry*, CIX, pp. 241–8.

Nelson, R.J. (1981). *Pascal: Adversary and Advocate*. Cambridge, Massachusetts and London, England: Harvard University Press.

Neruda, P. (1976). *Residence on Earth (Residencia en la tierra)*. Tr. D.D. Walsh. London: Souvenir Press.

———— (1977). *Memoirs*. Tr. H. St. Martin. London: Souvenir Press.

Nerval, G. de (1958). *Selected Writings*. Tr. G. Wagner. London: Peter Owen.

Nietzsche, F. (1973; orig. 1886). *Beyond Good and Evil (Jenseits von Gut und Böse)*. Tr. W. Kaufmann. New York: Vintage Books.

O'Neill, E. (1923). *Anna Christie*. London: Jonathan Cape.

—— (1932). *Mourning Becomes Electra*. London: Jonathan Cape.

—— (1956). *Long Day's Journey Into Night*. New Haven & London: Yale University Press.

Onarato, R. (1971). *Wordsworth in The Prelude*. Princeton University Press.

Oremland, J.D. (1983). 'Death and Transfiguration in *Hamlet*.' *Psychoanalytic Inquiry*, 3, III, pp. 485–512.

Osterweis, M., Solomon, E., Green, M., eds. (1984). *Bereavement: Reactions, Consequences, and Care*. Washington, D.C: National Academy Press.

Otto, R. (1930). *Mysticism, East and West: A Comparative Analysis of the Nature of Mysticism*. Tr. B.L. Bracey and R.C. Rayne. New York: Meridien Books.

Owen, W.J.B., and Smyser, J.W., eds. (1974). *The Prose Works of William Wordsworth*. 3 vols. Oxford University Press.

Oz, A. (1985; orig. 1982). *A Perfect Peace*. Tr. H. Halkin. London: Flamingo.

Pagis, D. (1981). *Points of Departure*. Tr. S. Mitchell. Philadelphia: Jewish Publication Society.

Painter, G. (1959, 1965). *Marcel Proust: a Biography*. 2 vols. London: Chatto and Windus.

Parkes, C.M. (1986; orig. 1972). *Bereavement: Studies of Grief in Adult Life*. London: Tavistock Publications.

Parkes, C.M., & Weiss, R.S. (1983). *Recovery from Bereavement*. New York: Basic Books.

Parrinder, G. (1976). *Mysticism and the World's Religions*. London: Sheldon Press.

Pascal, B. (1973; orig. 1670). *Pensées*. Tr. J. Warrington. London: Dent.

Pickering, G. (1974). *Creative Malady*. London: Allen and Unwin.

Plank, E.M., & Plank, R. (1978). 'Children and Death As Seen through Art and Autobiography.' *Psychoanalytic Study of the Child*, XXXIII, pp. 593–620.

Plath, S. (1963). *The Bell Jar*. London: Faber.

—— (1975). *Letters Home*. A.S. Plath, ed. London: Faber.

—— (1981). *Collected Poems*. T. Hughes, ed. London and Boston: Faber.

Poe, E.A. (1975). *Selected Writings*. D. Galloway, ed. London: Penguin Books.

—— (1984) *Poetry and Tales*, P.F. Quinn, ed. New York: The Library of America.

Pollock, G.H. (1978). 'On Siblings, Childhood Sibling Loss, and Creativity.' *The Annual of Psychoanalysis*, VI, pp. 443–81.

Prince, R., and Savage, C. (1965). 'Mystical States and the Concept of Regression.' In White, ed., pp. 114–34.

Proust, M. (1981; orig. 1913–27). *Remembrance of Things Past (A la recherche du temps perdu)*. Tr. C.K.S. Moncrieff *et al.* New York: Random House.

Purdy, R.L., & Millgate, M., eds. (1984). *The Collected Letters of Thomas Hardy, Vol. 4 1909–1913*. Oxford: Clarendon Press.

Raphael, B. (1984). *The Anatomy of Bereavement: A Handbook for the Caring Professions*. London: Hutchinson.

Ravnitzky, J.H. (1946). 'Notebook Jottings on Bialik' (Hebrew). *Reshumot*, II, pp. 182–7.

Rees, W.D. (1971). 'The Hallucinations of Widowhood'. *British Medical Journal*, IV, pp. 37–41.

Reid, F. (1926). *Apostate*. London: Constable & Co. Ltd.

Rilke, R.M. (1972). *Selected Poems*. Tr. J.B. Leishman. London: Penguin Modern European Poets.

—— (1975; orig. 1939). *Duino Elegies*. Tr. J.B. Leishman and S. Spender. London: Chatto and Windus.

Rimbaud, A. (1973; orig. 1873). *A Season in Hell and The Illuminations*. Tr. E. R. Peschel. Oxford University Press.

Riviere, J. (1955). 'The Unconscious Phantasy of an Inner World Reflected in Literature.' In *New Directions in Psycho-Analysis*. M. Klein *et al.*, eds. London: Tavistock Publications.

Robert, M. (1977). *From Oedipus to Moses: Freud's Jewish Identity*. Tr. R. Manheim. London: The Littman Library and Routledge & Kegan Paul.

Robertson, J., and Robertson, J. (1971). 'Young Children in Brief Separation: A Fresh Look.' *Psychoanalytic Study of the Child*, XXVI, pp. 264–315.

Rochlin, G. (1965). *Grief and Discontents: the Forces of Change*. London: J. & A. Churchill.

Rosenfeld, A. (1980). *A Double Dying*. Bloomington: Indiana University Press.

Roskies, D. (1984). *Against the Apocalypse*. Cambridge, Massachusetts: Harvard University Press.

Rousseau, J.J. (1977; orig. 1781). *The Confessions*. Tr. J.M. Cohen. London: Penguin Classics.

Rutter, M. (1966). *Children of Sick Parents*. Oxford University Press.

Sachs, N. (and Kovner, A.) (1971). *Selected Poems*. Tr. R. & M. Mead. London: Penguin Modern European Poets.

Sartre, J.P. (1975; orig. 1938). *Nausea (La Nausée)*. Tr R. Baldick. London: Penguin Modern Classics.

—— (1977; orig. 1964). *Words (Les Mots)*. Tr. I. Clephane. London: Penguin Books.

Saul, L.J., *et al.* (1956). 'On Earliest Memories'. *Psychoanalytical Quarterly*,

XXV, pp. 228–37.

Scharfstein, B. (1973). *Mystical Experience*. Oxford: Basil Blackwell.

—— (1980). *The Philosophers: Their Lives and the Nature of their Thought*. Oxford: Basil Blackwell.

Scholem, G.G. (1955). *Major Trends in Jewish Mysticism*. 3rd. edn. London: Thames & Hudson.

Segal, N. (1988). *Narcissus and Echo: Women in the French récit*. Manchester University Press.

de Selincourt, E., and Darbishire, H. (1947). *The Poetical Works of William Wordsworth*, vol IV. Oxford University Press.

Sexton, A. (1974). *The Death Notebooks*. Boston: Houghton, Mifflin Co.

Shand, A.F. (1914). *The Foundations of Character*. London: Macmillan.

Sheaffer, L. (1968). *O'Neill: Son and Playwright*. London: Dent.

Silbermann, I. (1973). 'Some Reflections on Spinoza and Freud.' *Psychoanalytic Quarterly*, XLII, pp. 601–24.

Silkin, J., ed. (1973). *Poetry of the Committed Individual*. London: Penguin Books.

Simon, B., Simon, N. (1972). 'The Pacifist Turn: An Episode of Mystic Illumination in the Autobiography of Bertrand Russell.' *Journal of the American Psychoanalytic Association*, XX, pp. 109–21.

Simpson, E. (1988). *Orphans: Real and Imaginary*. London: Weidenfeld & Nicolson.

Slater, M. (1983). *Dickens and Women*. London, Melbourne & Toronto: Dent.

Spender, S. (1951). *World Within World*. London: Hamish Hamilton.

Spinoza, B. (1970; orig. 1672?). *Ethics*. Tr. A. Boyle. London: Dent.

Spitz, R., and Cobliner, W.G. (1965). *The First Year of Life*. New York: International Universities Press.

Stace, W.T. (1960). *Mysticism and Philosophy*. London: Macmillan.

Starkie, E. (1971; orig. 1957). *Baudelaire*. London: Pelican Biographies.

—— (1973; orig. 1961). *Arthur Rimbaud*. London: Faber.

Steegmuller, F. (1970). *Cocteau*. London: Macmillan.

Steiner, G. (1967). *Language and Silence: Literature and the Inhuman*. New York: Atheneum.

Steiner, N.H. (1974). *A Closer Look at Ariel: a Memory of Sylvia Plath*.

Stengel, E. (1983; orig. 1964). *Suicide and Attempted Suicide*. London: Penguin Books.

Stern, K. (1966). *The Flight from Woman*. London: Allen & Unwin.

Storey, E. (1982). *A Right to Sing: The Life of John Clare*. London: Methuen.

Storr, A. (1973; orig. 1969). 'The Man' in *Churchill: Four Faces and the Man*. London: Pelican Books.

—— (1972). *The Dynamics of Creation*. London: Secker & Warburg.

—— (1988). *The School of Genius*. London: André Deutsch.

Swift, J. (1972; orig. 1726). *Gulliver's Travels*. New York: Dell.

Symons, J. (1978). *The Tell-Tale Heart: The Life and Works of Edgar Allan Poe*. London: Faber.

The Poems of Tennyson (1969). C. Ricks, ed. London: Longman.

Teresa of Jesus (1944, 1946; orig. 16th century). *Complete Works*. 2 vols. Tr. E.A. Peers. London and New York: Sheed & Ward.

Terr, L.C. (1987). 'Childhood Trauma and the Creative Product: A Look at the Early Lives and Later Works of Poe, Wharton, Magritte, Hitchcock, and Bergman.' *Psychoanalytic Study of the Child*, XLII, pp. 545–72.

Theobald, R. (1977). 'Charisma: A Critical Review.' Polytechnic of Central London, School of Social Sciences and Business Studies, Research Paper no. 5.

Thompson, L. (1966). *Robert Frost: The Early Years 1874–1915*. New York: Holt, Rinehart & Winston.

Ticho, E. (1974). 'Donald W. Winnicott, Martin Buber and the Theory of Personal Relationships.' *Psychiatry*, XXXVII, pp. 240–53.

Toland, J. (1976). *Adolf Hitler*. New York: Ballantine Books.

The Letters of J.R.R. Tolkien (1981). H. Carpenter, ed. London: Allen and Unwin.

Tolstoy, L. (1940; orig. 1882, 1884). *A Confession and What I Believe*. Tr. A. Maude. Oxford University Press.

—— (1973; orig. 1889). *The Kreutzer Sonata and Other Stories*. Tr. A. Maude. Oxford University Press.

—— (1987; orig. 1865–8). *War and Peace*. Tr. R. Edmonds. London: Penguin Books.

—— (1988; orig. 1874–6). *Anna Karenina*. Tr. R. Edmonds. London: Penguin Books.

Tomer, B. (1982; orig. 1963). *Children of the Shadow*. Tr. H. Halkin. Jerusalem: Institute for the Translation of Hebrew.

Trilling, L. (1970). *The Liberal Imagination*. London: Penguin Books.

Troyat, H. (1968; orig. 1965). *Tolstoy*. Tr. N. Amphoux. London: W.H. Allen.

Ungaretti, G. (1971). *Selected Poems*. Tr. P. Creagh. London: Penguin Modern European Classics.

Wainwright, W.J. (1981). *Mysticism: A Study of its Nature, Cognitive Value and Moral Implications*. Brighton: The Harvester Press.

Waite, R. (1977). *The Psychopathic God: Adolf Hitler*. New York: Basic Books.

Wapnick, K. (1969). 'Mysticism and Schizophrenia.' *Journal of Transpersonal Psychology*, 1, II, pp. 49–62. In Woods, ed., pp. 321–37.

Weatherby, W.J. (1977). *Conversations with Marilyn*. London: Sphere Books.

Weber, M. (1968). *On Charisma and Institution Building*. S.N. Eisenstadt, ed. Chicago and London: University of Chicago Press.

—— (1947; orig. 1922). *Theory of Social and Economic Organization* (*Wirtschaft und Gesellschaft*). Tr. A.M. Henderson and T. Parsons.

Weiss, D.A. (1962). *Oedipus in Nottingham: D.H. Lawrence*. Seattle: University of Washington Press.

White, J., ed. (1972). *The Higher State of Consciousness*. Garden City, New York: Doubleday Anchor Books.

Whitman, W. (1949; orig. 1855). *Leaves of Grass and Selected Prose*. S. Bradley, ed. New York: Holt, Rinehart and Winston, Inc.

Wiesel, E. (1960). *Night* Tr. S. Rodway. London: MacGibbon & Kee.

Wilson, B.R. (1975). *The Noble Savages: The Primitive Origins of Charisma and its Contemporary Survival*. Berkeley: University of California Press.

Wilson, E. (1947; orig. 1941). *The Wound and the Bow*. New York: Oxford University Press.

Winnicott, D.W. (1971). *Playing and Reality*. London: Tavistock Publications.

Wisdom, J.O. (1944). 'Three Dreams of Descartes.' *International Journal of Psychoanalysis*, XXVIII, pp. 11–18.

Wolf, E.S. (1983). 'Transience or Nothingness.' *Psychoanalytic Inquiry*, 3, III, pp. 529–42.

Wolfenstein, M. (1973). 'The Image of the Lost Parent.' *Psychoanalytic Study of the Child*, XXVIII, pp. 433–56.

Woods, R. ed. (1980). *Understanding Mysticism*. Garden City, New York: Image Books.

Woolf, S. (1969). *Children Under Stress*. London: Allen Lane, Penguin Books.

Wordsworth, J. (1982). *William Wordsworth: The Borders of Vision*. Oxford: Clarendon Press.

Wordsworth, W. (1973; orig. 1904). *Poetical Works*. T. Hutchinson, E. de Selincourt, eds. Oxford University Press.

—— (1975; orig. 1805, 1850). *The Prelude: A Parallel Text*. J.C. Maxwell, ed. London: Penguin Educational.

The Colleted Poems of W.B. Yeats (1973; orig. 1933). London: Macmillan.

Yehoshua, A.B. (1977). *The Lover*. Tr. P. Simpson. Garden City, New York: Doubleday.

Young-Bruehl, E. (1985). 'Psychoanalysis and Biography.' *Psychoanalytic Study of the Child*, XL, pp. 535–56.

Zaehner, R.C. (1957). *Mysticism: Sacred and Profane*. Oxford University Press.

Zolotow, M. (1961). *Marilyn Monroe*. London: W.H. Allen.

Zweig, P. (1984). *Walt Whitman: The Making of a Poet*. London: Viking; New York: Basic Books.

Name Index

Subject Index